AFRICA &
the WEST

Intellectual Responses to

European Culture

AFRICA &
the WEST

Intellectual Responses to
European Culture

Edited by PHILIP D. CURTIN

James W. Fernandez
Wyatt MacGaffey
Jean Herskovits
Leo Spitzer
G. Wesley Johnson, Jr.
Harold Scheub

THE UNIVERSITY OF WISCONSIN PRESS

The University of Wisconsin Press
1930 Monroe Street, 3rd floor
Madison, Wisconsin 53711-2059
uwpress.wisc.edu

3 Henrietta Street
London WC2E 8LU, England
eurospanbookstore.com

Printed in the United States of America

Library of Congress Cataloging in Publication Data
Curtin, Philip D/Africa & the West
Includes bibliographical references.
1. Africa, West—Civilization—European influences
—Addresses, essays, lectures. 2. Acculturation—
Addresses, essays, lectures. I. Fernandez, James W./II. Title.
DT474.C87/301.29'6'01821/77–176409

ISBN-13: 978-0-299-03894-6 (pbk: alk. paper)

CONTENTS

INTRODUCTION

Philip D. Curtin

Historians have recently begun to peer across the cultural barriers where only anthropologists ventured a few decades ago. The result is not merely the recent surge of nonwestern history by western historians; it extends to several kinds of cross-cultural history, including the history of people's views of one another across these same barriers. One kind of "image" literature surveys the western view of the non-West, while another is concerned with the nonwestern response to Europe.[1] This book is about African response to Europe—not the political response or the military response of the resistance movements opposing colonialism, but rather the intellectual response.

This response came in many different forms simply because the history of ideas is a very broad field indeed. It is properly concerned with any ideas that may influence or change human societies. This includes the vague sentiments of ordinary people alongside the most precise and intricate formal theories. The essays that follow explore several different themes in African intellectual history, rather than concentrating on any one of them. Common themes do, of course, occur. Africans, like other people at other times, began their assessment of the West by categorizing the westerners they met and fitting them into a pattern alongside other people. They also had to explain to themselves how their confrontation with the West came about.

But the problem of western civilization from the African point

1. See, for example, Ssu-yu Teng and John K. Fairbank, *China's Response to the West* (Cambridge, Mass., 1954); G. B. Sansom, *The Western World and Japan* (New York, 1950); Donald F. Lach, *Asia in the Making of Europe* (Chicago, 1965–); Philip D. Curtin, *The Image of Africa* (Madison, Wis., 1964); J. J. Waardenburg, *L'Islam dans le miroir de l'Occident* (Aix-en-Provence, 1963).

of view was not how the West got there, but what to do about it. This question carried a whole train of additional questions in its wake: what alien values were worth adopting? What local values were particularly worthy of preservation? What short-run changes seem to be dictated as the best intermediate stage toward a long-term goal? But, in fact, Africans, intellectual or otherwise, seldom wrote down explicit answers to these questions. Most people, for that matter, never come to grips with the central question and ask themselves what they would hope to find as the way of life of their grandchildren. Even those who do are not likely to write out an answer, but rather, to leave evidence by implication in a mass of other responses to short-range problems.

The detectable "reaction to the West" could therefore take at least three forms other than the desired statement of long-range goals. One reaction was not so much intellectual as political or military. The West, after all, appeared in Africa not as a "culture" (a social scientists' generalization in any event) but as some combination of traders and missionaries, followed later by soldiers and administrators. One very obvious reaction was either to welcome one or all of these groups, or else to try to get rid of them. In either case, the action is usually recorded, and the record is evidence of an intellectual attitude that can be read as either pro, con, or mixed.

A second and similar kind of evidence about response to an alien culture appeared in the life style of an individual. In the intense interaction of cultures that has marked recent African history, each person had to make day-to-day decisions about his own behavior. To wear European shoes or African? To become a Christian or not? If so, what kind of Christian? Many decisions implied a reaction to the West. Evidence about overt behavioral syncretism is one of the largest bodies of data we have, and it has the advantage of bridging the gap between the expressed thought of the intellectual leadership and the unrecorded thought of the masses. But this kind of evidence is very weak, as several of these essays will show. Overt cultural behavior may mean much, or very little. A peasant may want to have his society profit from the full benefit of the industrial revolution—but he may not show it for lack of money, enough even to buy a bicycle. A townsman may accept Christianity and still retain his African religion in another mental compartment. Other overt cultural behavior has more to do with the role model an individual may follow than it does with the cultural mixture he would advocate for society as a whole. President Senghor of Senegal may write according to the most cherished French literary standards; in his public life he may follow the completely western role model of behavior appropriate to a statesman; yet his expressed goal is a Senegalese culture that is far more African and less western than this behavior suggests.

A third type of intellectual reaction would be vastly different from either of these. Rather than expressing thought *about* western culture, an individual may take on new modes of thought, new perceptions of the world that result from new data introduced by a western presence in Africa. Some of the essays that follow give glimpses into this kind of reaction, though not as a part of the more overt response the authors set out to explore. To follow it systematically would lead very far afield—among other places into the vast maze of religious syncretism. It may be that religious thought will be the most significant area of cross-cultural intellectual history, but there are problems enough in the much less subtle and more overt reactions being considered here. We have therefore sought to avoid this intricate and tempting field of investigation.

In spite of the great variety of different evidence available, this collection has been molded (like other history) by that which has survived, conscious that writing is only one kind of evidence. Oral traditions help to fill the gap in many forms of African history, but oral traditions rarely tell as much as one might hope about past ideas or attitudes. Anthropologists, on the other hand, have evidence of African responses to western culture in more recent times, and these can sometimes be used for extrapolation into the past by a combination of present observation and the record of documentary history.

This volume grew out of a conference held in October 1969 and sponsored by the Joint Committee on African Studies of the Social Science Research Council and the American Council of

Learned Societies.[2] Three of the essays (those of James Fernandez, G. Wesley Johnson, and Leo Spitzer) are based on papers from that conference. The others were written by participants after the conference had taken place. In either case, the interdisciplinary approach was chosen as a way of trying to bridge the gap in Africa between the ideas of the acculturated elite and those of the illiterate masses—and, among western scholars, to bridge the gap between different ways of looking at similar phenomena.

The authors and the editor are grateful to the Joint Committee on African Studies[3] for its sponsorship of the conference that brought them together, and especially to the other participants for their valuable ideas and suggestions. They alone, however, are responsible for the opinions expressed here, which cannot be considered to have the approval or endorsement of either the Social Science Research Council or the American Council of Learned Societies.

2. For a report of the conference see P. D. Curtin, "Intellectual History and Comparative Studies: An Experimental Approach by the Joint Committee on African Studies," *Social Science Research Council Items* 24 (March, 1970):6–8.

3. Members of the Committee were: Elizabeth Colson, University of California, Berkeley (Chairman); L. Gray Cowan, Columbia University; Philip D. Curtin, University of Wisconsin; Walter Deshler, University of Maryland; William O. Jones, Stanford University; Roy Sieber, Indiana University; Robert F. Thompson, Yale University; staff, Roland L. Mitchell, Jr.

AFRICA &
the WEST

Intellectual Responses to

European Culture

FANG REPRESENTATIONS
UNDER ACCULTURATION

James W. Fernandez

The Fang are an ethnic and linguistic group of nearly a million people, belonging to the northwest cluster of Bantu-speaking peoples and forming the dominant culture in the hinterland of Gabon, Equatorial Guinea, and parts of southern Cameroon. In spite of their present location close to the Atlantic coast, their period of contact with the Europeans was short—hardly more than a century, compared to nearly five centuries for the Ba-Kongo (who will be treated below by Wyatt MacGaffey).

During the era when Afro-European relations mainly turned on maritime contact at a series of coastal points, the Fang lived well to the north and east of their present homeland. Though the slave trade reached far into some parts of the African interior, the Fang appear even to have escaped interference from slave raiders until they began moving to their present location in the course of the nineteenth century; by then the slave trade itself was coming to an end.

The earliest Fang contacts with the West were therefore through the missionaries who began to arrive toward the middle of that century, followed by colonial administrators a half-century later. Missionary and administrative writings make it possible for James Fernandez to examine Fang reactions to the West as they have changed through time, not merely as they were during his own ethnographic field work in Gabon.

James Fernandez has published widely in scholarly journals, including such other studies of the Fang as: "Affirmation of Things Past: Alar Ayong and Bwiti as Movements of Protest in Central and Northern Gabon," in R. Rotberg and A. A. Mazrui, eds., *Protest and Power in Black Africa* (London, 1970), and

3

"Unbelievably Subtle Words—Representation and Integration in the Sermons of an African Reformative Cult," *Journal of the History of Religions* 6 (1965):43–69.

P.D.C.

Purpose and Subject

I propose to examine here[1] the Fang response to pressure put upon their thinking about the world as a consequence of both administrative organization and missionary evangelization.[2] What impact has contact with the West had upon Fang thought styles and upon the mode and content of their representations? I will be concerned primarily with the reaction of the forest-villagers as they experienced the direct intervention of missionary and administrator in village affairs and not in the reactions of the intellectual elite in the trading centers and coastal cities. The intellectual elite have come under a much more diverse set of influences—and have been much more susceptible to being dislodged from their older conceptual centers of gravity.

This cannot, of course, be an absolute distinction, for most members of the educated elite have maintained village roots. Moreover, the introduction of widespread primary schooling[3] in

1. The research for this paper was made possible by a grant from the Foreign Area Fellowship Program of the Ford Foundation for research in Gabon, Cameroun, and Rio Muni (1958–60). Errol Hill has provided a valuable critique of the original version from which I have tried to profit.

2. By Fang I mean that population of Fang-Bulu speakers living in Gabon north of Ndjole, Lambarene, and Libreville, in eastern Rio Muni and in Cameroun south of Ambam. This population comprises speakers of the Ntumu, Mvae, Okak, Meke, and Fang-Fang dialects. The evangelical and administrative pressure put upon all these populations has been quite similar. My data were gathered in 1959 and early 1960, mainly in northern and central Gabon among the southern Ntumu, the Fang-Fang, and the Okak.

3. "Scolarization" in Gabon, the percentage of primary-school-age children (*enseignement primaire*) attending school (60–70 percent in the late 1950s, more than 80 percent today), has been very high in relation to comparable African countries.

Gabon since the Second World War and after the *loi cadre* has brought these educated elite influences directly into the villages. But the impact of intensive western-oriented education by its very recency and intensity poses a different set of problems,[4] for it has created a kind of crucible for the reworking of cognitions and evaluations that had not previously existed. In the situation of school learning the intellect is submitted to pressures to respond, to see, and to translate experience into language—pressures that are seldom present elsewhere, especially when the school is an agency of a foreign culture as until very recently was almost always the case in African primary education. Insofar as African cognitions and evaluations of experience differed from or were in conflict with the European previous to this widespread schooling, there was a much greater no man's land in which adjustments, adaptations, and syncretisms could be worked out.

Mentalities: Old Time and Old Testament

One should not underestimate the struggle for African minds going on previous to the introduction of schools. For example, we find in the Gabon colonial literature (and many times reiterated by Africans in my experience in the field) a deprecation of the African time sense. This was done by both administrators and missionaries alike. The African tendency to perceive time as periodically intensifying rather than as regular and perpetual frustrated both these groups in their attempts to impose specific time requirements.[5] The Gabonese missionary Briault[6] discusses Fang notions of time, the missionary pressure upon them, and some

4. It also offers the possibility of more exacting research on African response to the formal requirements of western education. See, for example, the John Gay and Michael Cole study of African responses to the New Math, *The New Mathematics and An Old Culture* (New York, 1968).

5. For a discussion of the time sense as periodically intensifying, see Edmund Leach, "Two Essays Concerning the Symbolic Representation of Time," in *Rethinking Anthropology* (London, 1961), pp. 124–36.

6. R. P. Briault, *Dans la Foret du Gabon* (Paris, 1930), eps. Chapter X, "La Notion du Temps chez les Noirs," pp. 107–120.

rather bizarre reactions on the Africans' part—among others, the importance to the young of possessing wristwatches as symbolic of their assimilation. In the Fang reformative cult of Bwiti, there is heavy emphasis upon the exact timings of ritual events. Alarm clocks are kept in practically all chapels of this widespread cult, though they run on a very local time. And it is sometimes the case that the leaders of these local groups will carry their clocks with them. In their passage through the forest they will periodically be brought to their knees in genuflection by the sound of the alarm—surely an intellectual reaction to the West!

The primary missionary instrument of intellectual coercion was, of course, the Bible and the catechisms and missals associated with it. By the 1860s both the Catholic and the Protestant missions circulated catechisms and biblical lessons in French and Fang[7] among the Fang of central western Gabon (the southwestern frontiers of their territory). As more and more of the Bible was translated, and particularly as the distinction between the religious cultures of the Old and the New Testaments became apparent, Fang reacted in favor of the Old Testament. This was contrary to missionary expectation but perfectly understandable in terms of African traditional religious culture. In one area in particular the Fang found themselves attracted to the Old Testament; this was the area of ritual regulations—taboos —as spelled out, for example, in the Books of Moses. The Fang themselves possessed a detailed and exigent system of ritual prohibitions (eki),[8] which gave a familiar look to that part of the

7. The earliest catechism in my collection was published by the American Presbyterian Mission in 1889. *Nteni osu Nteni Fanwe* (*First Book of Fang Readings* [Talaguga, 1889]). It contains 6 pages of lessons (*lesenyi*) —word recognition, phrase recognition, paragraph reading—followed by four biblical stories: Adam ye Ivi, Abi osua ("the first sin"), Jenesis 3: 14–24) Luki 1:26–55. The Bible, thanks to the prodigious efforts of the Swiss missionary Samuel Galley, was entirely translated into Fang by the end of the Second World War.

8. Cf. L. Martrou, "Les 'eke' des Fang," *Anthropos* 1 (1906):743–59. See also J. W. Fernandez, "Christian Acculturation and Fang Witchcraft," *Cahiers d'Etudes Africaines* 2 (1961):244–70.

Bible. Particularly for the Protestants, with their primary focus upon the Bible rather than upon the catechism and other accessory documents, this preference posed a problem. The missionary Grebert was already complaining in 1919 of his difficulty in evangelizing the Fang—how to pass from the *"mentalité juive"* to the *"mentalité greco-latine."*[9]

These two instances of incompatibility, time and Old Testament mentality, can stand for all the intellectual pressures brought to bear on village Fang. In order to obtain a theoretical frame of reference for the discussion, I would make the distinction between the way one represents experience to oneself—the cognitive models that one has in mind—on the one hand, and the emotional evaluation that one assigns to the various aspects of this modeled experience—the affective connotations of one's experiences—on the other. These representations can be of various kinds: enactive, iconic, and symbolic. Experience, first of all, can be represented in action, in our muscles so to speak, as we single out and learn to chain and hence reproduce certain sequences of action in such recurrent situations as playing a game or an instrument, in dancing or in typing. Experience, secondly, can be represented by certain mental images that we preserve out of our past experience and recollect in order to recognize a new experience. One may have such an image of "a man" collected out of past experiences that a long-haired male is disturbing: he doesn't look right; one doesn't recognize him. Finally, experience can be represented in abstract models. These are very much tied up with language skills of various kinds, whether everyday languages, one's mother tongue, or such formal languages as calculus or symbolic logic. Here men represent an experience in a set of language-explicit rules. Reference to these rules and the procedures they prescribe serves to solve problems presented by future occurrences of similar experiences. One states or codes the rules in one's language—the rules for integration in calculus, the rules for forming the past tenses in French, the rules for reading a book or a poem—and then one applies

9. Fernand Grebert, *Au Gabon*, 3ᵉ Ed. (Paris, 1948), p. 120.

the rules when confronted with a calculus problem, a perfectly past occurrence in Paris, or a book or a poem.[10]

All three modes of representation are employed by all men in all cultures. At the same time, I suggest that the amount of attention given to each mode differs from culture to culture and hence a shift in modes of representation is one of the important intellectual reactions to the contact of cultures—acculturation. In addition, the cognitive and emotional content of each mode of representation changes from culture to culture, hence changes in content—in the forms and feelings of representation within modes—is a second possible intellectual reaction.

Fang Matter-of-Factness

Like many communal societies, Fang culture had a narrow margin of existence. There was little surplus to free men to elaborate intellectual superstructures in any of the aspects of life, religious, economic, or social, hence the Fang representations of their experience were often just complicated enough to survive in that environment. It was an exuberant survival to be sure; since the early nineteenth century, they had been steadily moving south into Gabon, overwhelming the autochthonous peoples. The Fang were not given to extensive elaborations of their supernatural or their social experience, or their economic life, or their art and material culture. They lived matter-of-factly, worshipping ancestors about whose abode and way of life there was limited speculation. They had a segmentary lineage system in name but not in practice; levels of grouping beyond the village were vestigial. The extended family (*mvogabot*) was commonly the limit of

10. These three modes of representation correspond to those singled out by Jerome Bruner, "The Course of Cognitive Growth," *American Psychologist* 19 (1964):2. From an entirely different perspective but one I believe which relates to Bruner's distinction, I myself have discussed signal interaction, sign interaction, and symbol interaction as three modes of experiencing social and cultural life; signals are, I would argue, the elements of enactive representation, signs of iconic representation, and symbols of symbolic representation. See Fernandez, "Symbolic Concensus in a Fang Reformative Cult," *American Anthropologist* 67 (1965):902–927.

jural and moral authority, and only on occasion was the sense of community extended to the entire village. There were no regular courts, no specialists in jurisprudence, no regular markets. Material culture was finely done but quite functional. The powerful simplicity and realism of Fang sculpture is recognized[11] and appreciated. Only in the area of folklore, in troubador legends, does one find considerable elaboration.

Nothing should be concluded about Fang intelligence from this matter-of-factness. In the first place, even if they themselves did not systematize their various beliefs and activities into an intellectual superstructure, any student to whom system is important, such as an ethnographer, and who follows their beliefs and their actions from situation to situation—say in the realm of religion—can find a complex interlocking of elements. The Fang have invested more in their culture than they will say. Secondly, they were widely rated by practically all Europeans who came into contact with them in the nineteenth century as a sensitive and intelligent people who promised much for the future of Africa. Though frustrated in some respects, this judgment persisted until the end of the colonial period.[12]

The discussion of such matters makes relevant the distinction

11. Fang sculpture is almost always discussed in terms of its formal or balanced realism in books on African art. For some sense of the tensions out of which the vitality of this art arises see J. W. Fernandez, "Principles of Opposition and Vitality in Fang Aesthetics," *Journal of Aesthetics and Art Criticism* 25 (1966):53–64. I also discuss in that article aesthetic reaction on the part of the Fang to western art preferences.

12. The very high view of the Fang is discussed by me in "The Fall of the Noble Cannibal: The Fang Perceived 1840–1910" (unpub. MS).

Given the climate of the times, it is necessary to state that no genetic theory of racial differences is being put forth here. Nothing in my experience in Africa would incline me to such a theory. And in any case I am not made competent by the nature of my research either to discuss or adequately define intelligence as separate from the nurturance it has received and the particular challenges it experiences. My view is that different cultures or sub-cultures emphasize different modes of representation and modes of approach to problematic experiences. Should conditions change for that culture, other modes will correspondingly come to receive emphasis. A balanced statement on the problems involved in testing for intelligence with reference to African research is Leonard Doob, *Becoming More Civilized* (New Haven, 1960), Chapter 7.

between concrete and abstract forms of thinking, and the related distinction between the use of analogy and analysis in the approach to solving the problems presented by experience. Traditionally the Fang were more accustomed to concrete thinking and to assessment by analogy. To what degree has contact with the West moved the Fang towards the abstract thinking and analytic methods in which westerners take pride?[13] In the West, where scholasticism and the scientific method have produced academies, research laboratories, institutes, and other kinds of "think tanks" by the thousands, the sheer multitude of experiences men force themselves to contemplate and the problems they force themselves to solve have naturally resulted in high emphasis upon abstract deductive analysis of experience. But we can hardly blame the Fang if traditionally they found it intellectually quite adequate to scrutinize their experiences concretely and by analogy with previous experiences—relying primarily upon the actions and images of experiences previously represented in themselves to handle these new experiences.

Of course the Fang, like all men, possess a fully developed language which is inevitably an instrument for the generic coding of experience. But the Fang rarely self-consciously maximized this coding or concentratedly analyzed their experiences. They were not particularly intellectual in this sense, though I would reiterate that they were fully perceptive and complex enough in their definitions—their representations to themselves—of new experi-

13. Problem solving by genericizing is discussed by J. S. Bruner in his "Going Beyond the Information Given," in *Contemporary Approaches to Cognition: the Colorado Symposium* (Cambridge, Mass., 1957), esp. pp. 51–62.

The usefulness of characterizing the way people respond to problems along the continuum from abstractness to concreteness has been long argued, most insistently in Kurt Goldstein, *The Organism* (New York, 1939). Those high in concreteness tend to deal with new experiences in terms of their own specific identity and by analogy with previous experiences; there is little attempt to generalize what is learned, that is, to formulate an abstract generic code (a symbolic representation) in terms of which this experience and a whole class of previous experiences can be analyzed and rendered equivalent. Those high in abstractness, however, deal with the new experience not in terms of itself but as an instance of a more abstract generic category.

ences to respond quite adequately to all of the traditional environmental challenges.[14] Acculturation in recent decades has confronted them with the challenge of adapting to one degree or another to the civilization of theology, technology, and science, all of which boast abstract, analytic, and very self-conscious intellectual superstructures. Their intellectual responses to these are probably crucial to their modernization in any western sense.[15]

From Palabra House to Law Court

Western intellectual pressure has fallen upon several areas of traditional Fang life. The Fang language has changed in both grammar and lexicon. European difficulties with the copula and the consequent substitution in the early grammars of the facilitative, I am able to (*me ne ngu ye bo*), in place of the correct I am do (*me ne bo*), was widely picked up by the Fang themselves.[16] The impact of the vocabulary of the material culture—

14. Anthony F. C. Wallace has pointed out that in all cultures "far more subtle perceptions of situations are possible for men than their available neurological muscular and technical apparatus can permit them to recognize in response" ("Driving to Work," in *Context and Meaning in Cultural Anthropology*, ed. Melford Spiro [New York, 1965], pp. 277–92) and that all cultures usually manage to be just complicated enough in their responses for effective adaptation. Western man has created such a complicated environment for himself that he is forced to be perhaps much more "complicated" in the abstract analytic sense than the Fang. But "survival anywhere depends upon learned abstractions" (Doob, *Becoming More Civilized*, p. 186).

15. Professor L. H. Ofosu Appiah, the editor of the *Encyclopedia Africana*, has argued this in various articles and letters on science education in Ghana which appeared in the *Legon Observer* during the fall of 1966. It is not clear incidentally whether Ofosu Appiah is more concerned with "magical" mentality, i.e., the preoccupation with final rather than effective causes, or with the development of abstracting analytic attitudes. But he *is* very concerned that African responses to the western challenge not be seen simply in terms of economic or political structures.

16. George Bates, *Handbook of Bulu* (Ebolowa, 1928), p. 17. In my work with Bwiti "evangiles" I have noted a tendency to employ a missionary Fang. J. W. Fernandez, "Unbelievably Subtle Words: Representation and Integration in the Sermons of an African Reformative Cult," *Journal of the History of Religions* 6 (1966):43–69.

machis, kersini, and so on—is inevitable and not very interesting, but the entrance of the French word *politique* into Fang vocabulary gives us much more insight into their response to political processes in the late colonial period. It had an almost universally pejorative connotation, referring to machinations not in the interest of the people by a power elite in the coastal cities.

Let us look at a reaction, however, that relates to more theoretical distinctions. The Fang held no formal courts, except very rarely for interclan disputes.[17] But palabras (*adzo medzo*) were constant in village life. It was customary for several elders to be chosen to hear the dispute. Each side presented its views and cross-examination was allowed, often followed by restatement. The judges did little cross-examination themselves. They returned a verdict, if tempers weren't running too high, after some consultation among themselves. Indirection and proverbial statement were as characteristic of the shifting rhetoric of these verdicts as of the arguments themselves. Previous instances of similar disputes were referred to, usually without attempting to draw any explicit and direct parallels. Finally the judge, after subtly steering his way through a sea of diversities, came to the head of the matter (*nlo adzo*) and announced a verdict. Thus was the palabra carefully disentangled (*atia*) and neatly sliced (*akik*).

In the colonial district courts the pressures of the docket, the difficulties of translation, and the anxiety of the local administrator, who acted as judge, to cross-examine and to analyze the case before him in order to find a category in which it might be placed and on the basis of which he might make judgment, combined to produce in the eyes of Fang villagers a travesty of justice. It is clear that most administrators approached the cases that came before them with little interest in the cases themselves, but rather with the intentions of finding some generic category to which the particular case could be assigned and according to which, by reference to the colonial law books, a judgment could be made. The Fang often complained that such procedures of analysis and abstraction resulted in breaking the palabra (*abuk*

17. Some aspects of Fang jurisprudence, these rare clan courts as well as the village moots, are discussed in my "Redistributive Acculturation and Ritual Reintegration in Fang Culture" (Ph.D. Diss., Northwestern. 1963).

adzo) as opposed to untangling it and slicing it. In Fang thinking, the results of breaking a palabra are two jagged ends very difficult to rejoin. From their view, judgmental procedure of this kind can only be socially irresponsible.

The Fang themselves, elder judges and participants alike, have a much more consuming and concrete interest in the individual case. They certainly have an interest in handling it in such a way, with deliberation and indirection, that the two disputing parties will not be further exacerbated but will be brought closer together. Thus is village harmony preserved and restored. The amount of time devoted to the recollections of other disputes and even to the recollection of only faintly relevant experiences serves, of course, to suggest a continuity in village life beyond the immediacy of the dispute. But it is also an example of that second mode of representation in which the images of former experiences are recalled and exploited to provide the direction for the handling of present experiences. The use of proverbs is itself an example of this second mode of representation, for the reference of proverbs is almost always to everyday and usually domestic experiences which, it is proverbially implied though not directly stated, have in them some truth applicable to the experience one is presently struggling through. For example, an apt proverb heard frequently in palabras is "gravel thrown in the forest kills birds" (*bikok bi ake afan bi awiñ anwan*). It is usually used as an admonition in the sense of "wild accusations will eventually find a target," or in the sense of "wild accusations will surprise you with their results." Sometimes, since practically all proverbs are susceptible to multiple interpretation, it is taken to mean "one's case must be presented with greater diversity of argument if results are to be obtained." But in any case no abstract statement of the rule to be applied in the argument is needed. The similarity in the experiences compared by choice of proverb speak for themselves.

Who can deny the intelligence in the proverb? It parsimoniously codes several different rules about experience in general within an innocent enough domestic observation. The rule to be applied is, however, like all use of analogy, ambiguous and dependent upon context and inclination. In this tolerance of ambiguity it is not analytic. Nor is it essentially symbolic. It is iconic.

And the nature of iconic representation, as opposed to symbolic representation, is that it is not simply an abstracting and categorizing linguistic response to a situational dilemma; rather, it summons up imagery to deal with a dilemma of experience, and hence is itself exciting to the consciousness whose dilemmas it appears to resolve.

Africanists have long noted that during the late colonial period the law was one of the disciplines that most attracted young African students in their advanced work. It has been generally felt that, self-interest aside, this choice was an aspect of the drive towards independence and expressed a desire to obtain the tools of legal and jural power necessary to that drive. No doubt it was, but I would argue further from the Fang data that this choice represents: first, a reaction to the quite puzzling difference (as far as the Fang were concerned) between European and Fang jurisprudence, which made a challenging mystery out of the former; and second, a recognition that in spite of these differences the law in its forensic aspect at least was an arena in European life in which the modes of representation to which Africans were accustomed were most likely to be applied and appreciated. The law, after all, as contrasted to the district-administrator judges, remains interested in the details of the particular conflict experiences that come before it and in experiences precedent to it. The law is congenial to enactive and iconic thought styles.

Explanatory Models and Organizing Metaphors

Certain images were central in Fang experience and acted as models, as organizing metaphors,[18] in their approach to the experiences which came before them in their round of life. Horton

18. In metaphor we see the use of the essentials of one experience to grasp another. And it is interactive and integrative in the sense that both experiences have something in common. Strictly speaking, in the sciences the term "models" should apply only to such constructs as the Watson and Krick double helix mock-up of wire and plastic tubes and beads. Scientific models of this kind may be entirely factitious and hence are not interactive or unifying in the way metaphors are. When anthropologists talk about metaphors as models they generally do not make this distinction clear.

has made a very important general point in this regard, comparing the pre-scientific thought systems of Africa with the scientific thought systems of Europe.[19] He sees only one difference between African and scientific thought systems as patterns of reasoning. They both seek to explain and to predict, and they both work towards increasing levels of abstraction in explaining the problems of experience. But the African thought systems are not guided by any "body of explicit acceptance/rejection criteria," that is, by rules of scientific method. Both thought systems generate models (explanatory schemes) to explain the diversity of experiences within the world in which they live. These models are taken from prototype experiences that are already well understood.[20] Here, however, is the important difference. "Scientific thought tends to choose things rather than people as the basis of its explanatory models, while African thought systems by and large tend to make the opposite choice." This difference arises from the requirements of regularity and order in any explanatory scheme. "To qualify as a suitable prototype for a model, a set of phenomena needs not only to be thoroughly familiar, but also to be manifestly orderly and regular in its behavior."[21] For technologically advanced societies, nature has more regularity than society. For backward communities with little control or understanding of nature, the opposite condition holds true—their social life appears the most orderly and regular area of their experiences.

Though I intend to dispute some of Horton's conclusions, his point on different explanatory models seems crucial. It causes us to ask, in addressing the question of intellectual reactions of the Fang, whether we note any changes in their models. Let us remember that Fang changes to the models of scientific thought

19. Robin Horton, "Ritual Man in Africa," *Africa* 34 (1964):85–104.
20. Horton, "Ritual Man in Africa," p. 98. "The investigator (in either thought system) is impressed by an analogy between the puzzling observations he wants to explain and the structure of certain phenomena whose behavior has already been well explored. Because of this analogy he postulates a scheme of events with structure akin to that of the prototype phenomena, and equates that scheme with the reality behind the observations that 'puzzle' him."
21. Horton, "Ritual Man in Africa," p. 99.

are not likely to have occurred in the villages previous to intensive schooling, for neither missionary nor administrator was a particularly forceful advocate of this kind of thought, missionaries in fact being professionally committed to a mystical view of reality resting on a personal model of the universe.[22] But many new models of experience inevitably appeared among Africans as a consequence of their expanding horizons and of the new organizations set up by the colonial administrations.

Among the most fundamental of cognitive maps (the alternate psychological term for models) is the map of the space in which a people live. Here we see a shift in Fang thought from a representation of the various streams and tributaries as the crucial interstices of their landscape to a representation of the colonial road system with its thoroughfares and feeder routes and seasonal dirt track. In social life we see a shift from an image of the universe as an aglomeration of widely separated segments of clan lands each containing lineages at three levels (*ndebot, mvogabot,* and *abialebot*) coupled with an image of the village or town as the center of the Fang social universe, to an image of the *mvogabot* ("village of people") as the maximal social unit and of the village as an entity organized with others of its kind on the peripheries of the trading centers and great cities. These are only some of the ways in which Fang images were reordered as a consequence of colonial administration. There was, after all, in the administrative aspect of the colonial enterprise a compulsion to order. This determination had the compelling power of a religion in whose service the European, in his reverence for progress, was a prophet.[23] It would be surprising indeed if the Fang did not react to the new ordering of life presented to them in

22. For many centuries in Christendom, of course, there has been a stable dualism, or compartmentalization as between religions and scientific understanding or in terms of our discussion here between personal and natural explanatory models. Missionaries, naturally enough, rarely bothered to communicate that intellectual compromise to Africans, though it might have been highly desirable for them to do so. (See my "African Independent Christianity: Its Study and Its Future," *Journal of Asian and African Studies,* in press.)

23. Robert Delavignette, *Freedom and Authority in French West Africa* (Oxford, 1950).

such an evangelical spirit. They appear to have been mightily impressed even with the bureaucratic intricacies of colonial administration—intricacies of busywork and paperpushing which we find bizarrely imitated in the organization of a clan regroupment movement of the 1940s and 1950s (*alar ayong*). This movement in its periodic gatherings thrashed around under a top-heavy structure of "presidents, *adjoints, membres de conseil, secretaires,*" gendarmes and a flurry of pretentious paperpushing that seemed, in my experience, the perfect mockery of European organizationalism if it hadn't been taken so seriously.[24]

These were two main shifts in the model of social life: the first, from a relatively casual dispersal of clans over the landscape according to the accidents of watercourses to the rectangularization of colonial administration with villages strung out like beads upon the arteries of commerce; and the second from the traditional view of human affairs as relatively egalitarian, undifferentiated, and capable of being handled on the basis of kinship to one of social life as requiring the most complex kind of differentiation and structured planning. These shifts constitute some of the most basic intellectual reactions of the Fang. They include a shift from the nuclear family to the administrative organization as the basic explanatory model, and a shift towards treating social life with greater abstraction. The personal model of blood ties was replaced by a more abstract "natural" model of persons in structures. My data indicate that such changes occurred in many villagers and were occasioned by contact with the colonial adminstration even though that contact was never very intense (except around the *cheflieu*). For it was another characteristic of the French colonial administration that it had great difficulty in escaping its own bureaucratic entanglements and the settled routine and satisfactions of the *cercle.*[25]

If some reorderings of Fang cognitive maps were accomplished by an administration having occasional contacts with the

24. This movement and its bizarre embrace of the European organizational passion is discussed in my "The Affirmation of Things Past: Bwiti and Alar Ayong as Protest in Northern and Central Gabon," in *Black Protest in Africa*, ed. A. Mazrui and R. Rotberg (Oxford, forthcoming).

25. R. Delavignette, *Freedom and Authority*, passim.

village, how much greater should have been the influence of missionaries who itinerated among the Fang, who almost always spoke the language, and who worked concentratedly in translating their sacred works into the vernacular. In recent decades we have seen a kind of replete middle age of missions in which missionaries as well have experienced difficulty in escaping the satisfactions of the compound. But in the earlier days in Gabon all the missionaries made regular itinerations through the bush.[26]

The missionaries, moreover, had a thought system in respect both to personal models of the universe and for experience that was in many respects the same as the Africans'. The Africans' failing was that they believed in too many spirits, and in particular paid too much attention and gave to much credence to everyday evil spirits, witchcraft spirits (*evus* among the Fang). The missionaries' main task in bringing the *bonnes nouvelles* then was to curb very drastically this supernatural overpopulation as well as to reinvigorate what was to the Fang—as to most Central Africans—either an otiose diety, or at best a philosophical first principle useful only to lay inquiry to rest.

Of course the missionaries in spite of themselves were bearers of western culture and the missionary reports are full of accounts of African *emerveillement* before some gadget or another of European daily life: matches, collapsible drinking cups, bicycles.[27] Many missionaries succumbed to the temptation to credit these marvels of material culture to the Christian way of life, the *bonnes nouvelles* they were preaching. The compartmentalization between science and religion which had long prevailed in the West was overlooked and the word "science," which seems to have entered the Fang vocabulary early, came to be associated with the theological perspective of the missionaries. Thus

26. The first contact with the Fang, in fact, was made by an American Presbyterian, the Rev. Benjamin Griswold, on itineration in 1844. See my "Homage to the Rev. Benjamin Griswold: Class of 1837," *Dartmouth Alumni Magazine* 58 (1965):28–30. The itinerations of many of these early missionaries also constituted important acts of exploration.

27. Thus in the *Journal des Mission Evangeliques* [cited hereafter as *Journal*] 1 (1911):93, M. Cadier reports "une des femmes qui m'ont apporte de l'eau et des bananes me demande avec veneration si c'est Dieu lui-mene qui m'a donné cette belle machine . . . ma bicyclette."

we have M. Cadier writing enthusiastically of the thirst of the young Fang for more and more knowledge of the Word of God, "an astonishing zeal, always eager to penetrate further this mysterious science that gives this power to the white man."[28] Of course many missionaries may have believed that Christian revelation and a Protestant ethic lay behind western technological progress. But the consequence for Africans was that they labeled as science what was actually pre-scientific thought and thus set themselves up for the inevitable frustration inherent in the belief that pure piety would be materially productive. Many villagers, while convinced that the *bonnes nouvelles* was in some respects a fraud because it yielded no material benefit, were yet persistent in trying to penetrate this "mysterious science" which the whites possessed. In my own fieldwork many years later, I encountered numerous informants in the Fang reformative cult of Bwiti who described their cult as a *science des choses cachées*[29] and whose purpose was to penetrate to those hidden sources of power in the afterlife which the whites had kept hidden from them. It was futile to try to convince them that there was no such thing as a science of hidden things. I began to wish that instead of the Bible the missionaries had brought the collected papers of Michael Faraday as their *bonnes nouvelles*.

Religious faith in the West demands an acceptance of this contradiction between religion and science, and the maintenance of a will to believe despite the fact that, from a scientific point of view, these beliefs are manifestly absurd.[30] Missionaries, it seemed, were never anxious to communicate the skepticism inherent in their own culture that sorely tried and perhaps invigorated their faith. But for the Fang, as for the members of most pre-scientific communal societies, religion was not a matter of faith but a very pragmatic technique for understanding, predicting, and controlling, in short, a science or pre-science. To believe in something despite evidence to the contrary would be for-

28. *Journal* 1 (1910):125.
29. *Science ye mam me ne engan?*
30. These several points have been made by Melford Spiro, "Religion and the Irrational," in *Symposium on New Approaches to the Study of Religion, Proceedings of the 1964 Annual Spring Meeting of the American Ethnological Society* (Seattle, 1965), pp. 102–115.

eign to their attitudes. They had good evidence for their beliefs. The very failure of their ancestors to sustain them against western incursion was one of the main reasons why, as has often been the case in Africa, the Fang were trying to add Christian religious beliefs to or even substitute them for their former ancestor worship. It is very understandable that, given the vaguest understanding of the instrumental character of western science on the one hand, and the slightest suggestion by the missionaries that Christianity was a "mysterious science" on the other, the Fang should identify religion with science. Thus were the Fang caused to persist in a false empiricism despite the missionaries' monotheistic hostility to their magic and witchcraft.

In suggesting that both missionary and Fang acted on personalistic rather than naturalistic models of the universe, I do not mean to wipe out all distinctions and tensions between them. These are obvious. Nor is it surprising that the missionaries, under pressure to communicate their ideas to the Africans, sought those images which were familiar to their audience and in this respect reinforced the Fang preference for the iconic mode of representation—for concrete imagery rather than abstractions. Such an approach was no novel exercise: the Bible, after all, is a document largely concerned to make its points by parable, metaphor, and other forms of analogy. The analogies taken up by the missionaries ranged from the exceptional in experience to the very mundane. Thus in the *Journal* for 1919 H. Perrier[31] tells us how he used an eclipse of the sun as a parable—the moon of sin hiding the sun of justice and salvation. He had first tried valiantly, using his travel lamp, a man, and boy, to make for his auditors a natural model of the event but interest quickly flagged in such a conceit and he then turned the affair into a parable, which created a great stir in his audience.

The Fang are great hunters in the forest and the image of the *chasse* appears again and again in the missionary record. A newly converted Christian who is yet reluctant to return and spread the news to his brothers is asked what he would think of a hunter who had killed a fine antelope and instead of returning it to his village hid it in the forest to eat a bit of it alone day by

31. *Journal* 1 (1919):135.

day.[32] Trees of various kinds appear to have been important vehicles of missionary thought. The *oveng* (*Guiboutia tessmanni*),
one of the giant trees in the equatorial forest, subject, however, to being strangled by the parasitic *ekekam* (*Ficus hochstet-
eri*), is compared from time to time with Christianity, that ancient institution towering above all other life but always threatened by the suffocating encirclement of evil.[33] The oil palm
(*Elaeis guineensis*) and the hard battle it must wage against birds,
goats, grubs, and ants in order to reach a fruitful maturity is
compared to the life of a Christian who must ceaselessly combat
all kinds of impediments to his spiritual growth.[34]

This last image, developed by Samuel Galley, the lexicogra-
pher of the Fang, is considerably more suggestive than we make
it seem here. Not only was it used at a time when both Fang and
French were struggling to make oil palm cultivation a paying enterprise, Galley's mention of the inhabitation of the palm by certain kinds of birds was bound to suggest to the Fang a witchcraft
spirit (*evus*) often represented as a bird, *à l'oeil féroce,* taking
up residence in the human body.[35] This emphasis upon the use
of apt vernacular metaphor was not Protestant alone, though it
is in the Protestant literature that we get a detailed account of
the verbal strategies employed. Père Trilles, the early Catholic
student of the Fang, frequently prided himself on his grasp of
their figures of speech.[36] Accomplished missionaries of whatever
persuasion congratulated themselves, with good reason, on the
metaphore juste.

Thus in the nature of the missionary encounter with the Fang
we see an effort made to communicate to them according to
their intellectual preferences for concrete example and analogy.
This may have had the effect of increasing their delight in figures

32. *Journal* 2 (1907):448.
33. *Journal* 1 (1924):216.
34. *Journal* 1 (1930):41.
35. Another form that the *evus* takes is that of the palm squirrel: *rat
palmiste*. The goat has about the same connotation to the Fang as to the
European, a lecherous creature not in control of its appetites.
36. See the discussion of his exchanges of tales and riddles with the
Fang in his *Totemism Chez les Fang* (Munster, 1912), Chapter 1, et
passim.

of speech, if that were possible. Clearly, however, this intellectual style with its use of images was merely a means to the larger
end of a much more important image—that of the self. The
other side of the *bonnes nouvelles* was the need to convince the
Fang that they were morally inadequate and in need of just this
"good news" and the salvation it promised for their imperfect
selves.

Perhaps the phrase "need to convince" is not fully accurate.
Much of the missionary literature suggests a belief that the Fang
already possessed this sense of moral inadequacy. Early in the
mission experience we see the Fang described, usually in contrast to the coastal peoples contaminated by long contact with
the European, as a people of moral vigor fully conscious of their
shortcomings and their need for spiritual truth. "Never," says
the missionary Allegret on first arriving at his post, "have I better understood the basic human distress than in discovering
among these cannibal Fang an ardent desire for truth and life
mixed with the lamentable cry as of an abandoned child who
would never again discover his father's house."[37] Fang came forward and were convinced, or convinced the missionaries, that
their entire migration to the West was actually a search for their
Father God whom they had abandoned or who had abandoned
them. Many missionaries remained convinced of the remarkable
moral sensitivity of the Fang. The Fang custom which permits
men to cry when caught in a transgression was also interpreted
as evidence of deep feelings on moral issues.

But not so long after his arrival Allegret had changed his
tune. He found himself mocked by a villager with whom upon
his knees he had prayed in unison, *Je suis un pecheur.* He then
wrote that "the Fang know what is wrong but they are not bothered by it." "I may be mistaken perhaps but it seems that the
sense of sin, of culpability before God is entirely lacking. I
don't expect any real conversion among them despite their amiable dispositions. They think of God only as a powerful chief with
whom it would be desirable to establish a treaty of friendship."[38]
The migration towards the coast, first seen as a search for salva-

37. E. Allegret, *Les Idées Religieuses des Fang,* (Paris, 1904), p. 14.
38. *Journal* 2 (1893):435.

tion, was reexamined and admitted to be a search for goods, for merchandise.[39] It came to be recognized that the Fang are more a religious people than a moral people, and that their religion is more exterior than interior.[40] The missionaries were beginning to see their challenges clearly.

It is unlikely that the Fang were ever morally sensitive in the way that the missionaries expected them to be: afflicted, that is, by a perpetual sense of sinful self. Williamson's recent observations on the Akan seem helpful in relation to the Fang. "The Christian's preoccupation with man's need of salvation from sin by God's redemptive act," Williamson tells us, "evokes no significant response in the Akan." The Akan approach is to see human life in need of vitalizing rather than of changing from a sinful or fallen state. A *summum bonum* was bequeathed by the ancestors, evil and wrongdoing are a retreat from this state, and religion exists to appease the offended forces. Thus there is no concept of spiritual progress, but rather one of piety and obedience to a traditional pattern.[41]

Père Tempels' famous ontological resolution of the struggle between the Christian and the African view of the self is well known.[42] The Bantu view the world dynamically as a turbulent ebb and flow of powerful forces while the European sees it as static and structured. Hence the Bantu self is a vessel containing varying quantities of these powerful forces; the European self is a container with a relatively constant quantity of power whose quality, however, must undergo redemption. The object of religion to the Bantu must be to maximize the self's possession of power; to the European, religion's object is redemption, that is, a qualitative change in the uses of power.

We must be cautious that the materialism newly perceived in the Fang not be entirely ascribed to the African. For this materi-

39. It is the desire for trade goods that Balandier sees as the principal cause of Fang migration in his *Sociologie Actuelle d'Afrique Noire*, rev. ed. (Paris, 1962), p. 159.

40. Charles Cadier makes these distinctions in a letter to the *Journal* 2 (1924):179.

41. S. G. Williamson, *Akan Religion and the Christian Faith* (Accra, 1965), p. 144.

42. P. Tempels, *Bantu Philosophy* (Brussels, 1950).

alism, after all, was energetically promoted by the strongly mer-
cantile orientation of the early colonial enterprise. Moreover, the
increasing tendency on the part of the missionaries to ascribe
materialist and vitalist motives to African religions is suspect
both as a reassertion of the long-standing "fetish" stereotype,
and because it ignores evidence in these religions of a concern
with more "ultimate" things. Nevertheless, there were undenia-
ble differences in image. If missionaries like Allegret and Tempels had to struggle to come to analytic terms with the difference
in images of the world, the Fang in their more concrete terms
had long appreciated it. With respect to the missionary attempt
to turn them into good Christians they replied with a proverb:
Odjip e se zok mwan ("the small antelope [*Neotragus batesii*] is
not the child of the elephant").[43]

Just as the missionaries evolved in their reaction to the Fang,
so the Fang evolved in their reaction to the missionaries. Both
parties underwent profound feelings of disappointment with one
another: the Fang were disappointed in their hopes of obtaining
powerful and material benefits from the new religion; the missionaries were increasingly distressed that the Fang failed to develop that largeness of soul and need for redemption they themselves so valued. As early as 1899 the Fang had begun to refuse
to supply food to the missionaries,[44] who were themselves increasingly impressed with their charges' egotism, their avarice,
their impulsiveness.[45]

43. An intriguing proverb, for the elephant, often used to symbolize
the European, is slow, ponderous, committed, and predictable while the
odjip, the smallest of the antelopes, is quick, nervous, unpredictable, entirely fluid in its relationship to its environment. We should perhaps be
asking in our discussion here: if the Fang were not the child of the elephant, whose child were they? But we are not asking here the question
of the impact of child rearing on religious attitudes, always an area of
importance in the anthropological study of religion. Melford Spiro in his
recent study of *Burmese Supernaturalism* (Englewood Cliffs, N.J., 1967)
points out (p. 114), for example, how the principal teachings of Christianity—the redemptive power of God, the omnipotence of a female deity,
or the eternity of hellfire as a punishment for sin—are entirely inconsistent with the Burmese child's early experience.
    44. *Journal* 1 (1899):499.
    45. *Journal* 2 (1921):285–91.

In the 1920s *Journals* appear reports of widespread witchcraft among the Fang. This increase in witchcraft after contact has been often remarked by Africanists. It is a natural enough result of the pacification when such warlike people as the Fang begin redirecting their aggressive attentions from without to within. It is also a consequence of the fact that missionaries concentrated their early attacks upon what were, to them, the most blatant and unacceptable aspects of Fang religion—the ancestor cults which, as a repository of some of the more profound expressions of Fang religious sensibility, had acted to moderate the preoccupation with supernatural evil. The aggressive individuals within Fang society, who had been restrained by these cults, were thus freed and the Fang experienced a transitional anarchy.[46]

They also experienced a change in their concept of evil, almost an apotheosis of that principle.[47] The missionary and student of Fang demonology, A. Junod, remarks that the *evus*, which was formerly very much tied up with individual personalities, degenerated into "an impersonal power, a maleficent spirit, a demon in the New Testament sense of the word." Formerly easily controlled in the person who possessed it, it has become in recent decades, says Junod, a rampant force in the world threatening to sweep away all stable relations between men.[48] Since the Fang had early regarded the coming of the missionary with high hopes, one can imagine their sense of deception when not only were the expectations of material advantages disappointed

46. The inevitability of social anarchy in the contact between what they call the magical and the monotheistic world views is argued by Murray and Rosalie Way, "Magic and Monotheism," in *Proceedings of the American Ethnological Society* (Seattle, 1964), p. 55. For details on the increase in Fang witchcraft as a consequence of Christian missionizing, see J. W. F. and P. Bekale, "Fang Witchcraft and Christian Acculturation," *Cahiers d'Etudes Africaines* 6 (1961):244–70. This article contains a remarkable manuscript by Bekale on the apotheosis of evil in Fang life.

47. Cf. the Bekale manuscript in which *evus* is assimilated to the devil and almost given, in manichean fashion, his half of the universe.

48. A. Junod in *Journal* (April-May 1960), p. 78–79. In 1959 and 1960 I was present on several occasions at debates, shocking to older Fang, concerned with a national witchcraft conspiracy. It appeared clear that the political party system was being projected into the supernatural as a blueprint for the organization of generalized sorcery.

but there occurred a great increase in evil. Whereas earlier there had been a tendency to assimilate the Europeans, with their manifest material superiority, to the ancestors or to some other kind of supernatural status, there now appeared a tendency to assimilate them to the power of evil, and, in various myths, to ascribe their superiority to trickery and duplicity.[49]

The Fang began to react with an equivalent skepticism as regards Holy Scripture, not so much the scripture itself but the way the missionaries were explaining it. There seems to have been some condescension in their explanations. The Fang interpretations of the scriptural episodes had often amused the missionaries (though the Fang seemed to understand well enough Christ's sacrifice on behalf of mankind out of their own corporate experience of kinship: that of having to pay for the sins of others).[50] The Fang appear to have felt both deprecated and deceived in their Bible lessons. As regards the deprecation, there is considerable justification in arguments to the effect that the luxuriant growth of African independent churches in recent decades is a reaction to just this deprecation of African culture.[51] For that same reason the Old Testament, as the Africans slowly became aware of its content, proved particularly attractive; it was seen as a revindication of their culture whose worth had been brought into question by those evangelizing for the New Testament.

Fang, in short, were led to suspect that the missionaries had not been fully candid. It was not the parable, the allegory, and the indirect statement that troubled them; they were accustomed to these uses of language. It was rather that this document, the Bible, upon which all of western civilization was based was not yielding up its enormous secrets to them. For this reason the outpouring of occult literature from France had a flourishing market in Gabon, for it often offered keys to the interpretation of scripture or prayers and meditations said to have been lost

49. See Veronika Görög, "L'origine de l'inegality des races. Etude de trente sept contes africains," *Cahiers d'Etudes Africaines* 8 (1968):290–309. I have examined these Whiteman-Blackman legends in Mazrui and Rotberg, eds., *Protest and Power in Black Africa*.

50. Grebert, *Au Gabon*, p. 204.

51. David Barrett, "Reaction to Mission" (Ph.D. Diss., Columbia, 1965).

Bible chapters. And it is not surprising that one of the first works of Gabonese occult "literature," written by the Eshira "Prince" Birinda, was titled *La Bible Secrete des Noirs*.[52]

The Stages of Reaction

Missionary reactions to the Fang appear to have passed through five stages of spiritual colonization and decolonization,[53] perhaps equally appropriate for Protestant and Catholic:

1880–1920. The period of the manifest destiny of the civilizing mission. African fetishism and magic must be eradicated and Africans will no doubt welcome the *bonnes nouvelles*.

1920–1945. The period in which it is recognized that African "fetishism" runs deeper than previously suspected, and in which African materialism is fully perceived.

1945–1960. The period in which animism gradually becomes accepted as an authentic religion by the missions and in which many aspects of African religious cultures are recognized as worthy of incorporation into Christianity.

1960–1965. The period when a dialogue is begun with animism, in order to achieve as deep a penetration of Christianity into African culture as possible. African forms are incorporated into architecture, catechism, and liturgy.

1965–   . The period when the African view in the dialogue asserts itself as the two images of the world become confounded and their contradictions become evident. The ideal of celibacy confronts the ideal of procreation, eschatology confronts pragmatism, contractual worship confronts piety.

Surely this paradigm demonstrates a significant intellectual reaction on the part of missionaries to African religious culture.

52. Prince Birinda de Boudeguy, *La Bible Secrete des Noirs selon le Bouity* (Paris, 1952).

53. This scheme owes a good deal to L. V. Thomas and the last three stages are virtually his. See "l'Eglise Chretienne d'Afrique Noire," *Tam-Tam. Revue des etudiants catholiques africaines*, nos. 7–8 (Dec. 1963), pp. 7–21 (Dakar). David Goldenberg brought this article to my attention.

What about Fang reactions? I believe the reaction of the majority of Fang, some 75–80 percent of whom are nominally Christian, has been a compartmentalization, with a dominant or at least public commitment to Christian culture on the one hand and a recessive, often hidden, commitment to animism on the other. The evolution of Fang reactions would look something like this:

1880–1910. Period of conflict with administrative culture but of hospitable acceptance, even enthusiasm for the *bonnes nouvelles* as the secret to western power. Beginning of a tendency to identify the European in some way with the supernatural and to express dependence on him.

1910–1930. Period of acceptance of administrative control. Beginning of disillusionment with missionary culture and the "word" but continued cultivation of Christianity as politic and progressive. Period of considerable confusion and oscillation back and forth between the cultures in contact.

1930–1955. The high mystical expectations of the first period are now completely dissipated. Beginning of close scrutiny of the "word" and of missionary and administrative culture. Strong attraction towards the Old Testament as revindication of African culture. Administrative culture makes a strong impact, accompanied by a pervasive sense of cultural inferiority. Appearance among the majority of the Fang of a stable dualism or compartmentalization. Acceptance of Christianity for politic or progressive reasons along with adherence to the essentials of the old religious world view. Three minority developments: a small group of Fang (10 percent) entirely assimilated to Christianity; another group (25 percent) maintain the indigenous religion against all pressures, and a third group (10 percent) develop independent movements attempting in one way or another to syncretize or combine the two world views.

1955–1965. Indigenous religious beliefs, formerly the hidden half of the dualism, now made manifest. New confidence in African culture leads to pressures towards indigenization in religion and independence in politics and administration. The majority of Christians move towards the introduction of more African elements. Self-confident embarcation upon the creation of a national culture in the image of the Fang.

What we see in overall terms is an increasing understanding of mission and administrative culture and a decreasing value put on the missionary message. As far as Fang culture is concerned, not long after contact we find an emotional devaluation of it setting in and possibly, though I have no evidence for this, a decrease in the complexity of Fang cognitions of their own culture. I say this on the assumption that it is hardly worth wasting intellectual effort on that which is not emotionally valued.[54] There was a decrease within that culture of a philosophic concern with "ultimate things." This culture lingered on, however, as it could hardly fail to do, and, as the Fang came to terms with European culture, the claims of their own culture reasserted themselves and were emotionally reevaluated. New, more complex cognitions of this culture appeared in studies of folklore and in the independent cults.

This statement could hardly summarize all the complexities involved in "coming to terms" with European culture. It should be remembered that at least three cultures were interacting—the secular culture of administration, commerce, and technology, Christian culture, and the Fang animist culture. In the two-sided meeting of the two religions, four possible reactions have been noted—Christian, Christian-Pagan dualist, Nativist, and Independent Syncretist. If we add the third area of secular culture, additional combinations and permutations are possible as intellectual reactions. Even in the villages it is possible to find Fang like my landlord for a year and one-half in northern Gabon. He had turned highly skeptical about both animism and Christianity

54. There is probably a psychological principle involved here: that which is highly valued emotionally will be the object of more information search and organization. And there is an anthropological proposition involved, that of cultural focus: where a culture's interests lie, its value commitments in other words, there will be found the greatest cognitive complexity. M. J. Herskovits, the proponent of this proposition, has used African religion as an illustration of its operation. Herskovits, *Man and His Works* (New York, 1948), p. 548.

and was directing himself, acquisitively and instrumentally, towards the secular culture.

Even with this caution there yet remain many subleties in the Fang intellectual reactions which we have not made clear. I should like to turn to one example of these.

A New Representation: Bwiti

For the majority of Fang the intellectual reaction to the claims of Christian culture on the one hand and animism on the other was compartmentalization of these two belief systems and the respective world views they implied. Many other kinds of responses were possible, of course, and in the reformative cult of Bwiti we see combining and syncretizing processes which break down this compartmentalization. This cult, in existence since before the First World War, provides a wealth of data on intellectual reactions because its leadership at least is unusually self-conscious about its own thinking and about the structure of the cult.[55] They are much more given to symbolic representations than their animist predecessors, although, of course, the cult is also rich in enactive and iconic representations. And they organize the diverse materials presented to them out of tradition and from western culture in a variety of complexes. Elements may be grouped by contiguity, or chained together under a diversity of controlling concepts, or organized hierarchically under one. I would like to examine here just one feature of their intellectual reaction and another kind of dualism: institutionalized dualism.

The members of Bwiti (*asumege ening* branch) lay out their cult house in a very explicit manner with male and female sides, with a birth side and death side, with a life half and a death half, and with the sea beyond the altar (Fig. 1).[56] Ritual proceeds

55. Good examples of this self-conscious intellectuality are seen in my "Symbolic Consensus in a Fang Reformative Cult," *American Anthropologist* 65 (1965):902–8, and "Unbelievably Subtle Words: Representation and Integration in the Sermons of an African Reformative Cult."

56. Some cult leaders build the cult house with the altar facing west towards the actual ocean. In such cases the cult house is a microcosmic representation of the Fang migrating experience from northeast to southwest through the savannah to the sea.

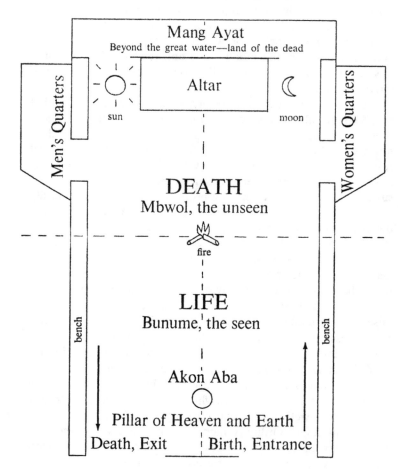

Fig. 1. Layout of Bwiti cult house.

through all quadrants of the cult house from front to rear and return, from female to male and return, etc. In so doing, it picks up the various connotations of these quadrants and creates a whole experience. But the basic axis of the entire intellectual structure of the chapel, upon which it is laid out, is that of right and left hand, sun and moon, male and female sides. And it is this set of oppositions I should like to examine as an example of intellectual reaction.

We can say of almost any society, even the simplest ones, that a "potential cultural reservoir of many possible values" is theoretically within the reach of every person.[57] Moreover there does not need to be consistency among the values within this cultural reservoir, and, in fact, in acts of valuation the individual is required to "compromise between several not necessarily commensurable values," so that ensuing problems in conduct are hardly avoidable.[58] Men may well strain towards consistency in their behavior, as is often argued in the social sciences, but they may still find incompatible and even contradictory values lying behind their day-by-day behavior. This variability may actually be necessary and the effective functioning of a society may depend upon the compromising of any given set of value derived rules. Life is perhaps best described as an unending series of compromises in a complex environment of contingencies which exert cross pressures and elicit contradictory responses.[59] Yet even if the behavioral situation be one of living through a series of minimax situations, men possess and seek to maintain a model—an image of themselves and their universe—in which there is some consistency. It is only the poet who proclaims: "Do I contradict myself?/Very well then I contradict myself,/(I am large, I contain multitudes.)" Ordinary men, it seems, as soon as they become aware of incompatibilities devise plans for dealing with them. One such plan is the institutionalization of dualism.

In traditional Fang culture, by the evidence I have and through a process we may call value distribution, complementar-

57. Otto von Mering, *A Grammar of Values* (Pittsburgh, 1962), p. 71.
58. von Mering, *A Grammar of Values*, p. 89.
59. D. T. Campbell, "Universal Values from Requisites of Social Systems" (unpub. MS).

ity was achieved between inconsistent even contradictory values. This was accomplished by systematic structural distribution of these values (or the behavior they prescribed) in time and place so that they did not conflict and hence had this complimentary manifestation. The fundamental question is not so much the fundamental values of a given culture but how these values are structurally distributed.

Since there is a clear opposition in Bwiti between the male and female—*mfa nga, mfa nom*—parts of the chapel, we may ask ourselves how maleness and femaleness, or the acting according to male and female characteristics, was distributed. Very likely it is universally the case that these are incompatible and contrasting values. On first glance the question of the distribution of these values hardly seems to arise. Is it not obvious that qualities of maleness are to be valued by the male sex, femaleness by the female sex? Yet anthropologists have enough data of semi-castration, of the *berdache* and "make man" ceremonies, and of blending in sex roles to make clear that the distribution of these values in nonconflictive fashion is by no means guaranteed. In the well-organized society, with an integrated culture, child training must act to distribute these values appropriately.[60] Complementarity of the sexes must be provided for, though this does not necessarily mean that the biological male will always follow the values of maleness or the female of femaleness. This distribution is not confined simply to sex roles, nor maleness and femaleness expressed solely in these roles. Among the Fang, these values are extended elsewhere into the social structure in an elementary but interesting way. What I am referring to may be called a kind of complementary filiation, that is, a distributing of maleness and femaleness in the social structure.

This works in the following way. Beyond the immediate nuclear family, for which there is no name, and within the widely

60. This statement is a bit too bald. I have, by reference to African folklore, tried to make a more detailed attempt to assess the responsibility facing all cultures to distribute in an appropriate way male and female influences on the growing child. See my "Filial Piety and Power: Psychosocial Dynamics in the Legends of Shaka and Sundiata," *Science and Psychoanalysis* 14 (1969): 47–60.

dispersed patrilineal group of kinsmen, the Fang clan (*ayong*), we find four grouping levels: the local extended family, *ndebot,* or house of people; the medial lineage, *mvogabot,* or village of people; the maximal lineages, *ayonabot* and *etungabot,* often referred to collectively as *abialebot,* "people of a common birth." The interesting fact is that by custom the Fang, though staunchly patrilineal, trace themselves alternatively to a female and a male ancestor as one rises from one grouping level to another within the clan. The *ndebot* is traced to a woman, the *mvogabot* to a man, any of the grouping levels subsumed under the category *abialebot* to a woman, and finally the clan itself to a man, its founder. It is well understood that in unilinear descent groups segmentation is often conceptualized on the basis of uterine and nonuterine sibling relationships in the nuclear polygynous family. In a polygynous family, in short, a single patrisegment can be divided into several matrisegments of a lower order if one chooses to focus on the respective female founders, the several wives of the male single founder. As the social structure is considered in increasingly wider perspective then, the succeeding levels of grouping are seen as alternatively enjoying the sanction of either common maternity or common paternity.

The interesting fact for our purposes is that the associated qualities or connotations of maleness or femaleness are characteristic of these various grouping levels according to their origin from a maternal or a paternal source. The *ndebot* is stable, placing emphasis upon the cooperation and mutuality of its members; the *mvogabot* is characterized by competitiveness and divisiveness in its constituent parts. One of the principal connotations of maleness, derived from the activities associated with it, is divisiveness and the competitive struggle for limited goods. In contrast, the principal connotations of femaleness are stability, unity, common purpose, and cooperativeness in the exploitation of the environment. Most of the women's day, for example, is devoted to cooperative agricultural activities while the men's principal activity, beside solitary hunting, is debate in the men's palabra house over such matters as bride-price and marriage arrangements.

It might be argued in a cultural-historical vein that what we see in this manipulation of maternal and paternal relationships is an unresolved bilateralism. Much more interesting to us here is this distribution of maleness and femaleness in the social structure so as to achieve a sense of complementarity. Conflictive contrast is avoided, for the culture carrier knows to what valued qualities to appeal by virtue of the context in which he is acting, the level of grouping that characterizes the specific social relationship of the moment. Is he interacting with someone of his same *ndebot,* or his same *mvogabot*? Or is it his same clan? The essential oppositions between maleness and femaleness are not perceived or contrasted directly in and of themselves but rather as complementary principles operating within a system, a larger unitary scheme of things.

The study of values has acquainted anthropologists with the fact that very often positive values constitute an interdependent set inextricably linked with others. When informants reason about what is good in life we frequently note a circularity. So other values come to be attached to the structural distribution I have just discussed. Fission and fusion, *angomela* and *angunge* (better translated as "dispersion" and "reunion") find themselves included with maleness and femaleness in this structural distribution. The house of people by reason of its femaleness exhibits knitting together; the *mvogabot* exhibits dispersion; and so on up the levels of grouping. The dominant value here may well be fusion or knitting together for thus is the lineage strengthened. Nevertheless, we cannot ignore (as the Fang do not ignore) that in certain circumstances and at certain levels fission is appropriate and is valued. The dispersion of antagonism at the *mvogabot* level, for example, avoids more serious conflict.

One final example to make the point of complementary distribution of incompatible values is the value set activity/tranquility —*elulua* and *mvwa'a*. Here too we find the interdependence of values, for maleness is characterized by activity, which leads to dispersion, and femaleness is characterized by tranquility, which leads to knitting together. Now activity is valued because it heats up the blood and illuminates the affairs of the kingroup which might otherwise fall into disrepute or be deprecated in the eyes of others. But tranquility is equally to be valued because too much activity leads to *ebiran* ("social disorder"). These values must be distributed, and this distribution is accomplished in the yearly cycle of ceremony and ritual, and in daily life as well, which has its appropriate fluctuation of activity and tranquility.

As we have learned to expect from the value studies of many nonliterate people such as the Fang, the moral code derived from the value system has a situational orientation. Judgments of behavior by the Fang rest not upon categorical but upon hypothetical imperatives. If one can, indeed, abstract any such thing as a moral code, the question is not (as Malinowski reminded us) how behavior conforms to the code but how the code is made to fit given situations. The consequences and context of behavior are important considerations in the judgment of that behavior. The value set activity/tranquility is very relevant to such judgment, and actions being judged are often referred to the active or passive quality of the situation in which action occurred. In times of activity, for example, such actions as adultery within lineage ranks or the appropriation without full consultation of disputed or communally held property could either be condemned because the act produced *ebiran* ("social disorder"), or excused as an act consonant with the heightened feeling of the time. While it is difficult to predict the exact way the situational context will be employed in judgment, it is important to note that the activity or tranquility of the situation is an important feature of the context to which judgment refers.

In fact, the moral excellence of the mature man, *nyamoro*, in part at least, lies in his recognition of the appropriate action for the appropriate situation. It is not too broad an interpretation of Fang thinking to say that his excellence lies in his ability to hold contradictory values in complementary opposition, distributing these values accordingly. He knows when to be active and when to be tranquil. This capacity has a physiologic counterpart. For the mature man most successfully combines the incompatibilities of the biological heritage of female blood, *meki,* and male seminal fluid, *meyom,* wilful determination and thoughtful direction. Youth tends to be too wilful and active, age too tranquil and thoughtful.

Fang culture, we see then, in its more traditional form achieved some freedom from contradiction by means of systematic complementarity. In one context it was appropriate that one follow female values and be tranquil, in another, male values and be active. In ritual relationships with the ancestors, it was the value of paternity that was foremost; in strife with other lineages, it was the principle of fraternity. Thus was the wholly satisfying fabric of social life woven together. The consequences of acculturation, however, were the redistribution of values and the creation of "cultural dilemmas," as inconsistent values were brought together in the same time and place making for situations of difficult choice.

It is possible to illustrate the way in which contrastive values once arranged so as to be complementary came to be perceived as conflictive in respect to any of the value sets we have discussed. This is manifested in generational conflicts, where the Fang feel themselves faced with a stark choice between fraternity and paternity. It is seen in increasing domestic squabbles, where the choice is polarized between maleness or femaleness in the household. In respect to the values of activity/tranquility, we see the consequences of redistribution particularly clearly. Here the introduction of cash crops and *corvée* and migrant labor have greatly redistributed old patterns. Older informants complain that "we no longer have tranquility in village life—always activity—and the result is *ebiran*, 'social disorder.' "

Whereas colonization imposed a political system much more complex than the original, with redistributive consequences in respect to the clan system, colonization offered a social structure much less complex than the traditional and thereby precipitated out of complementary suspension the value sets dispersion/knitting together, maleness/femaleness. The result in both cases was considerable confusion as to the nature and obligations of kin and clan behavior as values were redistributed and brought into contrast.

My own field work yields no good evidence that any of these value sets were perceived in traditional Fang culture as significant contraries.[61] For most purposes in traditional life these

61. My data may seem to disagree with that of early students of the Fang. Tessman (*Die Pangwe*, 2 vols. [Berlin, 1913], 2:Chapter 11) dis-

value sets acted more as allovalues, values that function in the same way in different contexts having the same kinds of structural use for purposes of rationalizing, judging, and controlling action. Their contrastive nature is not painfully apparent. So maleness and femaleness, fraternity and paternity can all be employed as structure-supporting values. Where conflicts were brought up for public debate in the palabra house, one or another of the complementary values might be appealed to, depending on the situation, in order to preserve the integrity of the area of the social structure in question. One situation, a dispute between nonuterine brothers for example, demanded that fraternal values by emphasized. In another situation, a generational struggle for example, the values of paternity were emphasized. The same variable appeal depending upon situation is characteristic of activity/tranquility. One or another of these values would be emphasized depending upon whether a given conflict was provoked by boredom or overexcitement. One might say, therefore, that maleness and femaleness were allovalues functioning in complementary fashion with respect to the preservation of domestic family structure, paternity and fraternity with respect to lineage structure, and activity/tranquility with respect to village structure.

---

cusses the even-handed representation of good and evil as a fundamental dualism in Fang religion while Trilles (*Totemism Chez les Fang* [Munster, 1912], pp. 388–89) sees as basic a dualism in the devotion to the totemic cult on the one hand and the ancestral cult on the other. Tessmann thus sees the Fang caught up in the strain of contrasting allegiance to the equally real principles of good and evil. Trilles sees the dilemma as contrasting allegiance to the principles of the spirit world on the one hand, the natural world on the other. In southern Gabon a male-female dualism seems to have been more pervasive in the traditional cults. We have a clear report of this from the mid-nineteenth century (Fleuriot de Langle, *Croisières au large du Gabon* [Paris, 1876], p. 270). The cultures of southern Gabon have had strong influence on Bwiti and quite probably on the institutionalized dualism we discuss here.

In the area of aesthetics, analysis does indeed reveal some working principles of opposition in Fang culture (see my "Principles of Opposition and Vitality in Fang Aesthetics") and some articulations of this, although the ethnologist must interpolate a good deal. But in any case the contraries were not felt as contradictions but as intentional difference.

In the cult of Bwiti, cult leaders explain ritual and ceremony to their followers in terms of opposing modes of conduct or opposing qualities or objects; a dichotomization or institutionalized dualism is produced with roughly the following set of contrasting qualities:

right hand	left hand
male	female
white	red
death	life
northeast	southwest
hot	cold
day	night
sky	earth
bone	flesh
sperm	blood
speech	silence
activity	tranquility
dispersion	knitting together
paternity	fraternity

I take it that this careful attention to matters of value distribution arises out of the dilemmas of acculturation, which has acted to redistribute values in confusing and conflicting ways. Among its other purposes, I think we can understand this cult as an attempt to reestablish some complementarity in values. Ritual becomes here in cult use an instrument for the harmonious redistribution of values: it maintains or recreates complementarity as maleness and femaleness, activity and tranquility, dispersion and knitting together are assigned their appropriate space and their appropriate period of manifestation in the night-long development of the ritual drama. At the same time this new dualistic complementarity has been produced out of an awareness of contrast in values much stronger than was formerly present in Fang culture. We see a move, thanks to the impetus found in cultural dilemmas, away from implicit value distribution. As is generally characteristic of such movements, we see on the part of cult leaders in this reformative cult a "quite conscious attempt to

recreate a satisfying culture."[62] I argue here that this consciousness is expressed with respect to a perceived contrast in values
and that this recreation is accomplished through the complementary redistribution of these values. This new cult is manipulating
many of the same elements characteristic of the older Fang culture but, due to the challenges of cultural dilemmas, it is doing
so on the whole much more consciously. At the same time, it seems
true that the old complementary scheme practiced by the Fang,
though not consciously manipulated, if systematically described
would turn out to be more complicated in its development than
the relatively simple dualism of the Bwiti cult. The consequences
of both solutions to the problem of value contrarieties is an integrity of system. But institutionalized dualism is the most elementary form of value distribution and, very likely, the simplest
solution to the problem of finding consistency in the face of the
value dilemmas of acculturation.

Some Analytic Representations

I would like to present here a set of analytic presentations of
changes in Fang representations of their experience. It is of interest that the Bwiti cult, in platitude at least, tries to make a
pan-tribal appeal. This is in sharp distinction from traditional
ceremonial, which was held in village or lineage exclusiveness.
This reminds us of significant shifts in Fang cognition of human relationships. We may point this up by examining the shifts
of hierarchical categorization within the domain of Fang experience of people (*mot, bot*), In Fig. 1.2 we indicate the categories that prevailed at the time of contact. We note that gorilla
and chimpanzee are included as types of men and that the two
categories of foreigners (*bilobolobo*), or those who speak gibberish, are blackmen and redmen. These categories, incidentally,
are taken largely from the Pahouin classic, *Dulu Bon be Afri
Kara* (*The Journey of the Children of Afri Kara*) written by the

62. A. F. C. Wallace, "Revitalization Movements," *American Anthropologist* 58 (1957):261–81.

Ntumu Ondoua Enguta in 1953 and published by the Presbyterian Mission Press in Ebolowa, Cameroun.

In Stage 2, which is the situation in the 1920s, the Fang have now split off the gorilla and the chimpanzee from the domain. They have made the pygmee a major category collateral, but not subsidiary to man and on the verge of being separated from the domain. Both the sub-categories of Fang and *bilobolobo* are more completely sub-divided. The whiteman appears in the domain replacing *mvele me bot,* the redmen.

The third stage of reaction, circa 1955, in the categorization of the domain (Fig. 1.4) shows us a more complex subdivision of the European category corresponding to Fang experience, with the three main European types, government administrator, missionary, and merchant. The difference, for example, between the Frenchman as missionary and the Frenchman as merchant or administrator is now well appreciated. It shows us a more complex categorization of the varieties of non-Fang Africans.

This particular analytic presentation—categories within domains—shows us a situation of increasing complexity of categories among the Fang. It contrasts, therefore, with our previous discussion in which we found the Fang moving from the complexities of multileveled complementary distribution to the relative simplicity of an institutionalized dualism. We may note here that in Bwiti a rather different categorization of the domain of people prevails than those more general ones we have presented. This categorization (Fig. 1.5) rests more directly on a physiological philosophy. Like the Bwiti chapel itself it is an intellectual reaction. But unlike our layout of the chapel, we present here an analytic abstraction based upon but not directly laid out in the following set of observations by members of this cult.

"Man is made of seen and unseen parts." "The seen is his body and the unseen is his spirit." "Men may also possess witchcraft (*evus*) which is both of the seen and the unseen." "The body is composed or combined of blood and sperm." "It has its share of the capacity over the unseen (*ki*) that comes down through the lineage from the creator gods." "The *evus* is combined of both the sperm for it dwells in the white portions of the

Fig. 2. Stage 1, to 1900.

Eyem Domestic Animals

MOT-BOT PEOPLE							
Ngi Gorilla	Waa Chimp	Bukwé Pygmee	Bon be Afri Kara Children of Afri Kara				Bilobolobo Strangers	
			Bulu	Fang	Ntum	Okak	Mvé	Bwele ni Bot Redmen	Nwt Mot Blackmen

Tsit Wild Animals	
ngi	waa

Fig. 3. Stage 2, to 1925.

Eyem Domestic Animals

MOT PEOPLE								
Bukwé Pygmee	Bon be Afri Kara Children of Afri Kara					Bilobolobo Speakers of Gibberish		
						Nsut Mot Blackmen	Niangan Whitemen	
	Bule	Ewondo	Ntum	Okak	Fang			
		Mvé		Betsi	Meké	Bekwel	Engon	Kofini	Fala

Tsit Wild Animals	
ngi	waa

Fig. 4. Stage 3, to 1955.

Bukwé Pygmee	MOT PEOPLE																								
	Bon be Afri Kara Children of Afri Kara										Nsut Mot Blackmen								Minie Missionary			Niangan Whiteman Government			Okira Strangers		
	Bulu	Ewondo	Mve	Ntum	Oka	Fang	Betsi	Meke	Osyeba	Meyong me Je Other Clans	Engom	Mfon	Bujeba	Sogo	Bekwel	Bubi	Kombe	Pongo	Fala	Puna	Merika	Fala	Pana	Kofini	Fala	Pana	Kofini

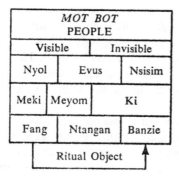

Fig. 5. Bwiti hierarchy, 1960.

body, and of *ki* for it gives capacity." "Of men we can say that they are more under the influence of one part of the body or another." "The whitemen are willfull and have capacity of the unseen." "There is much of the *evus* in him." "The members of Bwiti are of the spirit." And I may add to these notes the fact that it is the main object of Bwiti ritual to convert other Fang from their bloody and miserable lives to a higher spiritual status.

Conclusions: Being Better Represented

An almost inescapable reaction in Fang villagers as they have undergone acculturation is a greater self-consciousness, a greater awareness of their pattens of behavior. This consequence of acculturation is probably inescapable. Acculturation *means* a widening of the scale of relationships and hence a diversifying of the kinds of information available. Particularly in a situation of domination and subordination after colonial conquest do the ways of life of a dominant culture make the members of a subordinate culture such as the Fang self-conscious about their own way of life. They become anxious to explain it to themselves. This anxiety takes several forms. Various kinds of mythologies and legends appear, which explain the differences between, in our case, whiteman and blackman.[63] On the other hand, the Bwiti cult tried quite consciously to syncretize and harmonize the cultures in contact, to find a satisfactory explanatory network, in

63. See also on these legends the basic source: Henri Trilles. *Proverbes Legends et Contes Fang* (Neuchatel, 1905).

other words, for the anomalies produced by that contact. Other reactions included self-isolation so as to suppress the claims of the acculturated consciousness; but, in general, increasing self-consciousness is the lot of the acculturated. This must be labeled as an intellectual reaction, for at least in western tradition knowledge of self has been one of the hallmarks of the intellectual posture.

But the Fang experience was not simply a growing consciousness of patterns in their culture which were already there. In some areas new models were proffered and took their place beside, or were substituted for the old. Administrative control brought new models of the milieu, and of social interaction as structured rather than situational and familial. Missionaries brought an image of the supernatural as less populous and evil, and of the self as more stubbornly disabled.

It would be a mistake to think that these new models were always more complex than the old ones. In family structure and in cosmology, the new monotheism and nuclear familism were manifestly less complex than the old systems, however sparsely elaborated they may have been. In the Bwiti cult an intellectual structure took shape which lacks, in some respects, the subtlety of the former mode of thought, even though it is more fully articulated.

When one says this a specter in the social sciences rises up. For in saying that a consciously articulated structure in Bwiti is less subtle or less complex than the more traditional structure I am comparing a folk model with an analytic model—a systematization made by the culture carriers themselves, in the case of Bwiti, with a systematization made by the analyst, namely myself, of Fang traditional culture. As far as I know or was able to find out, no very elaborate systematization was on anybody's lips in the traditional society, even though a structure reveals itself to analysis of that more traditional culture. Systematization was buried in action and image. Those who feel that the social sciences are engaged in perpetual solipsism might ask: is this true? Does that abstract symbolic structure exist in any way relative to the informants' behavior and feelings? And customarily social scientists, anthropologists at least, have fought this out in relation to language analysis. Who but a language sophisticate appreciates the structure underlying his talk, and the importance of the phoneme in what he communicates? Significant structures do exist then and are commonly "understood" at some level: how else to account for language communication? But the problem still remains of getting at that structure which is "understood," if it is not articulated by those who "understand" it. Many contrary currents flow and false winds blow between that "understanding" and our analytic exposition of it. We may be compelled to accept the psychological reality of phonemes. We are more skeptical of the cultural structures exposed to us by Claude Levi-Strauss[64] or Marcel Griaule.[65] The point for us here is that acculturation with the West, with its penchant for symbolic representations and various kinds of abstract structures, can act to resolve the dilemma, in part at least, by encouraging an intellectual reaction in the members of these other cultures likely to produce, as in Bwiti, new structures out of their own self-awareness and cultural awareness.

At the same time I have pointed up how contact with missionaries and administrators not only subjected the Fang to contrary intellectual pressures but also confirmed the Fang villagers in a jurisprudence anchored in concrete experience, or in a pre-scientific supernatural empiricism. A transitional effect of evangelization was a net increase in objective evil, a development which continued to promote pre-scientific thought. In the very act of communication with the Africans missionaries prided themselves on their mastery of enactive and iconic representation and thereby reinforced this preference in the Fang. Since the Bible is also an instrument of indirection, however inspired it may be, one has cause to regret that the *bonnes nouvelles* were not in

64. As, for example, in the mythological structures detailed in Levi-Strauss, *Le Cru et la Cuite* (Paris, 1964).

65. As, for example, in the structures of Ogotemmeli's Mind (M. Griaule, *Dieu de l'Eau* [Paris, 1938]). The question here is the degree to which Griaule's own structures were reflected by Ogotemmeli, a remarkable man by any standard, in their long *entretien*.

equal part the works of that nineteenth-century untutored natural philosopher, Michael Faraday, whose smelling of truth might have more directly confronted the Fang with modern styles of thought.

Though Fang villagers perceived the European in many subtle ways—witness the many telling nicknames the Fang assigned to him[66]—they did not really ever perceive him as he was when he was discovering and creating those marvels of his material life. His organizationalism the Fang villagers perceived, but not his positivism and spirit of inquiry. By virtue of the marvels of his way of life, the European was early assimilated to the Fang supernatural. Though a general disillusion and even embitterment crept into the attitudes towards the European and the beliefs surrounding him, yet something of this aura of his supernaturalism persisted and was even still present during my fieldwork.[67] In the cult of Bwiti the European was often said to be a *revenant,* a blackman who had died and paid for his sins, learned the secret of the unseen, and returned purified and whitened.

We must still confront the distinction between concrete and abstract thinking. The distinction is too simple (or should the word be abstract?) as it stands, for there are such a variety of ways of thinking abstractly. And there is no simple movement from concrete to abstract. The proverb is a good example: here is a bit of domestic experience which contains a nugget of intelligence of wide applicability; it is not analytic, but it is an abstraction. Just as acculturation has not always added complexity to Fang culture, so we find areas in which the Fang were brought to a less abstract view of experience. A good example of this is their treatment of other tribes. In their more traditional culture, they had tended to treat all foreign tribes generically as *bilobo-*

66. A rather rotund missionary of a sedate and fastidious manner was known as the "elephant with clean feet" (*Nzok mebo mfuban*).

67. I have not had an opportunity to examine further in this paper the reactions in the Bwiti cult to the Christian doctrine of sin. This is worth a study in itself for one can see therein the doctrine of sin being assimilated to the traditional Fang notions of "bad body" (*nyol abe*), a ritual notion of uncleanliness.

lobo ("those who sputter gibberish"). But as colonial tranquility was imposed upon them, they began to intereact with and make many distinctions between these peoples, and many new names for these others came into their vocabulary, a shift towards concrete thinking. On the other hand the Fang traditionally possessed a quite complex categorization of their lineage structure into many levels. Recently there has been a tendency to abandon that conceptual structure and substitute for it the generic term *la famille*. Here generification simplified aboriginal complexities.

But it is only with caution that one can say that formerly the Fang were more committed to the details of their experience. If they seemed more committed to providing a sense of continuity or unity for these experiences and were less likely to view them outside the context in which they occurred, this was a contrast to the compartmentalization and institutionalized dualism they have often adopted when confronting modernization. Perhaps the best summary of their intellectual reactions is to say that in former days Fang communications tended towards that high semantic load characteristic of parables and proverbs; they tended to be low in the formal emphasis characteristic of the symbolic and abstracting style of mind. Modernization has tended to reverse that emphasis, but still in many ways the civilizing mission has contributed not only to a reinvigoration of a basically expressive and projective relation to reality but has contributed as well to enactive and iconic modes of representation.

I have discussed Horton's view that a major element in the change from nonliterate to western societies is a change from the personal or social model to the natural model. To connect Hortons arguments and the one made here, there is perhaps something in the personal model that inclines one toward concrete thinking, just as something in the natural model inclines one toward abstract thinking. That would be the case if we were able to accept Horton's distinctions in entirety. Unfortunately, not only is it doubtful that social life is really more predictable than nature for members of nonliterate societies (as opposed to the social anthropologist), but plenty of evidence in the institution of totemism suggests that nature stands as a model behind the social understanding of many peoples. Nature and its denizens, as Levi-Strauss puts it, are "good to think" rather than simply "good to eat."[68] Social classifications in this view take off from natural classifications rather than the reverse. And, in fact, it is just here that pressures were put upon Fang to shift their attention away from their natural emotional and intellectual involvement with the equatorial forest to the organizational exigencies, democratic trammels, and language anxieties of French colonial society—a society whose cultural center of gravity was in another country.

68. Claude Levi-Strauss, *Totemism* (Boston, 1963). This book explores at length the way that a natural model is used for social life in totemism.

THE WEST IN
CONGOLESE EXPERIENCE

Wyatt MacGaffey

Although the BaKongo and the Fang are both Bantu-speaking peoples sharing many profound cultural similarities and living only about six hundred miles apart, their historical experience has been very different. Where the Fang lived in the tropical forest, the BaKongo lived in the grasslands south of the equatorial belt. Where the Fang migrated to their present home during the nineteenth century, the BaKongo have lived in approximately the same region for at least 500 years and probably much longer. Where the Fang had no political units larger than the village, the Kingdom of Kongo goes back at least to the fourteenth century. This in turn implies a history of intercommunication among the BaKongo and between the BaKongo and others over a very long period—articulated at first through the traditional capital town of São Salvador, more recently through BaKongo communities in modern cities like Matadi and Kinshasa in Zaïre or Luanda in Angola.

This paper and the preceding one form a linked pair, like several articles that follow. They are not intended as a pair of comparable cases subject to the analytical rigor of comparative studies, but they serve to illustrate some of the similarity-in-diversity that can occur in the response of ordinary people, subject to foreign rule by men of an alien culture.

Wyatt MacGaffey has written *Custom and Government in the Lower Congo* (Los Angeles, 1970).

P.D.C.

Occidental folk recognize a category called "the West," which is defined by more general occidental concepts of space and time. Geographically, the West means western Europe and other parts of the world to which western Europeans have extended their culture by the historical process of migration and colonization. Occidentals evaluate their culture by reference to time; they refer to it as "modern," and compare it substantively with other cultures in terms of evolutionary progress. Western culture is deemed to be further advanced than others in especially two respects: having mastered scientific method, Europeans have developed industry and technology to unprecedented levels; having been endowed with the ethical insights of the Judaeo-Christian tradition, they have grasped more clearly than others the essential conditions of personal and social well-being, and to a greater extent than others they have been able to guarantee these conditions by means of the creation of democratic institutions. Congolese have entirely different concepts of space and time and see the components of "the West" in such radically different terms that "the West" to which they react is a complex entirely foreign to occidental thought.

The Congolese to whom I refer are the BaKongo, numbering some three million people and located on either side of the Congo River between Stanley Pool and the Atlantic. Because their territory, which they call Kongo, links the interior of Central Africa, the Congo basin, with the sea, the BaKongo have been longer and more closely in contact with Europeans and subject to European institutions than most Central Africans. Missionary and commercial activity in the coastal regions began at the end of the fifteenth century and continued sporadically until the European occupation of the interior in the late nineteenth century. During the colonial period the effect of European educational and economic institutions was probably more intense in the Lower Congo than anywhere in the interior. At present, nearly all BaKongo are professed Christians, and most men are literate to some extent in French and KiKongo.

In discussing Kongo intellectual reactions to the West we are spared the temptation to restrict the term "intellectual" to products of a minority conventionally recognized by Europeans as "intellectuals." With the possible exception of Affonso I, the great sixteenth-century king of Kongo, this part of Africa, unlike the coastal regions of West Africa, has only recently begun to produce men equipped to address themselves in writing to Europeans, using European languages and conventions. Most such men by the nature of their experience and training have been largely cut off from their ancestral philosophy and taught to evaluate it in inappropriate European terms. As long as cultural alienation of this kind persists, the indigenous intellectual is a poor guide to local social realities.

By "intellectual reactions" I mean the cognitive and speculative reactions of ordinary people, few of whom are accustomed to separating their thoughts from the context in which they occur. During my nearly two years of anthropological fieldwork, these reactions were made plain to me in the course of innumerable discussions centered on the experience of "the West" in the lives of individuals and small communities. I was especially interested in the political and ideological relations between the Belgian colonial regime and indigenous society, and as a foreigner myself I inevitably recapitulated in my own work some elements of those relations. The problem I confront now is to make explicit a number of ideas which the BaKongo themselves express implicitly in everyday conversation, but only occasionally and casually in writing. The phenomena are both obvious and impossible to demonstrate conclusively.[1]

The popular Kongo reaction to the West presumes a cosmology according to which the universe is divided into two complementary parts or phases that may be called "this world" and "the other world."[2] The division is not comparable to the modern oc-

1. Additional ethnographic information and some analyses of intellectual responses can be found in my publications listed in these notes. The fieldwork on which my conclusions are based was carried out from 1964 to 1966 under a Foreign Area Fellowship. The Foreign Area Fellowship Program bears no responsibility for the views expressed here.

2. See A. Fukiau, *Le Mukongo et le monde qui l'entourait*, Recherches et synthèses, no. 1 (Kinshasa: Office Nationale de la Recherche et du Développement, 1969).

cidental distinction between the natural and the supernatural, since there is no concept of natural law or natural forces; the contrast lies, rather, between perceived events and the unseen causes that give rise to them. This world is inhabited by black people who appear in it and leave it by the processes of birth and death. In this world they experience tribulations brought on largely by the operation of malicious forces against which they seek the protection of benevolent powers. Exceptional powers of both kinds, malicious and benevolent, belong naturally to the population of the other world, which is characterized by all that this world is not. In the other world there is neither disease nor injustice, neither birth nor death, nor any shortage of anything needful for prosperity. The other world is a world of clarity and order.

The powers of the other world, variously described as ancestors, ghosts, and spirits of several kinds, are colored white or red. They affect the lives of people in this world either directly or through the agencies of chiefs, prophets, magicians, and witches. Cult activity focusses on the two principal routes of communication between the worlds, which are water and the grave. Any real body of water, or any reflecting surface, may serve to represent in myth and ritual the ideal barrier spanned by spiritual communications; the land route is represented by graves in general, especially the grave of someone who manifested power in his lifetime, and also by crossroads, termite hills, caves, and large rocks.

Besides establishing the basis of religious ritual and symbolism, the model of the divided worlds is the foundation for cognitive and explanatory reactions to all unusual events. It is not possible to predict in every instance which events will be regarded by particular individuals or groups as "unusual," but in general the model will be applied to events or news considered to reveal the operation of exceptional powers, good or evil. Many types of events which the modern, rationalistic occidental mind would attribute to intelligence, luck, creative imagination, inspiration, emotional tension, and other "forces" thought of as largely internal or psychological, but not as supernatural, are usually considered by Congolese to show the influence of the other world.[3]

The results of this kind of thinking are very difficult to translate into occidental categories. Experiencing the difficulty, many observers have assumed that Africans are irrational. It has been a commonplace among European residents of Congo down to the present day that Congolese are incapable of abstract thought. On the other hand, Lévy-Bruhl, one of the few anthropologists to treat this problem seriously, took it for granted that "natives" were not intellectually inferior to Europeans.[4] His term "pre-logical," by which he meant "other-logical," is an improvement over "irrational," but his view that the "primitive" mentality is governed by "the law of participation" rather than "the law of contradiction" has not been accepted, and it does not fit Congolese intellectual behavior. For example, BaKongo assume that sickness, theft, and other misfortunes are likely to have been caused by witchcraft, but they approach the problem of identifying the witch in a forensic mode entirely familiar to occidentals.

The model of the divided worlds and the associated assumptions regarding other-worldy forces constitute an example of what Kuhn has called a paradigm,[5] an accepted framework of investigation that seems self-evident to the members of the community in which it is current. Members of other communities, including occidentals, regard the Kongo paradigm as a matter of belief because they do not share it. For the BaKongo, however, statements falling within the paradigm have much the same significance as the statements of natural or social science.[6] Speaking of the coastal religion that, for lack of a better word, she called "Fetish," Mary Kingsley acutely remarked:

3. See G. Lienhardt, *Divinity and Experience* (Oxford, 1961), p. 149; and M.-C. and E. Ortigues, *OEdipe africain* (Paris, 1966), p. 127.
    4. L. Lévy-Bruhl, *Primitive Mentality* (New York, 1923).
    5. T. S. Kuhn, *The Structure of Scientific Revolutions* (Chicago, 1962).
    6. Robin Horton, "African Traditional Thought and Western Science," *Africa* 37 (1967):50–71.

It may seem a paradox to say of people who are always seeing visions that they are not visionaries; but they are not . . . . The more you know the African, the more you study his laws and institutions, the more you must recognise that the main characteristic of his intellect is logical, and you see how in all things he uses this absolutely sound but narrow thoughtform. He is not a dreamer nor a doubter, everything is real, very real, horribly real to him.

It is this power of being able logically to account for everything that is, I believe, at the back of the tremendous permanency of Fetish in Africa, and the cause of many of the relapses into it by Africans converted to other religions.[7]

In explaining exceptional events, Kongo religious thought apparently imposes upon them the model of the divided worlds. The model is simultaneously structural and processual; that is, it arranges events in both space and time. Time, in this sense, is not calendrical but mythological, a medium in which relationships are displayed in narrative form giving the appearance of history at the expense of true history. Space can be employed in the same way at the expense of true geography. In both instances the medium, whether space or time, is not simultaneously available as a field for empirically verifiable events, and empirically oriented challenges appropriate to geography and history are rendered irrelevant.[8] Conversely, the materials of geography and history provide the content in terms of which the model of the divided worlds is apprehended by the BaKongo, since it does not exist abstractly but is implicit in their experience of the world.

The model of complementary opposition is applied by BaKongo to the spatial aspects of many situations and events in which they are interested. Modern myths contrast the northern and southern banks of the River Congo, for example, and the Upper and Lower regions of the Republic. In appropriate context, these oppositions are submerged in a higher opposition between Africa and Mputu. For most BaKongo, Mputu, the home of white people (*bamindele*), is a single continent including both

7. M. Kingsley, *West African Studies* (London, 1899), pp. 124–25.
8. W. MacGaffey, *Custom and Government in the Lower Congo* (Los Angeles, 1970), pp. 23n, 79.

Europe and America. The popular idea of the Atlantic Ocean's farther shore is confused and vague, but "America" is regarded as a single country (the United States), divided into "South America" and "North America." The dead go to America and have always done so.[9] The historical slave trade is recollected as a form of witchcraft, whereby large numbers of Africans were improperly and prematurely transported to the other shore; as such it continues to the present time. When ivory was being carried to the coast for export, stories were told of voices heard coming from inside the tusks begging passersby for drinks for the thirsty souls imprisoned within them.[10] Traders returning from the coast were asked for news of deceased relatives whom they might have seen on the shore, and themselves underwent a ritual to "return their souls" (*vutulwa nsala*) after such an expedition. "Gone to fetch salt in [the port of] Boma" was a euphemism for death."[11]

Since geographical space is being used metaphorically, the Atlantic Ocean is only one of a number of waters that may serve to represent the ideal barrier, which is called Kalunga. Boats of various kinds are vehicles for transporting souls or for returning to this shore such exceptional individuals as prophets, who are able to come and go. For that matter, any of the white man's vehicles may serve the same purpose. To dream of trains and trucks is to be warned of death, but the role of such vehicles is not simply symbolic, as in European thought; in the 1930s, according to my informants, BaKongo would hang about the stations of the Matadi-Léopoldville railway in the hope of seeing recently deceased relatives passing though on their way to Mputu.[12]

9. W. MacGaffey, "Kongo and the King of the Americans," *Journal of Modern African Studies* 6 (1968): 171–81.

10. W. H. Bentley, *Pioneering on the Congo*, 2 vols. (London, 1900), 1:278.

11. Bentley, *Pioneering*, 1:252; K. E. Laman, *The Kongo I*, Stud. ethnogr. upsal., no. 4 (Uppsala, 1953), p. 152; Laman, *The Kongo III*, Stud. ethnogr. upsal., no. 12 (Uppsala, 1962), p. 113.

12. A good example of the inappropriate empiricism of a European mind confronting African beliefs is Andersson's comment that popular expectations of the prophet Kimbangu's impending return to Kongo *in a*

Having crossed the water, the dead change their skin and become white. There is some doubt whether this transformation occurs immediately or gradually, and some suppose that "South America" is inhabited by blacks. Everybody is surprised to hear that black Americans do not speak KiKongo.

From an American point of view, America and Africa are separated by thousands of miles, but to Congolese the land of the dead is just beyond the horizon or even closer, as close as the cemetery or as nightfall. The ancestors live in the earth, in the forests and the waters, and in essence their world only differs from the ordinary world of daylight in being orderly and prosperous.[13] Gifted or fortunate persons experience a kind of shift of vision, usually while walking in the forest, and see about them the village of the ancestors. Likewise it is commonly believed that America is somewhere in Kongo although no one knows just where because, it is said, the Europeans make a point of concealing the routes by which they come and go.

Whenever their presence has been regarded as extraordinary, Europeans in Kongo have been classed as agents or incarnations of other-wordly powers. Their white skin is a sign of their other-worldly associations, as it is with albinos. An albino is thought to incarnate an ancestor or water spirit and to be exceptionally intelligent because he possesses both the wisdom of daylight (this world) and the wisdom of darkness (the other world); when he dies, his spirit returns not to the forest but to the water.[14] In practice, this idea is adduced to account for the success of a particular individual such as Mfumu Mpembe, chief of Kyanga village at the turn of the century, but omitted when an ordinary and undistinguished albino is the object of attention.

---

ship may have been a response to news of Marcus Garvey's Black Star Line (E. Andersson, *Messianic Popular Movements in the Lower Congo,* Stud. ethnogr. upsal., no 6 [Uppsala, 1958], p. 229n).

13. J. Van Wing, *Etudes Bakongo,* 2ª ed. (Brussels, 1959), p. 308.

14. J. H. Weeks, "Notes on Some Customs of the Lower Congo People," *Folklore* (London) 19 (1909):422–23; Van Wing, *Etudes Bakongo,* pp. 114, 318; K. E. Laman, *The Kongo II,* Stud. ethnogr. upsal., no. 8 (Uppsala, 1957), p. 8.

According to old men, *ndundu* ("albino") was a common term
for Europeans in the 1880s, when Europeans were believed not
to be born in the ordinary way but to come from the water, where
they returned at night to sleep. Some were specifically identified
as returned ancestors.[15] Protestant missionaries were still having
trouble at the beginning of this century in convincing their converts that white babies were born just like black babies,[16] and
even now there remains some doubt on the matter since white
babies are apparently not fed in the ordinary way but given powdered *miliki* instead. During the period of national independence,
as the KiKongo press of the time shows, *ndundu* was revived as a
popular term for European, and I have heard it applied to myself. The Europeans' curious custom of repairing periodically to
the ocean to bathe is regarded as a means of renewing their spiritual forces, and it is supposed that they bring back little bottles
of seawater as charms.

In Kongo popular sociology, people who manifest other-
worldly powers are assigned to one of four roles—chief, prophet,
magician, or witch—according to whether the powers are con-
structive or destructive, and whether they are exercised in the
public interest or not.[17] Europeans have been allocated to any
and all of the four roles, most often to those of witch (*ndoki*)
and magician (*nganga*). *Nganga* was until recently the ordinary
term for a missionary, and those who joined the church were
seen as having joined a purificatory or anti-witchcraft movement. As initiation fees they handed over, presumably, the souls
of relatives, which the missionaries in turn exported to Mputu;
in return initiates received schooling, or instruction in the new
magic, whereby in due course they might themselves become
rich.[18] To the extent that *nganga* causes death or misfortune he is

15. Van Wing, *Etudes Bakongo*, p. 309n.
16. C. L. Mabie, *Congo Cameos* (Philadelphia, 1952), p. 68.
17. W. MacGaffey, "The Religious Commissions of the BaKongo,"
Man, n.s. 5 (1970):27–38.
18. Andersson, *Messianic Popular Movements in the Lower Congo*, p.
44; Bentley, *Pioneering on the Congo*, 1:252; Mabie, *Congo Cameos*, p.
68; Van Wing, *Etudes Bakongo*, p. 273; Weeks, "Notes on Some Customs
of the Lower Congo People," p. 479.

simultaneously a witch (*ndoki*), but the primary significance of
nganga is that he is a technician employing his skills in order to
maximize his own material rewards; *nganga*, in fact, summarizes
the modern European's own view of western civilization, with
the difference that Congolese profoundly distrust the utilitarian
philosophy in which Europeans place such confidence, and suspect magicians of witchcraft.[19] The exercise of power in the interest of private individuals is deemed to promote social anarchy; in practice, a popular feeling of malaise gives rise to the
view that witches and magicians are operating unchecked. Nothing in their experience of colonialism could have led Congolese
to a better understanding of democratic freedoms; in any case
the prevailing Belgian colonial view that politics was an evil fitted very well the authoritarian indigenous theory of chiefship.[20]

According to the modern Kongo popular history of colonialism, the Europeans, as outstanding competitive technicians
themselves, made a point of destroying Congolese science by the
twin means of missionary teaching and state force, so that they
could monopolize the profits to be made. Destruction was concentrated in two areas in particular, medicine and metalworking.
The use of indigenous medicines (*min'kisi*, "fetishes") was pro-
scribed so that the sick would have to be brought to hospital,
where foreign doctors would profit by charging fees and by se-
lecting some souls as their victims in the spiritual slave trade.
Exported souls went to join the labor force "under the sea,"
helping to manufacture the European goods that the Congolese
were constrained to buy for lack of manufactures of their own.
It is known that the ancestors worked in metal (the first king of
Kongo is said to have been an ironworker), and after all the
Americans are themselves none other than the ancestors (*bam-*

19. This difference was brought home to me when a group of elders,
including myself as honorary elder, was discussing how to organize the
community to build new quarters for the local school. After I had suggested a competition between different sections of the community, each
vying with the others to make the largest contribution, one of the elders
said, "Yes, we could follow the route of jealousy (*nzila ya kimpala*),"
thus dismissing the suggestion. Jealousy is the chief cause and breeding-
ground of witchcraft.

20. MacGaffey, *Custom and Government in the Lower Congo*, p. 262.

buta). Stories are told of local geniuses who were prevented by the Belgians from making trucks or airplanes. Independence, it was thought in 1959, would mean the restoration of indigenous technology and indigenous medicine. Here is a description of independence (*kimpwanza*) from this point of view, as it appeared in the first issue of Daniel Kanza's newspaper *Kongo Dieto:*

When the missionaries came to Mbanza Kongo with the Word of God, our forefathers were already praying to Nzambi Mpungu Tulendo [Almighty God], and they had also extremely powerful charms [*n'kisi*], such as Mpungu, which is the Kodya itself [a large snail shell, symbol of Kongo nationalism]. The missionaries saw that the power of our elders exceeded their own, so they sought a way to burn all the charms in Mbanza Kongo and substitute the images of the saints. Then the chief called Ne Kongo took his Kodya and his sword Lulewu and fled with his following, the people of Kongo. On their journey the Kodya demonstrated many marvels. They crossed rivers on little things, for example, the clan Mbamba Kalunga crossed the River on a knife blade; others, on a raffia mat, or in the Kodya itself. In short, the Kodya had and has enormous power.[21]

In the second issue:

Independence will mean that our women and children will be healthy, sickness and death will no longer be as they are now, and our villages will be crowded. . . . Our elders knew how to make iron tools, guns, and many other things, but when [the Europeans] came to steal our freedom, the old [skills] disappeared.[22]

The foregoing selections express a widespread opinion; Congolese, in brief, do not see themselves as having benefited from the introduction of a form of civilization vastly superior to their own, nor do they share the European habit of distinguishing civilizations in racial terms, that is, in terms of the characteristic psychological, mental, and moral attributes of populations. The opinion as expressed may be naive, but there is a great deal of truth in it, as any serious student of, for example, either public health or economics in the Congo must recognize.

21. *Kongo Dieto* (Léopoldville, Kinshasa), n.d. [1959?].
22. *Kongo Dieto*, 25 October 1959.

If *nganga* is the technician, then *ndoki* ("witch") is very nearly the citizen voter, free-thinking and imbued with the spirit of capitalism. The BaKongo side with Hobbes rather than Locke and assume that the maintenance of social order requires a sovereign (*mfumu*) to set limits on liberty and to put down witchcraft. The ideal hierarchical order of the chief is heralded by the prophet (*ngunza*), whose mastery over witchcraft is demonstrated in the power to heal. The colonial regime, thought to be founded on the principles of magic and witchcraft, was first challenged in 1921 by the movement begun by the prophet Kimbangu and again in the 1950s by the Kongo political association ABAKO under the leadership of *le roi* Kasa-Vubu. Punning on his name, a front-page article in *Kongo Dieto*, 28 February 1960, referred to him as "the *nkasa* of hope" (*nkasa kuandi ya vuvu*). *Nkasa* is the poison of the witchfinding ordeal, expected in this instance to rid the country of the witchcraft of the whites (*kindoki kia bandundu*). Anti-colonialism was not primarily xenophobic, however, and many features of the movements of 1921 and 1959 had also appeared in the 1880s when many BaKongo apparently decided that the Europeans were the expected, idealized chiefs and prophets.[23]

The model of the divided worlds is applied to time as well as to space. BaKongo think of the course of civilization as an oscillation between two conditions, order and disorder, the former being one in which access to power and its benefits is guaranteed by an authoritarian chief who prevents witches from blocking the channels of power to their own advantage. They do not think of history as a record of linear progress in the accumulation of material and moral goods, and indeed do not appear to think historically at all. The insistent emphasis of the ABAKO party between 1956 and 1960 on the restoration of the old kingdom of Kongo was not so much secular revanchism as utopianism; a few of ABAKO's leaders had acquired in seminaries some historical sense of the old kingdom, but for most people to this day "Mbanza Kongo" is primarily a political and moral order. Independence, in 1959, meant the restoration of the kingdom, that

23. MacGaffey, *Custom and Government in the Lower Congo*, pp. 250–58.

is, of chiefship (*kimfumu,* "chiefship, freedom") as a moral principle; "our independence is not new but ancient," as a contributor to *Kongo Dieto* expressed it. Although there was apparently no standard doctrine, independence suggested to many people the *return* of the ancestors, the "Americans." Others expected that they would themselves become ancestors, that is, white people; the ABAKO newspaper *Kongo dia Ngunga* found it necessary to denounce this rumor in August 1956. The return of the "white" half of mankind is implicit in Kongo cosmology, in which the "original" population of the world was both black and white, the whites later separating from the blacks by crossing water.[24] This cosmology automatically generates the "prophecies" attributed to this or that distinguished elder, deceased just before the arrival of the Europeans, who is supposed to have foretold their coming.[25]

It is impossible to quantify the extent of this kind of thinking among the BaKongo, particularly since they live with it as Europeans live with their own geography, history, and other sciences. In 1966 a villager confessed to having killed six of his neighbors by witchcraft and sending their souls to Kinshasa in aircraft made of leaves; he was sentenced by the local court to 30 days in jail and people spoke of his crime with little more excitement than if he had stolen money. Belief in witchcraft is, I believe, a diagnostic symptom, so to speak, of the entire paradigm, and on that basis alone one would be justified in assuming that the kind of views of America (Europe) discussed above would seem at least plausible to 85 percent of the population.[26] The inevitable concomitant of belief in witchcraft is belief in the virtue of protective charms (*min'kisi*); wealthier and better-educated persons

24. See, for example, Laman, *The Kongo I,* p. 13.
25. See, for example, Mabie, *Congo Cameos,* p. 42.
26. Of Nigerian students who broke down at British universities in 1957, 90 percent showed clearcut evidence of beliefs in witchcraft and tended to regard their dream life as objective reality. "The African within his indigenous culture constantly asks the same existential questions posed by Heidegger. . . . The richness of his culture provides him with adequate answers" (T. A. Lambo, *African Traditional Beliefs and Concepts of Health and Medical Practice* [Ibadan, 1963], pp. 8–9).

are often distinguished from the common mass in this regard by their willingness and ability to buy European magical items or, for example, to subscribe to Rosicrucianism (whose meaning they understand in Congolese terms).

During a return visit to Congo in 1970 I ascertained that the view of myself as a returned Congolese and as a kind of scout for the millenary regime was even more widely entertained than I had previously thought. Many people came to inquire after their deceased relatives in America, to tell me that my arrival had been foretold in dreams, or to ask when the main force of "the Americans" would come. Others, mostly younger and better educated men, revealed their belief in the possibility by coming to interrogate me before deciding that the current rumor was false. One young man with enough education to speak good French stopped me in the street to ask if it were true that I was black, and others explained to their friends in the market that I had been sold to America by my "uncle" but that I had come back to accuse him of witchcraft before the elders. Even the members of the two communities in which I had lived longest shared this view almost unanimously.

Since the BaKongo have been subject to intensive European influence for eighty years, have nearly all been to primary schools run by Europeans, and have been exposed to continuous propaganda intended to explain and exalt the West and its ways at the expense of African culture, the modern popular readiness to identify America with the land of the dead is an intellectual phenomenon too substantial to be ignored or attributed to simple ignorance. I advance as important in this context three general considerations: first, that Kongo cosmology provides an adequate framework for the intellectual evaluation of Kongo experience in the modern world, it as did in the past; secondly, that the institutional position of literacy has not been such as to develop a consciousness of history; and thirdly, that Congolese experience of western culture has never been sufficiently different from popular expectations to cause a radical questioning of indigenous conceptual categories. I take up these three considerations in turn.

The theory of witchcraft as a philosophical system cannot be adequately assessed until a number of KiKongo texts on the subject have been made available in translation; to the best of my knowledge, none of these ideas has been published by Congolese in French or any other European language.[27] (By "witchcraft" I intend in a single term, substituted for Kingsley's "Fetish," to refer to Kongo thought as a whole.) European attention has always concentrated on witchcraft's more spectacularly unpleasant institutions, such as the poison ordeal, whose philosophical bases have been facilely reduced to a simple and obviously fallacious theory of cause and effect.

The ideas are mostly of the simpler forms, seldom passing the concretes of actual experience, generalisations being as a rule beyond their power . . . . Analogies are confined to the crudest forms, and a very simple figure of speech is apt to be unintelligible . . . . Take first the wizard, the ndochi, as he is called. No theory of occult art or magic, no diabolical attributes will enable us to understand the native's ideas on this subject. The only thing he knows, or thinks he knows, is that the ill-will of some people is physically detrimental to others.[28]

Kingsley, on the other hand, after a long conversation with a Kongo ritual specialist, concluded that the key to Fetish was provided by Goethe's "Prometheus."[29] Most commentators have displayed the curious ambivalence of Marichelle, for example, whose view, "Combien les coutumes des indigènes sont déplorables," is balanced by his suspicion that the witchdoctor's powers may be real after all;[30] to this day, I am reliably informed, there are American missionaries who will not stay in the same room with *kodya* and similar charms. Witchcraft is of course a de-

27. Tangential material can be found in Fukiau, *Le Mukongo et le monde qui l'entourait;* J. Malonga, *La légende de M'pfoumou Ma Mazono* (Paris, 1954); MacGaffey, "The Beloved City: Commentary on a Kinbanguist Text," *Journal of Religion in Africa* (Leiden) 2(1969):129–47; Van Wing, *Etudes Bakongo.*
28. R. C. Phillips, "The Lower Congo," *Journal of the Anthropological Institute* 17 (1888):214–37.
29. Kingsley, *West African Studies,* p. 121.
30. R. P. Marichelle, "Les tablettes d'un congolais: notice historique sur la mission et les indigènes du Loango," *Les Missions Catholiques* [Paris] 42 (1910), passim.

motic philosophy and should not be compared with the best products of specialists in other cultures; nevertheless, Kusikila's *Lufwa evo kimongie?* (1966) is a very respectable essay on the psychological and sociological effects of western influence on the BaKongo, employing the vocabulary and concepts of witchcraft.[31]

If the usual European appraisal of witchcraft were correct, Parrinder's expectation would be borne out: "In modern times these magical and witchcraft beliefs ought to disappear with the growth of education."[32] But the plain fact is that they do not. Witchcraft is part of a total mode of experiencing the world, inseparable from the ideas of chiefship, magic, and moral renewal. Cosmology creates the setting for these ideas, as the following incident illustrates. During my fieldwork I tried not to plant ideas in my informants' minds but on one occasion, in order to elicit comment, I drew a sketch of the universe as it appears in the traditional Kongo cosmology.[33] Those present included a retired pharmacist's assistant, a young man who was private secretary to one of the leading Kongo politicians, and an older man who was the master of a large railway station. Looking at my sketch the pharmacist remarked that he knew what I meant but that in school he had been taught another view of the world (that based on the usual globe) and now he didn't know which to believe. At this point, although witchcraft had not previously been mentioned, the station master broke in with this surprising comment: "When people accept the idea you heard about in school and forget the other, they will stop believing in witchcraft (*kindoki*)." In the ensuing discussion the younger man refused to agree that witchcraft was simply an idea; he had seen too much evidence, he said, of its truth. I myself gave several "geography lessons" to my neighbors, each time only to be asked the same questions a few days later: "Is it true that radios are manufactured down below (*ku nsi*)?" "Why don't South Americans speak KiKongo?" "Do you intermarry with them?"

31. Cf. P. Bohannan, "Extra-Processual Events in Tiv Political Institutions," *American Anthropologist* 60 (1958):1–12.
32. G. Parrinder, *Religion in Africa* (Baltimore, 1969), p. 65.
33. Fukiau, *Le Mukongo et le monde qui l'entourait.*

In reacting to other peoples' thought patterns, the occidental mind is itself likely to be governed by a series of conceptual oppositions forming a model not unlike that of the divided worlds. Westerners usually take it for granted that there are clear distinctions between primitive and modern, irrational and rational. They assume that the upholders of unscientific geographies and histories are not rational as "modern" men are, that irrationality will give way to education and experience, and that a "primitive" worldview is incompatible with the kind of instrumental rationality and "modernism" demanded of and usually exhibited by Africans occupied in the modern sectors of their national cultures. This occidental view seems to be founded on a double arrogance: a complacent expectation that since African culture is so obviously inadequate Africans themselves will want to adopt western ways as soon as possible, and a conviction that westerners are more rational than they really are. On the other hand, my experience with geography lessons in Congo is matched every year when I attempt to explain to American audiences simple facts of African history and politics. Nor is pre-logical thinking confined to the man in the street: the race history of Africa propounded until recently by distinguished scholars in white coats, brandishing calipers, statistics, and all the panoply of science, is in the strict sense a myth.[34]

Despite such similarities, there are important differences between Congolese and occidental thought whose origins lie in institutional contrasts, particularly in the institutionalization of literacy. In the 1950s the Belgian Congo had one of the highest literacy rates in Africa. In the Lower Congo in particular, primary education was virtually universal. A literate society is forced to recognize the past because it is not free to forget;[35] in a "traditional" society, whose experiences are almost entirely those of the present, the past is available as a medium for specu-

34. W. MacGaffey, "Concepts of Race in the Historiography of Northeast Africa," *Journal of African History* 7 (1966):1–17. Cf. W. Jordan, *White Over Black* (Baltimore, 1969).

35. J. R. Goody, *Literacy in Traditional Societies* (Cambridge, 1968), pp. 1–68.

lative discourse taking the form of myth. In the absence of maps, space is similarly available.

In the Congo the shift towards historical and empirical modes of thought that should accompany literacy has not taken place, for a number of reasons. One is that secondary education, except in seminaries, began to be available only in the mid-1950s. In the 1960s, most peoples' contacts with written material were limited to government documents and announcements, the Bible, hymnbooks, private letters, and occasional newspapers. A more important factor still is that although in recent years the small, largely urban, segment of the population entirely subject to statute law has rapidly increased, the personal affairs of most individuals—filiation, inheritance, marriage, jural liability and, in rural areas, access to land—are governed by customary law, rooted in oral tradition. This means that consciousness of social identity is formulated in mythical terms: ancestors, descent, *simbi* spirits, chiefship.[36] The role of tradition in modern Kongo is not itself entirely traditional; in some ways, the colonial policy of indirect rule served to intensify and elaborate oral tradition by endowing it with new political significance.[37]

Since independence, the written word has had a role in government practice, particularly in Kongo Central province, quite different from that allotted to it in Max Weber's model of bureaucratic organization: from 1962 to 1966, such documents as the provincial government produced, in the form of decrees, reports, policy statements and the like, served not to orient and describe the bureaucracy's real activities but to conceal them. Accordingly, the BaKongo have had little incentive to abandon their hermeneutic approach to the written word or their view that knowledge of the world is intrinsically an occult science.

The third point I wish to make, and the most difficult, is that Congolese have not seen anything like the strong contrast be-

36. "Though Kongo lacks gold and other material wealth, has it not tradition [*lusansu*]? Only Kongo has clans, which began in Kongo dia Ntotila [Mbanza Kongo] along with government [*luyalu*]. Chiefs with bracelets, and queen-mothers [*zindona*], are not known among the whites [*bandundu*]" (*Kongo dia Ntotila*, 30 June 1961).

37. MacGaffey, *Custom and Government in the Lower Congo*.

tween western culture and their own that occidental thought takes for granted. In the area of technology, where the contrast is surely extreme, BaKongo who believe in the *techniques* of witchcraft remain unfazed by mechanical miracles. A captain of police who was also a member of a prophetic congregation explained to me that the American-made FM radio in his jeep was merely a crude imitation of the spiritual communications system operated by his church.[38] Congolese experience with western technology has provided little challenge to the built-in assumption that the technology of Mputu is that of the ancestors; Congolese have been trained to operate but not to understand or to develop European machines and techniques imported ready-made.[39] It constantly perplexed a neighbor of mine, a self-taught mechanic, that although he could repair an internal combustion engine he could not imagine himself creating one. All public education has emphasized rote learning and the observance of rules, many of which Europeans themselves would now see in retrospect as arbitrary and unnecessary; analytical reasoning was not encouraged because, according to the theory of "the Bantu mentality," Congolese would not be capable of it for many generations.

In the field of health and healing the contrast is once again less clear than it should be. Between 1880 and 1920, as a direct result of the European occupation, the population of the Lower Congo declined drastically;[40] Congolese are more aware of this decline than of the subsequent benefits of colonial public health improvements. The profound cleavage between European and Congolese institutions and symbolic systems makes medical diagnosis extremely uncertain, and as Kusikila naively but representatively remarks, more people die in hospital than anywhere

38. This man had had some secondary education in the Protestant school at Nsona Mpangu.

39. For Europeans in Congo, according to popular belief, communication with the ancestors is maintained by the Catholic (not Protestant) clergy, who go to local cemeteries at night to perform the necessary rituals.

40. Van Wing, *Etudes Bakongo*, p. 82; G. Sautter, *De l'Atlantique au fleuve Congo: une géographie de sous-peuplement* (The Hague, 1966), pp. 986, 994.

else. The arrogant positivism of western medical practice has led to the neglect, until recently, of social and psychological factors in the etiology of disease to which African healers have always paid attention.[41] The disappointment BaKongo tend to feel with regard to European medicine is partly a function of their own standards of clinical efficiency; they assume that a genuine expert, like a genuine prophet or diviner, commands an absolute power, of which the x-ray photograph is one of the instruments, to "see" all hidden things and know the sources of all evil. Less than complete medical success confirms their suspicion that the practitioner's powers have been contaminated by his commercialism. It is a sign of the lack from the Congolese point of view of a clear contrast between the two cultures that of three men in one village who among them had accumulated more than 100 years of skilled service in Protestant mission hospitals only one, the youngest, did not believe in witchcraft.

The apparent absence of contrast between Congolese religion and Christianity is likely to be most shocking to occidental expectations although it is also the easiest aspect of the problem to demonstrate, particularly if we begin with the sixteenth century. It is even more difficult to know what people were thinking then than to know what they think now, but popular attitudes can scarcely have been less exotic in the kingdom of Kongo than in modern times. According to the evidence, there has been little change. It is consistent with the modern view of Europeans as other-worldly creatures that in Loango at the beginning of the seventeenth century they were required to be buried at sea.[42] The detailed similarities between the Antonine "heresy" of the

41. Horton, "African Traditional Thought and Western Science," p. 55. Cf. A. Kiev, *Magic, Faith and Healing* (Glencoe, 1964); L. Arden Almquist, M.D., "Medicine and Religion—A Missionary Perspective," *Practical Anthropology* 15 (1968):217–27.

The empiricism of western science is not universal in western thought. Mary Baker Eddy's definition of a miracle—"That which is divinely natural, but must be learned humanly; a phenomenon of science."—would be readily acceptable to most Congolese. The acceptability of Watchtower doctrines and various numerologies of the Book of Daniel has been demonstrated many times over.

42. Battel, in J. Pinkerton, ed., *A General Collection of the Best and Most Interesting Voyages and Travels,* 17 vols. (London, 1808–1814), 16:331.

first years of the eighteenth century and modern Kimbanguism are striking, and some of king's ritual gestures as described by the chroniclers can be seen today in the villages. The point I am making, however, does not require that continuity be demonstrated. Given the stubborn resistance of modern Congolese thinking to the concentrated western influences of recent decades, the obvious conclusion to be drawn from the apparent conversion to Christianity of large numbers of BaKongo in the sixteenth century is that the BaKongo saw in Christianity something with which they were already familiar, and that in terms of indigenous culture the new movement was simply one of the perennial revitalizations characteristic of this area.

Assuming religious expectations in the old kingdom to be much as they are now, we can see as no great surprise the arrival by sea of white strangers from another world who possessed a superior technology and proclaimed a religious doctrine that all men should abandon witchcraft and magic. The strangers brought with them the sign of the cross, but cruciform figures are implicit and explicit in many aspects of Kongo ideal culture, as indeed in that of West Central African peoples generally. As in the nineteenth century, not everybody saw the new movement as a good thing. Most eager to join were those, such as the Mani Soyo and Nzinga Mvemba, later known as Affonso I, who apparently saw an opportunity to link their ambitions to the theme of revitalization. After Affonso had justified his claim to close connections with the spirit world by successfully undergoing the traditional battle ordeal, the *nganga* Mani Kabunga, who had opposed him, became keeper of the holy water in the new regime. Vansina speaks of this as "a neat transposition of political function in a new religious idiom"[43] but it remains to be shown that the religious *idiom* was in fact new. Subsequently, the role of *nganga* at the king's coronation was taken over by the missionaries themselves; the papal bull authorizing the Capuchins to perform this rite became a charm (*n'kisi*) of the type called *dimbu kya luyaalu* or *Kiyaazi*.[44]

43. J. Vansina, *Kingdoms of the Savannah* (Madison, Wis., 1966), p. 46.

44. Merolla, in Pinkerton, ed., *A General Collection*, 16:283, 287. Cf. L. Jadin, "Le Congo et la secte des Antoniens," *Bulletin de l'Institut his-*

Virtually all of the historians of Kongo have shared the original missionary chroniclers' vested interest in evangelization.
Consequently, the "conversion" of the BaKongo has been taken
at the value put upon it by missionaries who knew little about
Kongo culture and rarely commanded the language. The later
religious history of the BaKongo is seen from this point of view
as a continuing struggle with superstition. Any ritual trait that is
apparently Christian in form, such as a demand for baptism, is
accepted without question as evidence of Christian belief; traits
obviously incompatible with Christianity are classed as atavistic
paganism. From Father Merolla's account of early-eighteenth-
century Kongo it is apparent that the people made no such distinction, and that what he regarded with great indignation as hypocrisy resulted simply from total misunderstanding of the Gospel. The difference in viewpoint is dramatically presented in one
of Merolla's experiences: in Noki he went to the local church,
which had a large wooden cross standing in front of it; inside he
discovered to his horror a great heap of sand, evidently a grave,
wherein was stuck a straight horn about five spans long, with
other material of superstitious worship besides.[45] From numerous incidents in Merolla's narrative it is evident that a major focus of Kongo religion, then as now, was a cult of the grave as a
means of communicating with the other world. As the Protestant
missionary W. H. Bentley later pointed out, the expression *nzo a
n'kisi,* which meant "church" to the missionaries, meant "grave"
to the Africans.[46]

Merolla himself was a particularly credulous and superstitious
individual, and his own teaching may not have been typical of
contemporary missionaries; only the eye of faith could distinguish many of his tenets from those of an indigenous *nganga.*
Among his recommendations were that women about to give
birth should wear religious relics instead of the wizards' mats,
and that instead of the magic guard planted to preserve corn and
render it fertile, consecrated palm branches and the sign of the

torique belge de Rome 33 (1961):505; W. G. L. Randles, *L'Ancien Roy-
aume du Congo* (Paris, 1968).
45. Pinkerton. ed., *A General Collection,* 16:280.
46. Bentley, *Pioneering on the Congo,* 1:236–37.

cross should be used. Most if not all of the early missionaries
accepted literally the local belief in witchcraft:

Since that nation has received the faith of Jesus Christ, there still
remain among them abundance of sorcerers and enchanters (as there
are heretics in Europe), who are the ruin of these people, otherwise
tractable enough. It is in a manner impossible for the King to root
them out, insomuch as that Prince, who is a very good Christian and
zealous Catholic, has given leave to several of his great men, who
know their lurking places, to fire their cottages; but they having spies
abroad, though they meet at night, make their escape and are very
seldom taken.[47]

Here is additional testimony to the homology between black
and white *banganga* in the early eighteenth century in the words
of Lawrence of Lucca:

Si nous recommandons de ne pas avoir recours aux féticheurs pour
recouvrer la santé, mais de s'addresser au Seigneur et à l'intercession
de ses saints comme on fait en nos pays (par exemple, en se recom-
mandant à Ste. Lucie pour les maux d'yeux, à Ste. Apolline pour les
maux de dents), quand on parle de la sorte, les féticheurs se mettent
à dire le contraire.[48]

It is clear from the missionary accounts, as it is from the political record, that the profession of Christian faith was seen by the
chiefs as a means to secure profitable trade contracts. In
Loango, Merolla asked the superintendent of foreign trade
whether he thought the King would be willing to be baptized;
"to which he, though a pagan, civilly answered, that he was certain he would, according to his promise, provided that trade
were settled within his dominions with the whites pursuant to
their contract."[49]

In the late nineteenth century, after almost all trace of early

47. Angelo and Carli, in Pinkerton, ed., *A General Collection*, 16:170.

48. "If we urge them not to resort to magicians to recover their health
but to address themselves to the Lord and to the intercession of his saints
as is done in our countries (for example, St. Lucia for eye trouble, St.
Apollinus for toothache), when we say such things the magicians start
saying the opposite." Quoted in J. Cuvelier, *Relations sur le Congo du
Père Laurent de Lucques (1700–1717)* (Brussels, 1953), p. 130.

49. Pinkerton, ed., *A General Collection*, 16:275.

Christianization had disappeared, missionaries who participated in the reconversion of the BaKongo soon discovered that they were regarded as visitors from the other world. It is not a contradiction that those who held this belief were also willing to be converted. Henry Richards, the first Protestant missionary to make converts in large numbers, attributed his success to a change in his preaching. For years he had preached "a sort of Judaism," emphasizing the law and the punishments for sin, but the heathen only began to show interest when he began to preach the gospel of the incarnation, life, death, resurrection and return of Christ.[50] This message closely conformed to the ideology of such revitalization cults as Kimpasi and Ndembo, which are known to have existed in approximately the same form from the seventeenth century to about 1900,[51] and of prophetic movements from the Antonine cult to modern Kimbanguism. These cults differ in important respects, but are similar in their guarantee to believers of special powers obtained by privileged communication with the other world, by death and rebirth.[52]

The impact of Christianity in recent decades is too complex a question to open here. Nearly all BaKongo call themselves Christian, either Protestant, Catholic, or Kimbanguist. Protestant and Catholic missionaries, like those of the seventeenth century, commonly complain that only such Christians as continue under close missionary supervision are free of pagan superstition. The persistence of traditional beliefs has already been shown. The people see themselves as confronting a choice between good and evil, not between African belief and Christian belief. Accepting Christianity means accepting some at least of the obligations of membership in a particular church, education being the principal mode of recruitment. To be a Catholic or a Protestant does not mean to cease to believe in the influence of

50. Richards' accounts are found in communications to *The Baptist Missionary Magazine* (Boston), March-April 1890.

51. Van Wing, *Etudes Bakongo,* pp. 474–78.

52. In recent years a number of younger Congolese Catholic clergy have begun serious investigations into the moral and philosophical bases of Congolese religions. See, for examples, the periodical *Cahiers des Religions Africaines* published by the Centre d'Etudes des Religions Africaines, Université Lovanium de Kinshasa.

ancestors or of witchcraft, since to the popular mind these forces are incontrovertible facts of experience. The Catholic and Protestant churches, however, offer little protection against witchcraft and refuse to discuss the subject officially; white men in general are of course immune to African witchcraft, although there is some question in the popular mind whether whites in Europe suffer from their local witchcraft.

From the European point of view, practical Congolese religion is syncretic, meaning that elements of Christianity are awkwardly and improperly combined with elements of African superstition which should, in time, wither away. From the Congolese point of view, European missionary Christianity is similarly syncretic and imperfect, contaminated by elements of particular European culture. According to one of the leading Congolese Protestant ministers, since 1960 there has been a move among the elders of the orthodox Protestant church to get rid of these extraneous elements, including, he said, the communion service. It is noteworthy that the Kimbanguist churches, whose rituals most closely follow those of orthodox Protestantism do not use the communion. Kimbanguist churches do, however, explicitly recognize witchcraft and provide protective rituals.

It is part of the intention of this paper to raise more questions than it answers. The intellectual history of the Lower Congo, in so far as it has been studied at all, has been studied in terms of irrelevant a priori categories constructed on the assumption that the world is as occidentals see it. The occidental view may in fact be correct in some or even all respects, but it is not shared by Congolese, who react to experience in terms of their own categories. Apart from Mary Kingsley, the first and virtually the only ethnographer of the BaKongo to perceive the existence of a system of categories in Kongo culture—that is, an intellectual basis for existential response—was Kingsley's friend Dennett, who indicated in the title of his book his discovery that there was after all something *At the Back of the Black Man's Mind* (1906). Dennett's methods, erratic in the extreme, have provided an excuse for ignoring his insights.[53]

53. See for example. L. Bittremieux, *La société secrète des Bakhimba au Mayombe* (Brussels, 1936), p. 138.

The Congolese worldview and the symbols associated with it must be studied as a whole; classification of traits in terms of their presumed origins tells us little about their present significance. Van Wing's remark on magic applies equally well to indigenous sociology and political science: "Le magicien-féticheur adopte tout, mais n'adapte rien; il ne change aucun de ses principes."[54] The persistence of fundamental ideal orientations evidently is not matched by any corresponding persistence in the quantitative aspects of social structure. Here anthropology has commonly been at fault in assuming that all "parts" of a culture are functionally determined and that immaterial notions are reducible to material realities of politics and economics. The structure of Kongo society underwent major transformations at the end of the seventeenth and nineteenth centuries; it is possible that a third transformation is in progress. Witchcraft, like democracy, has proved its viability in a variety of social contexts. As the contents of social relations in Congo change to resemble those familiar to occidentals, so the expression of witchcraft principles will come to appear less exotic. The transition is readily perceived in the conversation of intellectuals and in the now defunct KiKongo press. An issue of *Kongo dia Ntotila*, for example (11 December 1961), carried in the midst of impassioned appeals to Kongo tradition and apocalyptic Kimbanguist visions a blast against the ABAKO party, accusing some of its leaders of communism, Freemasonry, and Rosicrucianism, and of being secret agents of NATO and the European Common Market; the common denominator of these evils is the ordinary Kongo concept of witchcraft. Since the beginning of the twentieth century the BaKongo have been noted for their rapid adaptation to the material aspects of western culture, but the ideology that has guided this change has been essentially conservative.

54. Van Wing, *Etudes Bakongo,* p. 80.

THE SIERRA LEONEANS
OF YORUBALAND

Jean Herskovits

This article is comparable to the two that follow (Spitzer on Sierra Leone and Johnson on Senegal) in much the same way the first two contributions were a linked pair—similar but without rigorous comparison. Unlike the first two, this set of three has to do with people who were far from ordinary. It is concerned with those West Africans of the late nineteenth and early twentieth centuries who became literate in a western language and thus left a record of their responses to the West. Though these men are interesting and important in their own right, their responses may not be typical of their fellow-countrymen. Having been educated in western culture, and sometimes well educated, they were in a position to see the West almost as "insiders" who knew the West very well indeed. The picture would have another dimension if African writing in Hausa, Arabic, or some other languages written in Arabic characters could be included. Writing of this sort might be more truly representative of African attitudes, but such records have not yet been sufficiently studied by scholars, though they are known to exist.

The earliest generations of western-educated intellectuals were men drawn into the orbit of the European trading posts and forts along the West African coast. Some evidence about their responses dates from as far back as the sixteenth century; by the mid-nineteenth century, they had become a significant group.* Broadly speaking, they came into intensive contact with the West in one of three ways. Some were merchants or mer-

* See Robert July, *The Origins of Modern African Thought* (New York, 1967).

chants' agents who dealt with Europeans on the coast; they occasionally obtained a few years' education in England, France,
or the Netherlands for the sake of their business. A few of this
group in each generation were born to African mothers by European fathers, and the fathers often tried to see their sons established in commerce on the Coast.

A second source for the community of western-trained Africans was actual return from slavery in the New World. Returnees were never a large percentage of the slaves shipped overseas,
but they numbered in the thousands—Maroons from Jamaica,
United Empire Loyalists from the southern colonies of North
America after 1783, many Brazilians who returned to Dahomey
and western Nigeria, and the better-known groups of North
Americans who returned to found Liberia. Finally, a third category were the slaves-in-transit captured at sea after the legal abolition of the slave trade in 1808 and landed in either Liberia or
Sierra Leone. The chief center for these recaptives was Freetown
in Sierra Leone, and once landed they were subject to an intense
effort of acculturation and education by the British government
and missionary societies.

By the middle of the nineteenth century, the recaptives had
merged with earlier arrivals from the New World to form a
partly westernized African community called "Creole" (though
Creole originally meant simply American-born, and most Sierra
Leone Creoles were born in Africa). A later essay by Leo Spitzer deals with their intellectual responses to the West in the second half of the nineteenth century. Meanwhile, other Creoles began to move out from Sierra Leone toward their original homes.
If they originated close to Freetown, their exposure to the West
might have been brief, but one group was especially notable for
its impact on its homeland after it had acquired a western education in Freetown. They were the Yoruba returnees to present-
day western Nigeria. The Yoruba had made up a large proportion of those recaptured from the slave ships in the early century. When, from the 1840s, it became possible for them to sail
back down the coast to Nigeria, they settled in Lagos and its
hinterland and became a separate community, now returned to

their home area but with a western education and other attitudes learned abroad.

Jean Herskovits is the author of a full-length study of this community, published as Jean Herskovits Kopytoff, *A Preface to Modern Nigeria: The "Sierra Leonians" in Yoruba, 1830–1890* (Madison, Wis., 1965).

P.D.C.

The Sierra Leoneans of Yoruba descent who, through the last half of the nineteenth century, returned to Lagos and its hinterland and made that region their home, are an ideal, if distinctive, group to show the complex African responses to western culture in that period. They are ideal for several reasons, only some of which they share with other liberated Africans settled in Freetown and the villages around it.

Like the other recaptives, taken off slave ships seized by the British fleet and freed in Sierra Leone, these Yoruba were systematically exposed (certainly more systematically than other Africans from what would be the Nigerian interior) to both formal and informal ways of the West.

In the Sierra Leone setting, they were distinguishable from other recaptives. Because of historical circumstances—the Yoruba wars that provided captives who could be sold at the coast; the Fulani attacks against Oyo, which exacerbated conflict and increased further the numbers captured and sold; the actions of the British patrols that paradoxically increased the importance of Lagos and Badagry as points of export—for all these reasons large numbers of Yoruba were resettled in Sierra Leone in the 1820s, 1830s, and 1840s. In Freetown and the villages around it, they clung more tenaciously to their own way of life than did other groups, a feat possible largely because of their numerical strength.[1]

1. See John Peterson, *Province of Freedom, A History of Sierra Leone, 1787–1870* (London, 1969), esp. pp. 167–70; C. H. Fyfe, *A History of Sierra Leone* (London, 1962), passim.

Traditional Yoruba culture was rich and complex, with important regional variations. Islamic influence compounded historical differences in the religious sphere, though in this period Yoruba Muslims were only a small minority. Nevertheless, members of Yoruba sub-groups in Sierra Leone had a sense of "Yoruba-ness" and a desire to preserve their tradition. This common identification was especially strong for those who met non-Yoruba Africans, some for the first time, in Freetown. Their own cultural commitment, then, made the Yoruba in Freetown even less the *tabulae rasae* for British writing than missionaries and administrators often thought and always desired. It was partly because the size of the Yoruba community allowed its members to retain their cultural strength that they were the ones who moved in largest numbers back to their homelands.[2]

They returned, however, to a setting which was precarious from the start. Coming in 1845 to a region completely under African control, the first arrivals on the coast of present-day Nigeria, they found themselves lacking both British support and the possibility of British protection, since the closest British toeholds were Gold Coast forts to the west and Fernando Po in the Gulf of Guinea to the east. They were, indeed, returning to coastal points from which they had been sold as slaves. Continuing warfare might again make them its victims, for they could not expect their experiences in Freetown to carry any weight in unsettled Yorubaland. In Badagry, to which they first returned, their sights continued to turn elsewhere—inland, especially to the Egba city of Abeokuta. In contemplating a further move to the hinterland, they knew how much their way of life (if not their actual lives) depended on factors that were African, not European.

However these liberated Yoruba had chosen to react to western culture in Sierra Leone, that reaction would meet its primary test in Yorubaland. In this sense, their position was very different from that of the Creoles who remained in Freetown and its surrounding villages, and it continued to be different even after

2. Many factors contributed to the "repatriation." See Jean Herskovits Kopytoff, *A Preface to Modern Nigeria, The "Sierra Leonians" in Yoruba, 1830–1890* [cited hereafter as *Preface*] (Madison, 1965), pp. 36–43.

the British had established themselves in Lagos. In contrast to the *créoles* of Senegal or the Creoles of Freetown they were not cut off, either by racial mixture or by culture, from ethnic and family ties in the interior. None of this is to say that their experiences did not set them apart from the hinterland Yoruba, but the continuity of cultural and kinship ties gave them different options in their responses to the West.

Wherever the Sierra Leoneans found themselves in Yorubaland, several pressures affected their actions and their reasoned reactions. These pressures offered conflicting challenges, conflicting and sometimes irreconcilable choices; at the same time, they gave play to the Yoruba genius for compromise. One factor complicating the position of these Sierra Leoneans was their identification with the Yoruba in the hinterland, indeed, with one or another Yoruba sub-group. Another was British pressure to identify with Europeans culturally and politically. Finally there was the Sierra Leonean awareness that they had at least a partially separable identity of their own. All these contexts changed through time, which makes analysis both more difficult and more revealing.

Before their attitudes towards western-educated Africans changed in the 1880s, the British expected these men and women, both in Sierra Leone and down the coast, to become a homogeneous group of "Black Englishmen."[3] These expectations were simplistic. In Yorubaland reactions of the Sierra Leoneans and their children ran a gamut from rejecting all the ways of the West to cherishing the "Black English" ideal.[4] Within this range, behavior varied widely, and behavior is important here because it is closely tied to the way Sierra Leoneans saw their situation and thought about dealing with it. Naturally the cultural strands evident in the behavior of any individual will only tell something (not everything) about what he thinks.

From a European point of view, at the time and since, the Sierra Leoneans seemed a perfect example of the "western-educated elite," a category expected to exist and identified accordingly. Whatever reservations one may ordinarily have about this

3. See Leo Spitzer, "The Sierra Leone Creoles, 1870–1900," infra.
4. *Preface*, pp. 262–80.

use of the term "elite," it is particularly inapplicable in the setting of Lagos and its hinterland, in contrast to Freetown or the
four communes of Senegal. For, despite their early employment
by British missionary societies and later the consular and colonial administrations, the returned Sierra Leoneans had ties up-
country which forced them to recognize the power and greater
importance of long-established "elites," the traditional decision-
makers, themselves Yoruba.

Never in the years before the 1890s could those who returned
delude themselves into thinking that the British administration
and British standards *alone* determined their position and their
influence. All Sierra Leoneans in Yoruba country had to deal
with the fact that other Africans *did* identify them, to varying
degrees, with Europeans. An early term for the returnees was,
indeed, *Oyinbo,* the Yoruba name for white man. This identification then changed through time as differentiation took place.
Some emigrants were regarded as Europeans, some were not. It
depended largely on whether an individual chose to separate himself from the African context, or to support African interests
when such interests were seen to conflict with those of the Europeans.[5] Naturally, with human beings as complex as they are,
an individual's views of European culture were also affected by
the degree to which other Africans placed him in a European
camp and thus limited his possibilities of action and attitude.

The Sierra Leoneans in Lagos and its hinterland, then, perceived themselves as Sierra Leoneans—distinct from Europeans
whom they recognized as being different in all the obvious ways,
but also distinct from their fellow Yoruba who had not shared
their special experiences. Most of those who returned did not
immediately fall back into the societies from which they had
come, even after they had made contact. Both the British on one
side and the Yoruba on the other saw the Sierra Leoneans as
people apart, separate from the local Yoruba and also separate
from a second group of Yoruba ex-slaves returned from Brazil.
In his perceptions, everyone dealt with four major sub-divisions:
European (with its own internal sub-divisions), Yoruba (with
many more and more obvious internal variations), and two

5. *Preface,* pp. 268–72.

groups of Yoruba who were culturally but not racially mixed, those returned from Brazil and those returned from Sierra Leone.

It is impossible to stress too strongly the contrast between this situation and that of Senegal or Freetown. In Senegal, a four-part division into French, *créoles* (*métis*), the citizens of the communes, and the "other" Africans was racial as well as cultural. Sierra Leone presented a different situation. As in Lagos, there were Europeans, Africans, and the Creoles exposed to the West and thus culturally (though not racially) mixed. Though these Creoles in Freetown were African in their original culture, and though they preserved many of their traditions, the African components of their culture were not the same as those of their immediate neighbors, the Africans of the Sierra Leone hinterland. At no time did the Freetown Creoles see themselves—as the Yoruba Sierra Leoneans did—as culturally part way between the Europeans and the other Africans. Circumstances permitted them to remain aloof from the nearby Africans, as their counterparts in Lagos and its hinterland could not. Largely for this very reason, the position of the Sierra Leoneans in Nigeria was closer to that of most other Africans when they later faced the challenges of cultural contact.

The possibilities of cultural response to the West ranged along a continuum, paralleling intellectual responses. At one end was complete reassimilation, with its concurrent intellectual rejection of western culture. At the other was imitation of western ways by the staunchest advocates of Europeanization. In between came a range of "syncretisms," both practiced and prescribed, with varying cultural mixtures. Such syncretisms by definition merged Yoruba and western thought.

Vast reserves of scholarly writings can be used to illuminate the European component of this merger, but Yoruba ideas and ways of thinking have not been examined systematically. Yet none of the Sierra Leoneans, not even those most acculturated to western ways, was uninfluenced by Yoruba assumptions and the intellectual framework of Yoruba culture. The first generation of Sierra Leoneans had, after all, been brought up in their various Yoruba homelands; we may assume their enculturation.

Of the first returnees, only a few were born in Sierra Leone. Later generations, even if born into "westernized" Sierra Leonean families in Lagos, grew up in Yorubaland, and the possibility of being in a "pure" Europeanized environment diminished as families moved inland.

What, then, can we know about a nineteenth-century (or even twentieth-century) Yoruba view of historical process?[6] One formal history written in the late nineteenth century allows us to infer Yoruba answers to fundamental historical questions, especially that of causation. The book is *The History of the Yorubas,* begun by the Sierra Leonean clergyman, Samuel Johnson, in the 1880s, or possibly earlier. It has several distinctive features which both contribute to and detract from its usefulness. Its pronounced Oyo bias[7] is not, for our purposes, a drawback. Indeed, in showing the author's commitment, it may suggest a persistence in him of Oyo views as well as Oyo loyalty. More important are his ordination as a Christian minister and his long years with the Church Missionary Society (C.M.S.). Under these circumstances, one might expect Johnson's interpretations to reflect Christian views of historical process. He tried, however, from "a

6. I plan to do continuing research on the historical views of the peoples of the West African forest states, and I hope that anthropological work in progress and in the future will yield essential data so necessary for such problems of historical interpretation.

7. In 1901, Obadaiah Johnson (younger brother of Samuel Johnson and compiler and editor of *The History of the Yorubas,* working from his brother's notes after the original manuscript had been lost) gave a talk on Yoruba history at a meeting in Lagos. In the discussion afterwards, several Sierra Leoneans, who with other western-educated Yoruba, made up most of the audience, criticized Johnson's bias, one he shared with his brother. Most pointed were the comments of C. A. Sapara Williams, of Ijesha origin and born in Sierra Leone: "I deny that Oyo is the capital city of Yoruba land. Ife, the cradle home of the whole Yorubas and the land of the deified Oduduwa, has been recognised by every Interior tribe (including Benin and Ketu) for all intents and purposes as the capital city." He regretted further that Johnson "has certainly gone into debatable ground in his enquiry into some of the causes that have led to the disruption of the Yorubas kingdoms," and he regretted that there was no time to take up such matters just then (C. A. Sapara Williams, commenting on Hon. Dr. O. Johnson, "Lagos Past" [Duplication of a paper read before the Lagos Institute, 20 November 1901]).

purely patriotic motive" to record Yoruba history from its oral tradition.[8] This conscious purpose would presumably counter some of the possible Christian influence, and the book itself bears out this expectation.

Johnson, in this book a chronicler reminiscent of Froissart, reveals a Yoruba philosophy of history only by implication. In explaining the origins of the Sixteen Years' War (1877–1893), for example, Johnson writes first of the high expectations held at the accession of Adeyemi, a new "king" of Oyo:

But no sooner had he ascended the throne than an evil reign was prognosticated for him. As usual the divination was sent from the sacred city of Ile Ife. The "Igba Iwa" consisting of two covered calabashes identical in shape and size, similarly draped but the contents of which were different were brought before him. The one contained money (cowries), cloth, beads, etc., indicating a happy and prosperous reign, the other gunpowder, bullets, razor, knife, miniature spears and arrows, indicating wars and turmoils. He was to choose one and by his choice detemine the fate of the Yoruba kingdom. Unfortunately he chose the latter and from that time evil days were held to be in store for the country. This was fulfilled by the troubles initiated by the Are of Ibadan, which culminated in the protracted 16 years' war which involved the whole of the Yoruba country and ended by the British protectorate and the loss of the Yoruba People of their absolute independence.[9]

8. Samuel Johnson writes in the "Author's Preface": "With respect to the ancient and mythological period he [the author] has stated the facts as they are given by the bards, and with respect to the History of comparatively recent dates, viz. from the time of King Abiodun downwards, from eye-witnesses of the events which they narrate, or from those who had actually taken part in them. He has thus endeavoured to present a reliable record of events" (Samuel Johnson, *The History of the Yorubas, from the Earliest Times to the Beginning of the British Protectorate* [London, 1921], p. vii).

9. Johnson, *History of the Yorubas*, pp. 402–3. Another example is a passage in which Johnson reports "opinions freely exchanged and conjectures made in those days [at the end of the Sixteen Years' War] as to what would have happened had the British Government not interfered in the interior wars." The "unbiassed observer" (presumably Johnson speaks for himself here) thought the prospects of Ibadan better than those of the Ekitiparapo "for the following reasons: (1) If the Ekitis could have driven them, they had the best chance of doing so when they were fur-

In this, as in others of Johnson's all too few explanations of historical causation, the roles of divination and prophecy loom large, and they show a combination of determinism and free will that follows from Yoruba religious tradition.[10] Whether Adeyemi had a real option to choose the other calabash and change the course of history is left ambiguous, but Yoruba ideas of causality do allow a role for both divination and human choice. A proverb puts the complex interaction succinctly: " 'A Chief is calling you and you are casting Ifa; if Ifa speaks of blessing and the chief speaks of evil, what then?' "[11]

Johnson explains the voluminous trans-Atlantic slave trade in similarly Yoruba terms. He quotes Alafin Awole Arogangan, betrayed in the turmoils of the years just before 1800:

before he committed suicide, he stepped out into the palace quad-

nished with thousands of rifles, and the roads being closed, the Ibadans had not even ammunition for their old flint-lock guns. . . . But latterly when the Ijebus were able to acquire a few scores of rifles, their chances became more even, and the Ekitis were no longer able to assume the offensive. It was only a matter of time; and the Ibadans would eventually have increased their stock of rifles, and then the Ekitis would have had no chance against them. (2) The Ibadans moreover were inspired with hopes of a future success by the following circumstance derived from experience. In all their previous wars, whenever in a difficult campaign, while holding their foes in check they were able to send out a detachment for a subsidiary punitive expedition, which proved successful, victory ultimately rested with them. . . . The victory at Ile Ife showed it would be the same in the Kiriji campaign. (3) The next ground of hope was of a more solid nature. Ogedemgbe was the only leader in whom the Ekitiparapos relied to hold their different sections together. . . . It was not unlikely that the Ibadans, having acquired rifles, a stray bullet might one day put him out of action. . . .

The Ibadans on the other hand could count upon scores of men willing and able to take the lead. In fact *they attributed their non-success to the disobedience to the voice of their national oracle which bestowed the office of Balogun on Akintola, but which the Are was not inclined to follow, consequently the fall of their own leader was not likely to have a bad effect upon them but probably just the contrary*" (pp. 635–36). (Italics mine.)

10. William Bascom, *Ifa Divination, Communication Between Gods and Men in West Africa* (Bloomington, Ind., 1969), pp. 103–119.

11. Quoted in Bascom, *Ifa Divination, Communication Between Gods and Men in West Africa*, p. 119.

rangle with face stern and resolute, carrying in his hands an earthen-
ware dish and three arrows. He shot one to the North, one to the
South, and one to the West uttering those ever-memorable impre-
cations, "My curse be on ye for your disloyalty and disobedience,
so let your children disobey you. If you send them on an errand, let
them never return to bring you word again. To all the points I shot
my arrows will ye be carried as slaves. My curse will carry you to
the sea and beyond the seas, slaves will rule over you, and you their
masters will become slaves."

Johnson concludes, "With this he raised and dashed the earthen-
ware dish on the ground smashing it into pieces, saying . . . a
broken calabash can be mended, but not a broken dish; so let
my words be—irrevocable!"[12]

These basic and very general ideas about causation and process may provide the context in which the Yoruba would have
explained whatever happened to them. Recent anthropological
writings support this interpretation.[13] William Bascom, dealing
with Yoruba divination, concludes his account of the system of
belief:

The ancestral guardian soul, the deities, evil spirits, witches, charms
and medicines, curses, oaths, and ordeals were matters of serious
belief, and religion in its various forms permeated all aspects of
Yoruba life. Yet it would be wrong to conclude that the Yoruba were
resigned to uncontrollable destinies, or that they were content to rely
on divination and other religious practices to solve all their problems.
Several Yoruba proverbs clearly convey the message that "God helps
those who help themselves," and some show an almost skeptical

12. S. Johnson, *History of the Yorubas*, p. 192.
13. The ideas set forth below grow out of passages gleaned from recent anthropological writings on other aspects of Yoruba belief. One can
also gain a few insights, though of course not hard evidence, from the
work of other anthropologists among West African groups geographically
or culturally close to the Yoruba. For example, see R. Horton, "The Ka-
labari World-View: An Outline and Interpretation," *Africa* 3 (1962):
197–219; and M. J. and F. S. Herskovits, *Dahomean Narrative* (Evans-
ton, 1958), Finally, further insights about Yoruba ways of thinking come
from such diverse sources as Wole Soyinka, *A Dance of the Forests*
(London, 1963), and T. A. Lambo, *African Traditional Beliefs. Concepts
of Health and Medical Practice* (Ibadan, 1963). Lambo is writing particularly about the Yoruba.

attitude toward these religious beliefs: "Bravery by itself is as good as magic." . . . "A charm for invisibility is no better than finding a big forest to hide in; a sacrifice is no better than many supporters; and a deity to lift me on to a platform is no better than having a horse to ride away on."[14]

Peter Morton-Williams, discussing the Ogboni cult in Oyo, makes the following revealing analysis:

In discussions of Yoruba religion, contemplative Ogboni men will often introduce such phrases as "I know that everything must have its cause," meaning that whatever the *orisa* do for mankind is a consequence of human action; implicit is a denial of the ordinary man's conviction that there is an element of irresponsibility or of chance in events; implicit also is the awareness that Elegbara, the Trickster deity, cannot lead a man into misfortune unless he himself or an enemy provokes the event.[15]

Again the combination of human will and foreordained destiny is clear, however ambiguously divided.

In analyzing Yoruba views of death, Morton-Williams makes the following comment: "Mankind and the gods can participate in maintaining a social life only under the assurance that the cosmos is eternal in its structure and that *change is growth*— whether it be the ageing of the individual, the development of towns, or new varaitions [*sic*] in culture, change must not be thought random or obliterating."[16]

It would seem, then, that the confrontation with the West would be explained, not in terms of Europeans' characteristics, however different or powerful, but in relation to a Yoruba destiny. And such Yoruba explanations persisted among the Sierra Leoneans, some of whom, it is important to stress, became members on their return of the Ogboni Society,[17] clearly a Yo-

14. Bascom, *Ifa Divination*, p. 119.

15. P. Morton-Williams, "The Yoruba Ogboni Cult in Oyọ," *Africa* 30 (1960): 373.

16. P. Morton-Williams, "Yoruba Responses to the Fear of Death," *Africa* 30 (1960):40. (Italics mine.)

17. See *Preface*, pp. 126–27. In addition, George W. Johnson was in the 1880s described by some of his Egba compatriots as "true Ogboni." Private letter (unsigned) to Johnson, Abeokuta, 16 May 1888, encl. in Moloney to Knutsford, Lagos, 22 April 1888. CO 806/299, quoted, *Preface*, p. 349, n. 63.

ruba "elite." Even so Christianized a Sierra Leonean as Samuel
Johnson explained the coming of the Europeans, and especially
the missionaries, by Yoruba prophecy. Of the arrival of the first
English C.M.S. missionary in Abeokuta in 1845 he wrote:

Thus light began to dawn on the Yoruba country from the south,
when there was nothing but darkness, idolatry, superstition, blood
shedding and slavehunting all over the rest of the country. There
was an old tradition in the country of a prophecy that as ruin and
desolation spread from the interior to the coast, so light and restoration will be from the coast interiorwards. This was a tradition of
ages. Is not this event [the Rev. Henry Townsend's arrival] the beginning of its fulfillment?[18]

For Johnson Christianity brought "light and restoration," not
merely because of the truth of its revelation but also because of
Yoruba, not Christian, inevitability.

Against this background of a shared Yoruba world view, individual Sierra Leoneans undoubtedly understood and explained
the Europeans and the continuing British presence in a variety
of ways. Intellectual reactions were implicit in the actual cultural
mixture each individual made in his own life style and we cannot
categorize for the Sierra Leoneans as a whole either the life style
as practiced or as prescribed for others. We may distinguish sub-
groups according to the degree of exposure to western culture
and western values.

One group consisted of missionaries. They had the most intense and continuing contact with Europeans, not only in the
church but with English government officials and traders in
Freetown and later in Lagos. The decision to become a missionary was a kind of cultural choice, and these men, the most devout of the Christian converts in Sierra Leone, also had special
exposure to western education to fit them for the ministry.

Three careers are especially illuminating here—those of Sam-
uel Crowther, of Egba origin; James Johnson, born in Sierra
Leone of Ijebu parents; and Samuel Johnson, also born in Sierra
Leone, probably of Oyo parents.[19] Although their views differed,

18. S. Johnson, *History of Yorubas,* p. 296.
19. See *Preface,* Appendix A, for additional biographical information
on these and other individuals mentioned.

especially in later years and especially about the best way to meet the western challenge, these men classified and evaluated Europeans similarly. All three distinguished missionaries from government officials, and both of these groups from traders. All tended to associate themselves with what one might call standard missionary views, shared by white missionaries—that both government officials and traders should be judged by whether or not they facilitated the Christianizing and "civilizing" mission. They appeared in a favorable light if their projects furthered agricultural progress and "legitimate trade"; thus could they join the missionaries to bring the beneficent results expected from "the Bible and the Plough" as the missionaries phrased their solution to Africa's problems.[20]

In spite of their similar perceptions, the Sierra Leonean missionaries took different directions on the question of what should be done about the Europeans. Samuel Crowther's position was the most extreme. He, more than anyone else, tended to view African and European ways and outlooks as mutually exclusive, and to choose the European culture. His most famous statement of his position came in a charge to his clergy at Lokoja in 1869:

Africa for the Africans, the rest of the world for the rest of mankind, indeed. If we have any regard for the elevation of Africa, or any real interest for evangelization of her children, our wisdom would be to cry to those Christian nations which have been so long labouring for our conversion, to redouble their Christian efforts.[21]

As E. A. Ayandele has summarized his position, Crowther was:

accommodating to European civilization . . . and saw no conflict in Nigerians' interest in the penetration of the country by it, but rather hoped that the country would derive cultural, social and above all, religious advantages from it. . . . [H]e had no intention of studying African institutions and religion with the hope of understanding them and grafting Christianity on their healthy parts. Rather, he had the worst epithets for these institutions and the Delta peoples.[22]

20. *Preface*, esp. Chaps. 6 and 11.
21. Bishop Crowther, Charge delivered to his Clergy, 1869. CMS: CA 3/04, quoted in *Preface*, p. 255.
22. E. A. Ayandele, *The Missionary Impact on Modern Nigeria* (London, 1967), p. 206.

It is not clear that Crowther ever changed these views, not even after his humiliating removal from the episcopacy of the Niger in 1891. He certainly was not a leader in the movement for African self-assertion that broke with the C.M.S. over the incident.

James Johnson, though sharing some attitudes with Crowther, took a different position. Less willing to assume European cultural superiority (though he was a devout Christian and a key C.M.S. missionary both in Sierra Leone and in Yorubaland), he saw, as Crowther did not, that elements in African culture not only did not need to be destroyed, but *should not* be destroyed. Indeed, they should even be reasserted in the face of the western challenge. African names, African dress—such continuities did not interfere with the practice of Christianity, and Johnson saw no reason why they should be discarded. He even supported African marriage customs, and did not believe in excluding "polygamists" from the church.[23] Politically, he wanted to keep Africa independent of British control. Possibly because of his Ijebu ties (the Ijebu resisted colonial domination through the 1880s until that resistance was broken by British force in 1892), he argued, as Crowther did not, against British penetration into the interior.[24]

Samuel Johnson had a background of experience similar to that of Crowther and James Johnson, but he had a slightly different position from either of them. Never rising so high in the C.M.S. hierarchy (and therefore not so severely thwarted in attempts to assert his own authority and influence), he was nonetheless an ordained minister. Interested in the Yoruba language and history, he also worked, as they did not, on behalf of the British government as a mediator in negotating an end to the Sixteen Years' War in the hinterland.[25]

Though that role might make him appear to show less concern for African independence than had James Johnson, Samuel

23. *Preface,* pp. 240–41, 251–52. See also Spitzer, "The Sierra Leone Creoles," infra.

24. On the Lagos Legislative Council (1886–1894), Johnson argued consistently in debate in support of African independence in the hinterland. See Minutes of the Legislative Council, 1886–94, *passim,* Nigerian Record Office: CSO 32/1377.

25. See S. Johnson, *History of the Yorubas,* pp. 508ff.

Johnson was often acting within a Yoruba context, as his historical writings indicate. His *History of the Yorubas* is a volume of
over 650 pages. Some two-thirds of the book deal with the
events of the nineteenth century, but until page 494, the point
where discussion begins of actual British mediation in the hinterland wars, only a few dozen pages even mention the European
presence, despite the facts that C.M.S. missionaries were in Yorubaland from 1845, and that British political intervention on
the coast began in 1852.

Johnson's mediation grew out of his knowledge of Yoruba
diplomacy and an earlier Yoruba initiative. In 1881, the Alafin
of Oyo had (through another C.M.S. agent, Daniel Olubi) written to the Lagos governor:

I have several times undertaken to bring about the long-desired
peace, but my efforts have from time to time been frustrated. Instead of terminating the war is extending, to threaten the utter extinction of the Yoruba race. . . . With all possible speed I beg that
the Imperial Government . . . come to my help. I crave your assist-
ance both to come to settle this unfortunate war between the bel-
ligerent powers, and to stop the Dahomians who have made an in-
road into my kingdom.[26]

Attempts at mediation in the succeeding years had failed; it is
not surprising that Johnson (and Charles Phillips, who under-
took the mission with him), agreed to participate in another attempt. It was possible, in other words, to view such mediation
within a basically Yoruba framework. Johnson does not appear,
from the evidence in hand, to have thought of himself as an
agent of British power.

Though Samuel Johnson had not maintained close family ties
in the hinterland, he must later have come to see himself—as he
certainly was seen after the implications of British intervention
in the interior became clear—as having facilitated European
penetration. However ambivalent he may have felt in the early
1880s, by the time he had finished the book in 1897 his views
were clear. Looking back on the turmoils of Yorubaland and the

26. Adeyemi, King of the Yorubas to Gov. W. B. Griffiths, Oyo, Oct.
15, 1881, quoted in Johnson, *History*, p. 463.

establishment of the British protectorate, he concluded his work
with the following sentences:

When we have allowed for all the difficulties of a transition stage,
the disadvantages that must of necessity arise by the application of
rules and ideas of a highly civilized people to one of another race,
degree of civilization, and of different ideas, we should hope the net
result will be a distinct gain to the country. But that peace should
reign universally, with prosperity and advancement, and that the
disjointed units should all be once more welded into one under one
head from the Niger to the coast as in the happy days of Abiodun, so
dear to our fathers, that clannish spirit disappear, and above all that
Christianity should be the principal religion in the land—paganism
and Mohammedanism having had their full trial—should be the
wish and prayer of every true son of Yoruba.[27]

Though he talked of a "new era," he also suggested that it might
have finite length; only the future could tell how long it would
last.

A second group along the continuum of Sierra Leonean views
and behavior were less inclined to set forth their intellectual responses in formal writings. Also products of missionary influence in Freetown, such men as Henry Robbin (of liberated
Egba parents) and J. A. Otonba Payne (whose parents were
freed Ijebu) were, at most, lay leaders in Christian congrega-
tions. As vocations, they had chosen trade like Robbin or administration like Payne, and they were successful in their careers.

They too distinguished between Europeans, tending to evaluate them according to what may be called (too simply perhaps)
self-interest, and their interests were not only intellectual and religious but also consciously political. Each was committed to the
cause of his particular Yoruba sub-group in the interior. Robbin's attitudes towards missionaries and administrators reflected
a profound concern for Egba interests; Payne had a similar commitment to the Ijebu.[28] Neither was prolific in his writings (despite Payne's editing of a many-volume *Lagos Almanack*), and

27. Johnson, *History,* pp. 641–42.
28. *Preface,* pp. 143, 179, 189, 234 (Robbin); 156–57, 177, 191–93
(Payne).

these men show their attitudes most clearly in their actions. Both
were important men in the category Europeans generally called
"Black Englishmen." Both worked with the European community of traders and administrators and could not have failed to
gain similar impressions of how the British behaved.[29] Yet, because of the experiences of their respective Yoruba sub-groups
in the interior, their approaches to dealing with the British presence differed.

Henry Robbin spent most of his time in Abeokuta, where he
involved himself in politics as well as trade. He asserted the need
for Africans to be independent of European commercial ven-
tures, and he joined his fellow Egba in their passion for political
autonomy. He was willing to be consulted by Lagos administrators, but he never worked on their behalf. He was not prepared
to help Abeokuta oppose Lagos' encroachment by supporting
structural changes of the kind proposed by the Sierra Leonean
politician, G. W. Johnson, but this position did not destroy his
considerable influence among the Egba. He, like many other Sierra Leoneans, could not anticipate in the 1860s, 1870s and
even early 1880s the overtly expansionist British policy that
would come.[30]

Payne's position among the Ijebu was different. For one thing,
he was for decades a key and constant figure in the otherwise
changing Lagos administration—a British administration that,
by its very proximity, menaced Ijebu independence. For another, though the Egba may have wavered about trusting Sierra
Leonean returnees, making different judgments in specific cases,
the Ijebu were consistently hostile. James Johnson wrote:

I had long heard of the stubborn dislike of my Countrymen the Jebus
to the Gospel and to English customs. . . . Their dislike of European
missionaries and suspicion of natives who had associated themselves
with Europeans and who use their costumes and whom they like
others are fond of designating "White Men" are partly based upon
the fear they entertain that Europeans would take away their country from them.[31]

29. *Preface*, p. 193. Payne entertained in at least partly English style.
30. *Preface*, pp. 97, 197, 188.
31. *Preface*, p. 192.

Against a background of such fears, it is not surprising that
Payne should have felt a distance between himself and his compatriots that limited his room for maneuver. Though his position
made it impossible to take a stand in favor of African independence from British control, he supported the preservation or restoration of certain African practices. His own public life style
was classically "Black English," starting with his two-storied,
colonial-style home, Orange House in Tinubu Square, but, he
declared: "The unanimous opinion of intelligent Africans is, that
health in West Africa is impaired, and lives shortened by the
adoption of European tastes, customs and habits, materials and
forms of dress."[32]

Payne, is, indeed, a striking case of a human but important
inconsistency. Though he himself had adopted many western
practices, this fact did not necessarily mean that he wanted European culture to prevail throughout the country. We must be
careful, in other words, not to deduce prescription solely from
behavior. Payne was not atypical; the incongruities between his
personal actions and his pronouncements are no more striking
than those of other Sierra Leoneans who took other positions.
Their inconsistencies are simply different from his. In politics
and religions, however, Payne accommodated himself to what he
must have seen as the realities of Lagos life. Despite protests at
Crowther's treatment by the C.M.S., he, like James Johnson, did
not cut ties with the church. Nor did he resign from the Lagos
administration after Governor Carter seized Ijebuland in 1892.

Sierra Leoneans in the two groups just described felt their
connection with the English more strongly than did their compatriots farther along the spectrum. They also knew those Yoruba
in the interior who most often associated them with Europeans.
Because other Yoruba made this connection and because men
like Johnson and Payne had advanced farthest in the Europeans'
sphere, they reacted most strongly to a changed western attitude
toward them. Beginning in the 1880s, whites grew more hostile
towards educated Africans because of competition, fear, and the
broader racist currents feeding that fear. The Sierra Leoneans

32. J.A.O. Payne and others, *Views of Some Native Christians on
Polygamy* (Lagos, 1887), p. 24.

were bound to respond with a new assessment and evaluation of the Europeans. They also became at times assertive in defense of African ways.

By passing intermediate positions, we come to a last example on the Sierra Leonean continuum—men and women far less acculturated to western ways, whether by choice or by chance, people who also lacked a continuing and insistent contact with Europeans. The main figure in such a grouping is George W. Johnson—or Osokele Tejumade Johnson as he preferred to be called after 1885. Born in Freetown of Egba parents, he came to Abeokuta where he played an unusual political role. Exposed only to the rudiments of missionary schooling in Freetown, Johnson had less continuing contact with whites than the others, and he felt less cultural pressure. He took little part in work the European presence made possible. He was never employed by the missions or the colonial government, nor was he ever a successful merchant in touch with European traders. However he may have distinguished among Europeans, he dealt with them as a single cohesive force.[33] He actively sought to differentiate himself from them, most strikingly by denying in 1885 that he was a British subject and changing his name.[34]

Johnson's reaction to the western presence was to oppose it. He regarded it as a clear and present danger that the authorities of Abeokuta, the Egba capital, must resist. He sought to guide that resistance himself in ways hardly divorced from his personal ambitions. Nonetheless, he hoped to further both those ambitions and the independence of the Egba by structural changes in the government of Abeokuta, changes that depended on his knowledge of traditional practices but, even more important, on what he had learned from his contact with the British.

From the time G. W. Johnson moved to Abeokuta in 1865, he worked to entrench the authority of the Egba United Board of Management (E.U.B.M.), a political group created to parallel and support the traditional Egba political authority. He was, of course, to be the key person—the secretary of the Board, and

33. *Preface,* pp. 178–81.
34. Notice, Abeokuta, 1 May 1885, in G. W. Johnson papers, Egba Documents, Ibadan University Library.

principal advisor of the Alake. Like the missionaries before him, he believed that Egba independence could be preserved only through centralized authority, especially that of a stronger Alake, but not just any Alake. As it turned out, Johnson became involved in partisan Egba politics with his own candidates and enjoyed a greater personal influence when they were successful.

Here we see another example of inconsistency between action and attitude. John A. Otonba Payne, to recall the first case, was clearly affected by western ways in his personal life style, yet he came to be a staunch and vocal advocate of preserving aspects of African culture; he did not seek, certainly, to bring about structural changes within an African framework. Johnson, in contrast, was himself much less influenced by the West; yet it was he who advocated far-reaching structural modifications in the traditional Egba way of ordering life.[35] He sought to use his knowledge of western political techniques and diplomatic formalities to thwart western penetration. He opposed missionary influence (hence Samuel Crowther, among others, opposed him). He too was against European names and styles, but unlike the Sierra Leoneans in Lagos, for whom such stances have been described in the similar Freetown context as "defensive Africanization," his position on such issues was more aggressive; one might even call it "offensive Africanization," an attack of anticipation, not reaction.

Johnson did not have united Egba support. He, no more than others, Egba or Sierra Leonean Egba, was able to avoid partisan politics. Working within a purely traditional framework, he faced the opposition of those vested interests he threatened (the political power of the trading society, the Parakoyi, for instance), and of factions other than his own. Henry Robbin refused to support the E.U.B.M. at least partly because he and Johnson had at times favored opposing candidates for Alake.[36]

It is not difficult to set forth what different Sierra Leonean groups or individuals (or other Africans) proposed to do when

35. *Preface,* pp. 182–86, 349–50, notes 63–4.
36. *Preface,* p. 188.

faced with the European presence. Their plans emerge, explicitly or implicitly, from their actions and, when historians are fortunate, their writings. It is harder to be certain what these statements and actions really meant. As the late J. R. Levenson pointed out in his work on Chinese intellectual history, " 'a body of knowledge consists not of "propositions," "statements," or "judgments" . . . but of those together with the questions they are meant to answer.' By this token, a proposition's meaning is relative to the question it answers."[37] It is therefore important to know what implicit question or problem lies behind a particular suggestion.

What principal problems were the Sierra Leoneans trying to solve? Their perception of the relative significance of the problems facing them is in some respects as important an intellectual reaction as the solutions they suggested. We cannot assume that they asked simply, "How do we best adapt to this culture and power from the outside?" That question itself assumes some superiority in western culture or power that would force some adaptation. The Africans may not have seen it that way.[38] They may have been asking different questions, or additional questions. Is it not possible that in some cases even the extreme behavior of "Black Englishmen" could have been tactical? In logic,

37. J. R. Levenson, " 'History' and 'Value': The Tensions of Intellectual Choice in Modern China," in A. F. Wright, ed., *Studies in Chinese Thought* (Chicago, 1953), p. 147. Levenson is quoting R. Collingwood and citing Suzanne Langer in this passage. Levenson demonstrates this point (p. 147) with an example of eighteenth- and nineteenth-century European assessments of Asian civilization.

38. Indeed, does not assuming that question parallel the assumption Englishmen made about Africans in the nineteenth century? The phrasing would have been different; it might have run as follows. Africans, recognizing the superiority of Europe and its culture, are seeking to emulate Europeans. They do so by imitation. They will *inevitably* try to imitate. If they fail, it is because they cannot succeed (a view of western-educated Africans that came to be held more and more strongly towards the end of the nineteenth century). If Africans champion certain African ways (marriage customs, names, dress, for instance), it is, in this view, because they have no alternative. They are *unable* to follow the "superior," that is, European, route. Such views were based on unexamined European assumptions about African aims, assumptions certainly not derived empirically.

at least, it could have been an answer to the question, "How do
we best learn about those who threaten us, in order to oppose
their domination effectively?" If so, the same response—apparent mimicry of western ways—would have quite a different
meaning.

And if Sierra Leoneans took up the defense of African ways
(the name and dress changes of Lagos and Freetown, for example), they may not have been responding to the question, "How
can we assert our sagging self-respect in the face of European
attacks on our ability to master their culture?" Might it not as
easily answer another: "How can we assert our identity, or at
least our ties, with our own people and their interests in the hinterland?" Or it could be a response to the long-range problem:
"What, ideally, should be the ultimate culture adopted by Africans?"

In the specific cases, there are the frustrating limitations of
evidence about individual intent. But probably, of the individuals considered here, only Samuel Crowther seems to have posed
for himself only the single question: "How do we best adapt to
outside culture and power?" Certainly James Johnson went beyond it; he may have been trying to find an answer to one more
complex: "How can we take what seems to us useful, appropriate, necessary, even good from the West but still maintain cultural and political independence?" He wrote: "Here [in Lagos],
people are truly loyal British subjects; but this loyalty does not
lessen or destroy their particular love for and interests in their
independent countries, their original homes, the birthplaces of
their parents or their own, and their desire to see their independence maintained."[39] If one assumed, as Johnson did obliquely
in this statement and others did more emphatically, that the
preservation of African independence was possible, it must have
made a difference in the measures he and they proposed.

The most explicit reaction along these "proto-nationalist"
lines was G. W. Johnson's. There are other examples, such as
J. P. Haastrup, a Sierra Leonean who lived in Lagos and described
himself as the "nephew" of the *Owa* of Ilesha. We have little

39. Quoted in *Preface*, pp. 273–74.

record of his thought, but from his actions in the 1880s in the hinterland conflicts we can conclude that he saw British mediation and intervention in the wars of those years as aiding Ijesha's fight for independence from Ibadan's control.[40] Action that might look like political accommodation to Lagos seems clearly to have been for Haastrup a pragmatic answer to a problem in Yoruba balance-of-power politics.

We have virtually no data, unfortunately, on a final group of Sierra Leoneans who chose to react to the West by rejecting it completely. They merged into traditional Yoruba culture, sometimes even becoming members of one or another traditional elite.[41] The bias of the evidence is obvious. Those men and women, who chose not to remember or accept what they learned in Sierra Leone, left no written record, even of their rejection of the West. For this reason, it can only be said that they did exist, acknowledging that the range of positions firmly substantiated does not reflect a true statistical breakdown.

To assess fully African intellectual reactions to the western impact, then, one must examine closely the relation between European influence and education on one side and African cultural influence on the other. One must know in each case how distinct were the ties; how strong and durable were the connections; how close and how frequent was the contact? Changes in those variables produced different responses among Yoruba Sierra Leoneans. Such changes surely affected the questions individual Africans were asking and the assumptions (including the all-important one about historical process) on which those questions were based. It is only, finally, through determining just what Africans were asking, what problems they were seeking to solve, that we can draw valid conclusions about the responses.

40. *Preface,* p. 275.
41. *Preface,* p. 183.

THE SIERRA LEONE CREOLES
1870–1900

Leo Spitzer

The Creole community of Sierra Leone was the source from which the "Sierra Leoneans" of Nigeria emerged, but the two were far from identical. In some respects, the Creoles' position in Nigeria was closer to that of the Afro-French community in Senegal than it was to that of the Creoles in Sierra Leone itself. The key point here was the culture of the neighborhood. Where Creoles in Lagos and western-influenced townsmen in Senegal could see their own roots in the African culture of the surrounding rural areas, no matter how complete their western-style education, the Creoles in Sierra Leone were cut off from their African roots. They were resettled in Africa, but in a part of Africa where the local culture was almost as alien as that of the Europeans. They were also subject to a more intensive assimilationist campaign by government and missions than was attempted in either Senegal or nineteenth-century Nigeria.

These conditions help to explain why they moved so far in the direction of western culture. They dropped their original home languages after a time and took up a conglomerate language, which became modern Krio, combining English with several African languages. Krio often became their only African language, while the Senegalese continued to speak Wolof, and the returnees to Nigeria spoke Yoruba as well as English. Leo Spitzer's article explains, however, why even the Creoles of Sierra Leone were not willing to respond to the West simply by becoming western.

He is author of a forthcoming book which will trace the changing responses of Sierra Leone Creoles from the mid-nineteenth century to the mid-twentieth.

P.D.C.

Love and Betrayal

"We must lay a good foundation," he said, adding, "when you start school you must study hard, and if you do, who knows but you may go to England one day!"

England! I was really interested now. For even in those my early days, England was a magic word to us. It was the country where our bishop, our governor, the women missionaries, and the white men in the shops all came from, and where our own people had to go to become doctors and lawyers. It was almost as far as heaven in our imagination, except that heaven was above the clouds.

(R. W. Cole, *Kossoh Town Boy*, p. 77)

The upset of the Sierra Leonean began with the upset of thought of his white rulers concerning him. A day came when white thought began to be changed, white feeling began to be altered, and white action began to be fitted to the thought and feeling. The commencement of the period coincided with the rise of imperialistic ideas and of the rediscovery of Africa. Those who had been fathers now rose to arms, and in many and strange ways proclaimed that Arcady was gone, and the idyllic must be superseded by a reality which must go hand in hand with sternness. Segregation was the first blast of the trumpet; then other things and other things.

(Editorial, *Sierra Leone Weekly News*, 8 April 1916)

Sierra Leone Creoles were long called "Black English."[1] Initially

1. A. J. Shorunkeh Sawyerr, "The Social and Political Relations of Sierra Leone Natives to the English People," *Sierra Leone Weekly News* [cited hereafter as *SLWN*], 15 April 1893. Although it has on occasion been used to refer to the racially mixed offspring of a liaison between an African and a European, the term "Creole" is generally defined differently in Sierra Leone. At first, "Creole" was only applied to the colony-born children of liberated Africans. Intermarriage and cultural blending between the various groups which had been settled in Sierra Leone—the Poor Black, Nova Scotians, Maroons—gradually erased the distinctions

they understood the term to have no pejorative connotations. Upper-class Creoles took it as a confirmation of fact: they were black and they felt like English, and to be English during the reign of Queen Victoria was something of which to be proud. To be called "Black English," moreover, was recognition of their successful Europeanization—of having shed the manners and customs which they and Europeans associated with the "less civilized" peoples of the interior of Africa. For a large number of Creoles, living, dressing, speaking and acting like Englishmen— or as they believed the English to do these things—was "the inevitable outcome of the civilization and enlightenment" which had been brought to bear on Sierra Leone Colony since its inception.[2] The Sierra Leone experiment, after all, had originally set out to create "Black English," persons who were educated in the European manner, preferably Christian, disdainful of superstition, abhorring slavery, willing to accept the values of Victorian England, and to keep its faith.

England was the focus of attention for educated Creoles. They were drawn to the island physically and, like true lovers, tended to idealize her virtues and minimize her faults. For many of the wealthier Creoles England was a second home—a place to which one could journey during the rainy season, a country where one completed his education, where young women were polished into genteel ladies and young men became gentlemen. Indeed, many Creoles attended some of the best schools in Britain, graduated with degrees from Oxford and Cambridge, studied law and medicine, joined societies like the Royal Colonial Institute, dressed in the latest fashions, and mixed freely, if at

---

which had originally existed among them; "Creole" then came to describe the descendants of all the black African groups which were settled in Sierra Leone after 1787. "Creole" in Sierra Leone eventually took on a wider, cultural definition as well. The Creole community came to include persons of black African stock, usually from one of the neighboring ethnic groups or from the Sierra Leone hinterland, who emulated the "Creole way of life" by adopting the language, habits, standards of behavior, and outlooks with which Creoles identified.

2. "Our Native Manners and Customs," *Sierra Leone Times* [cited hereafter as *SLT*], 23 June 1894.

times self-consciously, with the English on the latter's own home grounds.[3]

At a time near the mid-nineteenth century when the color bar and racial discrimination in Britain were as yet relatively uncommon, it had been easy for Sierra Leoneans to see England as utopia achieved. Creoles felt then that theirs was a special association with Britain, that their relationship had been made exceptional by historical events. Proud of Sierra Leone's place among the oldest of British possessions, Creoles came to view their homeland as somehow more loyal to the British crown than other colonies. They were grateful to British philanthropy for freeing their ancestors from slavery, for educating them and placing them at what they believed to be the vanguard of black peoples on the African continent. It was reassuring to imagine themselves as Britain's favorite and favored Africans.

Queen Victoria had a special place in their hearts, symbolizing all that was good in the relationship between Britons and Sierra Leoneans. Locally, she was called "We Mammy," "Our Mother."[4] The Queen's Golden Jubilee in 1887 coincided with the centenary of the first settlement of Sierra Leone and both events were celebrated in the colony with an enthusiasm which bordered on ecstasy. E. W. Blyden composed a centenary ode and wrote a historical play depicting the settlement of the colony. Fireworks, parades, balls, and entertainments marked the festivities. Many female children born during 1887 were named "Jubilee" or "Victoria."

A number of the more enlightened deputies of the British government in the colony were also regarded with great affection. Governor Sir Charles MacCarthy, who later lost his head fighting the Ashanti, was called "We Daddie," "Our Father," during his sixteen years in Sierra Leone.[5] Sir Arthur Kennedy, who had

---

3. For examples, see M. C. F. Easmon, "Sierra Leone Doctors," *Sierra Leone Studies* n.s. no. 6 (June, 1956), pp. 81–96; *Royal Colonial Institute, Proceedings* 13 (1881–82):56–90; Christopher Fyfe, *History of Sierra Leone* (Oxford, 1962), pp. 406, 433.

4. *SLWN*, 10 June 1911.

5. *West Africa* (London), 28 February 1920, p. 185; A. B. C. Sibthorpe, *History of Sierra Leone* (London, 1881), p. 23.

begun his career as an unpopular governor, ultimately redeemed himself and was commemorated by the "Kennedy Leaf," an indispensable home remedy whose medicinal good effects were beyond question, and by the song popular among women:

> Who reign? Governor Kennedy!
> Who reign? Beloved Kennedy![6]

Sir John Pope-Hennessy, perhaps the most popular of all Sierra Leone governors not only for his abolition of the resented House and Land Tax but also because of his championing of African capabilities, was remembered long after his death with a yearly celebration of "Pope-Hennessy Day," a public holiday, and with the Krio song:

> All dem Governor do bereh well
> All dem Governor do bereh well;
> Pope Hennessy do pass dem,
> Pope Hennessy—Pope Hennessy do pass dem.[7]

Creole sympathies for Britain, however, went even beyond their near adulation of Queen Victoria and the handful of British governors who had pleased them. After the Congress of Berlin and during the accelerating scramble for Africa, for example, educated Sierra Leoneans felt a genuine identity with the aims of British imperialism and the white man's burden. Creole children recited Kipling by heart and sang "Britannia Rules the Waves."[8] Similarly, their parents, who had grown up learning a great deal about European history and geography and little or nothing about Africa and its past, took pride in Britain's imperial victories and mourned her defeats. Many Creoles were genuinely saddened when General Gordon lost his life at Khartoum and did not show the slightest sympathy for the aims of the Mahdi, a fellow African.[9]

Creoles rationalized their sympathy and support for Britain's

---

6. Article by D. T. Akibo-Betts in *SLWN*, 27 October 1934.
7. Recorded in Freetown, September 1965.
8. Robert Wellesley Cole, *Kossoh Town Boy* (Cambridge, 1960), p. 91.
9. *SLWN*, 11 April 1885.

imperial aims in a number of ways. They could not forget what
Britain had done in the past for their ancestors and for Sierra
Leone Colony. Not only had Britain put a stop to "tribal wars"
that had been a byproduct of the slave trade, but also, according
to some Sierra Leoneans, "by patience, perseverance, by sacrifice, by expenditure, by wise administration, in spite of some de-
plorable mistakes," Britain restored order and peace to Africa,
stopped the trade in human beings, and gave the opportunity to
millions of Africans "for growth in civilization." "We are largely
indebted to England," argued an editorial in the *Sierra Leone
Weekly News,* "for material, intellectual, and it may be, ultimately, spiritual salvation."[10] Most important of all, Creoles
were favorably inclined toward the imperial movement because
they still liked to see themselves in much the same way as the
missionaries and philanthropists had viewed them in the early
decades of the nineteenth century—as an important and privileged arm of British penetration and "civilization" into the interior of the continent, and as the living examples of successful
British ideas and actions in Africa.

The Creole attitude toward Britain had an obverse side as well.
Love stood back to back with hate. Having for decades been
nurtured in the belief that they were somehow special—better
than those Africans who had never been exposed to the benefits
of European culture and as good as any Englishman who, like
them, was a Christian and a gentleman—Creoles were psychologically little prepared for the changes that were taking place in
European ideas about Africans after the 1860s. With racist ideas
coming into vogue, few in Europe still believed that "lower
races" could even grasp the complexities of the European way of
life, to say nothing of mastering it well enough to act as carriers
of European culture among their own people.[11] While physical
anthropologists were proclaiming the inferiority of black peoples, and Darwin's work was being used to bolster the proposition that superior races were marked by their material superior-

10. *SLWN,* 25 November 1899.
11. Philip D. Curtin, *The Image of Africa* (Madison, 1964), pp. 238–
40, 414–15, 425–26.

ity, the noble savage stereotype was replaced by the popular image of an ape-like black man in top hat and dark suit. As paternalism came to displace the ideal of equality through conversion too many Britons made Creoles feel like parodies rather than equals. Under these circumstances, it was difficult for Creoles to maintain without blemishes of disillusionment their love for Britain.

When British deeds and attitudes toward educated Africans became more negative as the century progressed, educated Creoles increasingly deviated from the starry-eyed idealization of Britain and her aims. They began to feel betrayed, scorned. By 1887, the year of Queen Victoria's Golden Jubilee and the centenary of the settlement of Sierra Leone, a number of Creoles were already certain that the days of beneficent British philanthropists who had worked along with other Europeans for the cultural transformation of Africans through Christianity, education, and commerce were forgotten, or at least obscured. "Now-a-days," complained a writer in the *Sierra Leone Weekly News,* "we may expect to meet with antipathy where in by-gone days we met with support. The successors of those who forty years ago believed in giving us every opportunity to rise in the world now believe that every effort on our part should be nipped in the bud or regarded with indifference bordering on contempt."[12] Having striven for an identity with Britain and Britons in all phases of their lives, these Sierra Leoneans repeatedly saw themselves relegated to subordinate positions, spurned by the very people whose cultural wards they had become.

As the catalogue of actions unfavorable to Creoles expanded in the 1890s, Sierra Leoneans found it ever more difficult to rationalize British behavior. Some of the iniquities in the catalogue were minor—a haughty tone of voice, a murmured insult, a shove in the streets, an arrogant gesture.[13] They were inflicted on

12. *SLWN,* 26 February 1887. See also "Some of Our Drawbacks," *SLWN,* 5 February 1887; "My View of Things," *SLWN,* 25 June 1887; "Origins and Purpose of Sierra Leone," *West African Reporter,* 4 June 1888.

13. See *SLWN,* 16 February 1896, for a Creole reaction to the word "nigger."

an individual basis, person-to-person, and their impact, although cumulative, was not sufficient to arouse a mass response. Such occurrences deviated markedly from the good will, courtesy, and tact which Creoles believed to have characterized interracial relationships in former days; still, many upper-class Sierra Leoneans passed over these incidents as the product of a "lower type of Englishman," less educated and certainly more boorish, but to be pitied for his actions if not forgiven altogether.

Other incidents, however, either affected or became known to a greater number of people and were less easily dismissed as uncharacteristic slips. Creoles met discrimination in the professional fields, in the civil service, and in commerce. Each aberration added fuel to a fire which, for a significant element of Creole society, was burning up the old associations between themselves and the British.[14]

Defensive Africanization: Cultural

Some Sierra Leoneans, ever charitable toward Europeans, responded to the growing alienation from the British with anxiety and insecurity, blaming the turn of events not on external factors but on weaknesses in Creole society. Examining their own culture they agreed that something was amiss, that a "lack of progress" had become the curse of their lives and that they were bordering on degeneracy.

Creole responses of this type varied considerably in sophistication and depth of analysis. The old, standard, Victorian assumptions which blamed the ills of soul and body on "vicious indulgence," "intemperate habits," and "fast living" all seemed inadequate, especially since many of the people who were most affected by the changed British attitudes could be counted among the colony's finest citizens.[15] One man attributed the situ-

14. See Leo Spitzer, "Sierra Leone Creole Reactions to Westernization, 1870–1925" (Ph.D. Diss., Wisconsin, 1969), pp. 72–82; Spitzer, "The Mosquito and Segregation in Sierra Leone," *Canadian Journal of African Studies* 2 (1968):49–61.

15. J. H. Spaine's lecture, "The Youths of Sierra Leone, Their Condition and Prospects," *The Independent*, 22 July 1875; Editorial, "Early

ation to "inexorable decrees" by an "offended Creator" who had meted out punishments to Sierra Leoneans for "misused and abused advantages."[16] Others interpreted their state of being in terms of the survival of the fittest. Comparing their own felt lack of vitality, health, and strength with the vigor of the up-country-men, or even with that of their fathers and grandfathers, these Creoles believed themselves to be growing weaker, fading in mind and body, rapidly being surpassed by the vigorous Mende, Timne, and Limba.[17] Still others explained their situation as a vestige from their "slave past." "The slave mind," stated an editorial in the *Sierra Leone Weekly News,* "is one of the evil things which have come to us by inheritance from the inhuman traffic. . . . All the qualities of mind which are mighty [*sic*] to obstruct progress both of individuals and communities may be reasonably included in this evil property."[18]

In order to soothe anxieties about their own situation and to assess in less deprecating terms why things had turned out the way they did, a number of Creoles took an altogether different tack. Feeling themselves to have been historically manipulated by a multitude of forces over which they had little control, these Sierra Leoneans looked within their own society to examine afresh its character and values and to question the very premise on which their culture rested—the validity of the African assimilation of European ways.

The Creoles given to this type of introspection had a great deal in common. The majority of them were at the peak, or very near the peak of the Creole class structure, star products of Britain's imperial mission in Sierra Leone, and in firm possession of

---

Mortality of Influential Natives of Sierra Leone," *West African Reporter,* 3 June 1882; Dulcie Nicolls, "The Effects of Western Education on the Social Attitudes of the Creoles in Sierra Leone" (Dip. ed. Diss., Durham Univ., 1960), p. 45.

16. "The Passing Away of the Creole Element," *Colonial and Provincial Reporter,* 17 January 1914.

17. "One Thing and Another," *SLT,* 24 June 1893, 28 August 1897; Letter to the Editor by Abdul Mortales, *SLWN,* 8 January 1898; Editorial, *SLWN,* 4 January 1902; Editorial, *SLWN,* 22 June 1912; *Sierra Leone Guardian and Foreign Mail,* 18 October 1912.

18. Editorial, *SLWN,* 4 March 1911.

European knowledge, techniques, and outlooks. As the persons most exposed to westernization, they were extremely sensitive and vulnerable to changes in European attitudes toward them. Culturally Europeanized but racially black African, they suffered a crisis of identity when rejected by the British on whom they modeled themselves.

The group was numerically small. But it included the most literate and vocal members of Creole society, men with direct access to the Sierra Leone press and other vehicles of communication. Occupying the top rung of the social hierarchy, they set fashions, shaped opinions, and exerted an influence far exceeding their numerical strength.

For the most part they were conservative in social outlook, advocating moral rather than political reforms in the way of life as they knew it. Caught up in the British idea of fair play, they were upset when their mentors deviated from the rules. But, when pressed, they were Victorian gentlemen looking for amelioration rather than revolution. Barricade fighting was alien to the tradition they had come to love and accept; to them, composing cleverly worded protest letters to the editor of the *Weekly News,* while sitting in an easy chair and sipping afternoon tea, seemed much more civilized and less foreign.

Edward Wilmot Blyden, although not a Creole himself, was one of their primary intellectual influences and spokesmen.[19] Early in life Blyden fashioned an ideology which combined a teleological belief in the perfectibility of man with a conviction about the uniqueness of races. Influenced by his Christian upbringing, his training as a minister, and his connection with the New York Colonization Society, he had no doubt that the mil-

19. For biographical information see E. W. Blyden, Taylor Lewis, Theodore Dwight, et. al., *The People of Africa—A Series of Papers on Their Character, Condition, and Future Prospects* (New York, 1871), biographical note by H. M. S., pp. 1–3; *Journal of the African Society* 11 (1912):362–64; *SLWN,* 10 February 1912; Obituary, *Sierra Leone Guardian and Foreign Mail,* 16 February 1912; Hollis R. Lynch, *Edward Wilmot Blyden, Pan-Negro Patriot, 1832–1912* (London, 1967); Edith Holden, *Blyden of Liberia, An Account of the Life and Labors of Edward Wilmot Blyden, LL.D., As Recorded in Letters and in Print* (New York, 1967).

lennium would ultimately come, but only after each race had fulfilled its divinely ordained destiny. "Each race is endowed with peculiar talents," he wrote in *Christianity, Islam and the Negro Race*, "and watchful to the last degree is the great Creator over the individuality, the freedom and independence of each. In the music of the universe each shall give a different sound, but necessary to the grand symphony."[20] In Blyden's conception, differences between races did not mean that any one race was inferior or superior, either physically, intellectually, or morally. Each was capable of equal, but not identical, development and progress. Europeans in this racially determined universe became God's rulers, God's soldiers, and God's policemen to keep order. In the divine plan, it was their role to work for the material and temporal advancement of humanity. Science and politics were their racial fortes; individualism was the basis of their society.[21] African blacks, on the other hand, possessed a different racial "personality" (Blyden used the now popular term "Negro Personality"). They were members of a "spiritual" race, communal and cooperative rather than "egotistic and competitive" in social organization, and polygynous rather than monogamous in family life. Unlike the whites, their divine "gift" did not lie in the realm of political life but in spiritual advancement through church, school, farm, and workshop.[22] And, perhaps because they were by nature the less aggressive people, the qualities uniquely inherent in their race had to be nurtured, pro-

20. E. W. Blyden, *Christianity, Islam and the Negro Race*, 2nd ed. (London, 1889), pp. 317–18. John R. Schott, "Edward Wilmot Blyden: First Pan Africanist?" (Paper presented at the 9th Annual African Studies Association Meeting, Bloomington, Indiana, 1967) gives an interesting interpretation of the influences of Christianity and the ideology of the New York Colonization Society on Blyden's thought.

21. E. W. Blyden, *Proceedings at the Banquet in Honour of Edward Wilmot Blyden, LL.D., on the Occasion of his Retirement . . . January 24th 1907* (London, 1907), pp. 40–41; "Banquet in Honor of C. E. Wright," *SLWN*, 28 November 1903.

22. E. W. Blyden, *Africa and the Africans, Proceedings on the Occasion of a Banquet Given to E. W. Blyden by West Africans in London, August 15, 1903* (London, 1903), p. 44; E. W. Blyden, *African Life and Customs* (London, 1908), pp. 9–36; Obituary, *Sierra Leone Guardian and Foreign Mail*, 16 February 1912.

tected, and developed if they were to contribute their share to the total uplifting of mankind. As Blyden saw it, no man benefitted from the dilution or destruction of the black African personality through the wholesale introduction and acceptance of European culture.

All these ideas, of course, had particular relevance for Creoles. Blyden shared the pessimism which some Creoles held about their own society. He explained the Creole lack of initiative or "African manhood," their superficial attainments, lack of progress, "artificial emotions," and their easily caricatured appearance, by blaming their European education and training. Since the races were divinely ordained to move along "parallel lines," and not "in the same groove," no amount of cultural interaction or tutelage would ever make Europeans from black Africans or black Africans from Europeans.[23] At best, those Africans who thought of themselves as Europeans were imitators unable to achieve a viable hybrid culture; at worst they became "apes" and parasites, men without identity who had lost "the flavor of their race."[24] Speaking to the Freetown Unity Club, Blyden made himself quite clear on this point:

Your first duty is to be *yourselves.* . . . You need to be told to keep constantly before yourselves the fact that you are African, not Europeans—black men, not white men—that you were created with the physical qualities which distinguish you for the glory of the Creator, and for the happiness and perfection of humanity; and that in your endeavors to make yourselves something else you are not only spoiling your nature and turning aside from your destiny, but you are robbing humanity of the part you ought to contribute to its complete development and welfare, and you become as salt, which has lost its savour—good for nothing, but to be cast out and trodden down by others.[25]

23. "Banquet in Honor of C. E. Wright," *SLWN*, 28 November 1903. See also CO 267/324, Blyden to Earl Kimberley, 1873; Blyden, *Christianity, Islam and the Negro Race*, pp. 76–77, 254, 317–18; Blyden, *Aims and Methods of a Liberal Education for Africans, Inaugural Address delivered by E. W. Blyden, LL.D., President of Liberia College, Jan. 5, 1881* (Cambridge, Mass., 1882), pp. 6–11
24. Blyden, *Christianity, Islam and the Negro Race.*
25. *SLWN,* 20 June 1891.

Blyden had made a series of trips to the interior both in Liberia and Sierra Leone, and he often met with Muslim traders from up-country with whom he conversed in Arabic. To contrast with the coastal, educated, Europeanized Africans—ironically, the group to which he himself belonged—Blyden celebrated the people of Africa's interior as prototypes who possessed the true "Negro Personality." He wrote:

In the European settlements on the coast, there are visible the melancholy effects of the fatal contagion of a mimic or spurious Europeanism. [Those] who have been to Europe, bring back and diffuse among their people a reverence for some of their customs of that country [Europe], of which the more cultivated are trying to get rid. But, happily, the inhospitable and inexorable climate prevents this pseudo-civilization, called "progress," from spreading to the interior. The tribes still retain their simplicity and remain unaffected.[26]

Undoubtedly, through his contacts, he should have had firsthand information about the customs and ways of the hinterland. But his writings belie this. Not particularly drawn to ethnographic study or description, Blyden built his "interior Africans" into an abstraction—as removed from an African reality as the noble savage of eighteenth-century Europe had been false to the character, appearance, and ways of the American Indians.[27]

Blyden's efforts to make West African blacks more conscious of their "true" racial identity and his challenge to their wholesale

26. Blyden, *Christianity, Islam and the Negro Race*, p. 400.
27. Even he, of course, considered the interior to be far from perfect. Like other Europeanized Africans of his time, Blyden looked contemptuously on "paganism, with all its horrors and abominations," which was practiced by interior peoples. He admitted that up-countrymen lived a "savage existence" in "quiescent and stagnant barbarism" but only because of the "cruel conditions" of their environment. Nonetheless, the good far outweighed the bad; Reprint of a letter from Blyden to the *Christian Advocate* in New York (the official organ of the Methodist Episcopal Church in the United States), *SLWN*, 15 July 1899; Article reprinted from *The Charleston World*, *SLWN*, 8 January 1890; "Blyden in Lagos," *SLWN*, 14 February 1891; *West African Reporter*, 28 November 1876; Blyden speaking about Sierra Leone in Lagos, *SLWN*, 20 September 1884; "Address Delivered at the Celebration of the 20th Anniversary of the Educational Institute, L. J. Leopold, Principal," *SLWN*, 20 September 1903.

assimilation of European ways struck an exposed nerve among all Creoles concerned with the state of their own society. His uncomplimentary views about Europeanized Africans hit painfully hard, to be sure, but they were nonetheless the views of an educated fellow black and, as such, more easily received than if they had been articulated by a European. Moreover, no matter how harsh their implications for Creoles, his ideas were also extremely attractive: to believe in the distinctiveness and uniqueness of the black race and its destiny was an effective psychological salve against the pain inflicted by European insults and discrimination.

Influenced by Blyden, some Sierra Leoneans began to attribute the ills of their society to the perversion of their true black African racial personality by means of their indiscriminate Europeanization. In their anxiety and depression they looked again at themselves—at their educational achievements, their social life and occupations, their dwellings and diet, their trousers, coats, top hats, and boots, their woolly hair parted in the European style—and were displeased to find a community of captive intellect, one that had grown up "aping the white man," blindly imitating manners and customs that were racially alien and, in any case, unsuitable to the African environment.[28] A few expressed themselves in terms of Blyden's teleological vision, repudiating their emulation of European customs and manners as a falsification of a divinely ordained separation of races.[29] Others put their views in more secular terms:

Nature must have her way. She is always insuperable. She will triumph over all our false aims and aspirations. Some say that we

28. See, for example, James H. Spaine, "The Youths of Sierra Leone, Their Condition and Prospects," *The Independent*, 22 July 1875; Letter to the Editor, *Methodist Herald*, 10 December 1884; Letter to the Editor by Latonday of Abeokuta, *SLWN*, 12 December 1885; "First of a Series of Articles on 'The Degeneracy of the Civilized Blacks of West Africa'," *SLWN*, 14 July 1906; Editorial, *SLWN*, 8 June 1901; "One Thing and Another," *SLT*, 28 August, 20 November 1897.

29. "Notes by the Way," *SLWN*, 28 July 1888; also read the comments about the pageant which Blyden wrote for the festivities celebrating the centenary of the founding of Sierra Leone in *SLWN*, 23 June 1887; *Memorial of the Jubilee of Her Majesty's Reign and the Centenary of Sierra Leone, 1887* (London, 1887), pp. 92–108.

are now in a transition state, and that the process of all transitions is painful and sometimes destructive. . . . But, under our climatic and racial conditions, the transition only leads to death. . . . The fact is, that not only is there a want of adjustment between the two states of things, but an invincible incompatibility. The facts of European civilization will never fit in with the everlasting facts of African conditions. . . . If Nature demands the continuation of the domestic and social customs of the natives as the price of the preservation of the race in this climate, the price must, of course, be paid or extinction will supervene.[30]

Still others, however, decided to break through the tyranny of foreign customs by direct reversion to traits, manners, and identifications which they felt were inherently black African. William J. Davis, for example, who was senior master at the Wesleyan High School and the first Sierra Leonean to receive a B.A. from London University, changed his name to Orishatukah Faduma, a name which he derived from the Yoruba divinity Orisha and the oracle Ifa.[31] A letter to the editor of the *Sierra Leone Weekly News* written by Kufileh Tubohku, a man who himself had probably "Africanized" his name, explained Davis' action:

We have received an education and a civilization that have instilled into us an element of doubt as to our own capacity and destiny, that have implanted in us falsehoods about ourselves, which, instead of producing in us self-respect, efficiency, and self-reliance, with a sense of our own individuality—the outcome of a correct education—have rendered us self-detractors, self-depreciators, distrustful of our own possibilities, striving to escape from our own individuality if possible, contemptuous and doubtful of every native element, and indifferent to everything of our own originality.

Those who censured Faduma for changing a name by which he had been known from his birth should remember that every one of our Liberated Negro Parents had a name given him in the land of his nativity by which he was called and known from his birth up to the time he arrived in the land of his exile. He had a name full of meaning . . . preserving a tribal or racial individuality. When transported through the baneful traffic of the Slave Trade to this land,

30. *SLWN*, 12 January 1901.
31. Letter to the Editor, *SLWN*, 1 October 1887; *Methodist Herald*, 24 August 1887; G. Parrinder, *West African Religion* (London, 1961), pp. 12, 26, 96.

that name was exchanged for a foreign one . . . void of meaning and insignificant to him.

It is nought but a profound and crass ignorance that thinks a man who would be civilized must forsake all that belongs and is natural to him, in exchange for what is foreign and unnatural.[32]

A number of Creoles joined Faduma and "reformed" their names as well, either shedding their "foreign" surname to adopt one with an African sound, or adding an African name to their European one. Thus A. E. Metzger became Tobuku-Metzger when he added his father's Yoruba name to the name which the family had taken from his father's German missionary pastor at Kissy.[33] O. T. George became O. T. Nana; Claude George, the man who had written *The Rise of British West Africa,* became Esu Biyi; Isaac Augustus Johnson changed to Algerine Kefallah Sankoh, and Africanus Matthew Goodman became Eyahjemi Moondia.

But perhaps more important than name reform among these Sierra Leone Creoles was the establishment of dress reform. A Dress Reform Society which could claim E. W. Blyden, Rev. James Johnson, and Rev. J. R. Frederick as associates, was founded in 1887 by some of the most socially prominent Creoles in the colony. James Hasting Spaine, the colonial postmaster, was president, A. E. Toboku-Metzger was the secretary; Cornelius May, editor of the *Methodist Herald* and later editor and owner of the *Sierra Leone Weekly News,* was a founding member along with Orishatukah Faduma, and Enoch Faulkner, chief clerk at the colonial secretary's office and later assistant colonial secretary.[34] Unlike such other nonwestern peoples as the Japa-

32. Letter to the Editor by Kufileh Tubohku, *SLWN,* 1 October 1887.
33. See Fyfe, *History of Sierra Leone,* p. 468.
34. Other founding members were: J. C. Sawyerr, N. F. Browne, C. E. Wright, J. B. Mends, M. Benson-Nicol, J. W. M. Horton, E. Beccles Davies. Others who subsequently joined were: J. C. May, publisher of the *Methodist Herald* and principal of the Wesleyan Boys' High School; J. B. M'Carthy, a well-to-do merchant; J. Langley Grant, T. Taylor, S. G. Roberts, R. Smith, T. Dundas, J. S. T. Davies, P. A. Bickersteth, S. O. Lardner, E. C. Lisk. See *The Artisan,* 31 December 1887, Supplement; *Methodist Herald,* 21 December 1887.

nese, Chinese, and Indians, whose retention of their individual clothing styles highlighted what Blyden would have called "their separate racial identity," Creoles in the Dress Reform Society were convinced that their addiction to the "Religion of the Frock Coat and Tall Hat" was yet another mark of their cultural subordination.[35] The Society saw the elimination of the most obvious badge of Europeanization—European dress—as the first, and most important step in bringing about a gradual independence from *all* European customs.

It should be presumption to state that the intended sphere of the Dress Reform Society is unlimited. It would set itself as time advances to grapple with other social and local questions. Its intention is to become the line of advance of all social improvements. . . . It is a society that could become more and more the rallying point for all who long for and are zealous for the independent national existence of Africa and the Negro.[36]

To counteract the perversion of their "racial personality," and to safeguard their health, the members of the Dress Reform Society adopted a new wardrobe. Instead of trousers with belt and braces, shirt, waistcoat, collar, and tie, they devised an "undertunic" and gown, somewhat like a Turkish kaftan, to be worn over a pair of breeches reaching down to the knees, similar to European knickerbockers but free at the bottom to admit the flow of air. Female fashions, however, were not altered at all. In the age of Victoria, reform bowed to discretion.[37]

35. *SLWN,* 10 August 1907, Letter to the Editor by C. W. Farquhar contains the phrase "Religion of the Frock Coat and Tall Hat" to describe the Creole habit of wearing European-style clothing.
   36. *Methodist Herald,* 21 December 1887.
   37. *Methodist Herald,* 21 December 1887. The high, starched collars, ties, silk top hats, and heavy woolen suits worn by the men, the corsets or tight lacings, long dresses, and bonnets in style with the ladies, had all been designed for colder weather and were not loose enough to allow for the free circulation of air needed in the tropics. See *SLWN,* 19 May 1888, reprint of a paper given to the Dress Reform Society by Surgeon J. J. Lamprey, Senior Medical Officer of the Army Medical Staff of the West Coast of Africa, on clothing to be worn in the tropics. See also Letter by J. J. Lamprey, *SLWN,* 4 August 1888; *SLWN,* 9 February 1889.

At no time did the members of the Dress Reform Society or the individuals who Africanized their name view their activities as steps to initiate direct cultural links between themselves and the African peoples in the immediate hinterland of Sierra Leone. The adopted names were generally in the language of the Creoles' forefathers, most usually in Yoruba, or, like the name "Africanus," were manufactured to sound African. They were not names generally found in Sierra Leone's up-country. The Dress Reform Society's wardrobe was an invention as well, somewhat like the short trousers and sleeveless country-cloth gowns of up-countrymen to be sure, but still different enough not to be confused with them. All this, of course, served a distinct psychological function. In defining elements of the black African personality as they saw fit—far enough removed from up-country realities so that no confusion would arise—they were able both to have their cake and to eat it: they could believe that they were no longer wholesale imitators of the Europeans and were shaping their culture more in keeping with their "racial destiny," without, at the same time, being frightened that they were in any way reverting to the ways of up-country "barbarian aborigines."

Dress reform was shorter-lived than name reform. The members of the Dress Reform Society wore their costumes to the relatively infrequent meetings which were held in 1887 and 1888. But, although their convictions may have been strong in a closed gathering, they were not strong enough to induce them to wear their dress every day in public. A basic reason for the failure of the Society to catch on was that its members were apparently too proud of their high status within Creole society to risk being laughed at and socially demoted for nonconformity, both by other Creoles and by the trend-setting Europeans.[38] Name changes, on the other hand, were less visible and thus less prone

38. *Methodist Herald,* 21 December 1887; *The Artisan,* 6 October 1887, ridiculed name and dress reform in one of its articles; "The Degeneracy of the Civilized Blacks of West Africa," *SLWN,* 21 July 1906; J. R. Renner-Maxwell, *The Negro Question, or Hints for the Physical Improvement of the Negro Race with Special Reference to West Africa* (London, 1892), p. 30.

to come under attack. Europeans seemed less amused by the decision of a few Creoles to Africanize their names than they were by the Creoles' choice of unusual Greek, Latin, or Biblical first names and by their seemingly pretentious inclination to add a hypenated second name to their surname.[39] But even name-changing did not escape derision completely and the practice, while remaining a characteristic of Creole society long after the 1880s, became much less publicized.[40]

Defensive Africanization: History and Myth

Unable to escape the disparagement cast on their way of life, their past, and their achievements, it was essential for Creoles to regain their self-respect and to heal their battered race pride by restoring their heritage to a place of honor. In order to achieve this—to convince both themselves and their European detractors—they began to search back in history and, through a filter dictated by their own needs and expectations, sought evidence of great deeds and past glories.

The look back in history was not without obstructions. The direct ancestors of the Creoles had been torn from their traditional societies by the shattering experience of slavery. Although a number of them remembered the histories of their people from preslavery days, their links with the past had nevertheless been broken and, with the passage of time, even these memories tended to fade.[41] Thus the Creoles, a conglomerate community originating from the intermarriage of settler Africans from diverse ethnic groups, knew even less about the histories of their ancestors. Furthermore, since their formal education largely derived from European books and teachers, they had little opportunity to acquire this information outside the home. Knowing so

39. "Familiar Talks on Familiar Subjects," *SLWN*, 25 September 1915, discusses European attitudes to so-called "double-barrelled" names.
40. *The Artisan*, 6 October 1887; Fyfe, *History of Sierra Leone*, p. 468; *SLWN*, 19 June 1909, 13 August 1910, 25 September 1915, 23 June 1923. Many other examples of name-changing exist as well.
41. See P. D. Curtin, ed., *Africa Remembered: Narratives by West Africans from the Era of the Slave Trade* (Madison, 1967), pp. 317–33.

little about the historical deeds of the people from whom they descended, Creoles could hardly be expected to rely exclusively on this material in order to impress skeptics. On occasion they did glorify their Settler and liberated African ancestors—"those giants of our race," as a writer in the *Sierra Leone Weekly News* called them.[42] The same man wrote:

> How some of these men who like the ancient people of God, the Israelites, though kept in the house of bondage for hundreds of years, and made to serve their task-masters with rigour, yet on being enfranchised and liberated, became in a few years the equals of their benefactors and liberators, stood head and shoulders above the aboriginal inhabitants of this Peninsula, and laid the foundation for the social, religious, and political prosperity of the race, seems indeed miraculous.[43]

Praise of this sort, however, was infrequent. Tainted by the indignities of their past slavery, these ancestors were not the ideal example of unqualified historical success.

Alternate sources for the kind of historical material the Creoles sought did, of course, exist outside their own immediate society. The histories of their neighbors in the interior of Africa could have presented them with deeds and stout heroes sufficient to belie European slander and to ensure the greatness of the black African past. They could have invoked the attainments of past West African Empires like Ghana, Mali, and Songhai, or great African warriors and kings like Sundiata and Mansa Musa. But this they did not do. Undoubtedly, given the cultural gulf that had grown up between themselves and the African ethnic groups of the interior, some Creoles were unsure that the people surrounding them even had a history, to say nothing of its being worthy of exaltation. Others, products of a Eurocentric educational system, knew relatively little African history. While many of them had indeed heard of men like Uthman dan Fodio, Sheikh Al-Hadj Omar, and other African leaders from the near and distant past, their knowledge was spotty and inaccurate. More contemporary accomplishments, like the British defeats by

42. "Some Notables of Sierra Leone in the Past by DeeTee," *SLWN*, 4 January 1899.
43. *SLWN*, 15 July 1899.

the Ashanti and Zulu and the French setbacks by Samori Toure, might be taken as indubitable proof of black African military prowess, but, at a time when European imperial expansion in Africa was at a high point, the honor and reputation of a race could hardly be made to depend on such isolated triumphs.[44]

Since they lacked the factual tools to reconstruct African history and to make it acceptable on its own terms, these Creoles had another alternative, one which would not only satisfy their own quest for honor but also be most likely to impress Europeans. European racial slurs were often made about black Africans in general, not just Creoles in particular. Creoles, therefore, responded as black Africans—as members of a large and wronged African community, rather than as individuals belonging to a particular group. Having been educated by Europeans, they used that education as an instrument of combat,[45] as evidence to show that they, as black Africans, not only possessed a great past but were in fact the originators of the civilization cherished by the West. In this way a number of Creoles traced their cultural genealogy not to any contemporary group of Africans, nor their history to recent deeds or traditions, but back to what they believed to be the general black African past—back to the glories of Roman Africa, ancient Egypt, and the greatness of the biblical middle east.

Blyden's influence on some of these endeavors, exerted through his activities in Sierra Leone and through his many speeches and writings, is quite apparent. In his essay "The Negro in Ancient History" and in his travel account *From West Africa to Palestine,* his reconstruction of the glories of Negro antiquity anticipated the aims, concerns, and the methods of Creole writers like A. B. C. Merriman-Labor. In *From West Africa to Palestine,* Blyden described his visit to the great pyramids of Egypt. He saw these as the work of "the enterprising sons of

44. "The Fall of Ashanti," a poem, *SLWN,* 4 May 1901; *SLWN,* 28 January 1899; Blyden, *Christianity, Islam and the Negro Race,* p. 10: Speech by Blyden to the Freetown Unity Club, *SLWN,* 20 June 1891; Claude George, *The Rise of British West Africa,* 5 parts (London, 1902–3), pt. V, Appendix Z, pp. 455–56.

45. "Education . . . as an instrument of combat" is a phrase used by Georges Balandier, *Afrique Ambigue* (Paris, 1957), p. 280.

Ham," the racial progenitors of his contemporary "Negro-Africans," men who had sent civilization into Greece and thus had been teachers of the ancient poets, historians, and mathematicians. Standing in the central hall of a pyramid, his fervent dream had been that Negro Africans would retake their fame. And, in an aside to Europeans—as much if not more the intended audience for his writings than educated Africans—he hoped that they would accept the Negroes' participation in the great deeds of history.[46]

Even before Blyden, however, Dr. Africanus Horton had written of "Africa's Great Past" in his *West African Countries and Peoples,* a book which he revealingly subtitled "A Vindication of the African Race." The book was a direct response to a Select Committee of the House of Commons which, in 1865, had studied British involvement in West Africa and had recommended imperial retrenchment everywhere "except, probably, Sierra Leone," and the preparation of educated Africans for self-government.[47] Horton sought to counteract the detrimental evidence given to the Committee by such Creole haters as Richard Burton, and was particularly concerned with obliterating the infamous slurs cast on the entire community of educated West Africans, especially through the pseudoscientific racism expounded by organizations like the British Anthropological Society.[48] In antiquity, Horton believed, Africa had been the nursery of science and literature. Both Greece and Rome acquired these arts by means of the pilgrimages which men like Solon, Plato, and Pythagoras made to that continent in search of knowledge. Christianity, moreover, owed something of its development to

46. E. W. Blyden, *From West Africa to Palestine* (Freetown, 1873), pp. 104–110. Visiting the Sphinx, he commented (p. 114): "Her [the Sphinx's] features are decidedly of the African or Negro type, with 'expanded nostrils.' Is not the Sphinx clear evidence," he therefore asked, "as to the peculiar type or race to which that king [of Egypt] belonged?"

47. Great Britain, Parliament, *Parliamentary Papers* (House of Commons), Report from the Select Committee Appointed to Consider the State of the British Settlements on the Western Coast of Africa, 1865 (412), vol. 1:8513–19, 2045–46.

48. Known formally as "The Anthropological Society of London," this organization had Richard Burton as a vice president. Using "science," it sought to demonstrate the inferiority of nonwhites. See Fyfe, *History of Sierra Leone*, p. 335.

Africa because such men as "Origen, Tertullian, Augustin, Cle-
mens, Alexandrinus, and Cyril who were fathers and writers of
the Primitive Church, were tawny African bishops of Apostolic
renown."[49]

Charles Marke, a Wesleyan Native Minister in Sierra Leone,
paraphrased Horton's statements but embellished them when he
stated that Africa was once adorned "with churches, colleges,
and repositories of learning . . . and . . . was the seat of a most
powerful government which contended with Rome for the sover-
eignty of the world." J. Augustus Cole, who eventually Africanized his name to Abayomi Cole, lectured before a crowded
house at the Wesleyan Methodist Church when he visited Richmond, Indiana, that the ancient Egyptians were black Africans.[50]
Likewise, a Creole writer in *The Watchman and West African
Record* reminded Sierra Leoneans: "Let it not be forgotten that
we are the direct descendants of men that have built those stu-
pendous Pyramids which have in all ages exacted wonder and
admiration, and have baffled the most skillful of modern archi-
tects."[51]

A. B. C. Merriman-Labor, who had grown up at the height of
British disdain for educated Africans, was satisfied in his *Epitome of a Series of Lectures on the Negro Race* that West African Negroes descended from Ethiopians because both "practice
circumcision," "are in the same branch of language," and "are
identical in physique, physiognomy, and colour." Ethiopians, in
turn, "are descendants of Cush, the Son of Ham, the grandson of
Noah, the ninth patriarch in descent from Adam, the father of
all mankind. Therefore, in Adam through Cush . . . is the origin
of the Negro Race."[52] Having established this pedigree, Merriman-Labor then used it to link blacks to the great deeds which

49. J. A. B. Horton, *West African Countries and Peoples, British and
Native. With the Requirements Necessary for Establishing That Self-
Government Recommended by the Committee of the House of Commons,
1865; and a Vindication of the African Race* (London, 1865), p. 67.

50. Charles Marke, *Africa and the Africans* (Freetown, 1881), pp.
26–28; *Methodist Herald*, 27 April 1887, reprinted an account of Cole's
lecture from the *Richmond Daily Telegram*, 19 March 1887.

51. *The Watchman and West African Record*, 30 October 1887.

52. A. B. C. Merriman-Labor, *An Epitome of a Series of Lectures on
The Negro Race* (Manchester, 1899), pp. 11–12.

Europeans generally associated with "ancient civilizations." According to Genesis, which he pointed out to be divinely revealed and therefore unerring, the Cushites ("let us call them Ethiopians or ancient Negroes, just as we choose"[53]) achieved great distinctions. They founded Nineveh and other great cities and, under their leader Nimrod, built Babylon, the world's first kingdom. The ancient Negroes were, furthermore, chosen by God "to be the primitive leaders of the van of civilization and to teach mankind the first principles of good government." Before Nimrod there had existed no governmental authority except that of a father over his household. Under him, families and tribes were united into a commonwealth. These people, in turn, went on to teach "the elementary principles of government to the Egyptians, from whom Greece and . . . Rome . . . Europe and America, borrowed much that was profitable."[54]

After constructing a magnificent past for the Negro race, however, Creole intellectuals needed to rationalize its subsequent decline in Africa. God, according to Merriman-Labor, having employed blacks as the primitive leaders of the world, "knew what evils a continued leadership would entail." He thus took the "sun of civilization" away from them, in much the same way that He had taken it away from Moses and the Israelites, and allowed it to move westwards, first over Greece, then Rome, and ultimately over Britain. This idea combined religious determinism with the concept, old and persistent among European historians, of the "westward flow of civilization."[55] Abayomi Cole fit the downfall of Negro greatness within the framework of a cyclical theory of history. "When a race has reached its zenith of physical intellectuality," he wrote, "and developed its highest civilization and can go no more in its own cycle, there is a tendency for it to progress to absolute evil. This has been the case with the Black Race who inhabited the ancient Continents—and no other race will escape it." Similarly, Africanus Horton discussed Negro decline in terms of the rise and fall of nations and the tendency for human affairs to undergo gradual and progres-

53. Merriman-Labor, *Negro Race*, p. 13
54. Merriman-Labor, *Negro Race*, pp. 13–15.
55. For a study of this idea see Loren Baritz, "The Idea of the West," *American Historical Review* 66 (1961):618–40; Curtin, *Image of Africa*, pp. 249–50, 375–76.

sive deterioration. But in no case did these writers want to convey the impression that blacks, having declined from past greatness, were now doomed to perpetual stagnation. The contemporary state of affairs in Africa was seen as transitory—as a historical setback and not a permanent condition. "The race which is backward today," wrote Cole, "can be drawn by a new current of evolution and come again into prominence, when those in advance are descending." And, according to Horton, "those who have lived in utter barbarism, after a lapse of time become the standing nation." Since nations were subject to a cyclical law of history, West Africans could well hope that, in time, they would again "occupy a prominent position in the world's history, and . . . command a voice in the council of nations."[56]

As black Africans, most Creole writers felt that they would be able to view historical events relating to Africans from a different perspective than Europeans. A. B. C. Merriman-Labor's *An Epitome of a Series of Lectures on the Negro Race,* for example, was a child of its age, a reaction to the educational system then prevalent in British colonies which concentrated entirely on a Eurocentric curriculum and refused to acknowledge that Africans had a historical past worth studying.[57] "It is a matter for 'regret,' " wrote Merriman-Labor in the first chapter of this work, "that every intelligent schoolboy in our country knows much of the Caucasian Race, and at the same time little of the Negro section of mankind. Even the limited knowledge which he possesses of the Negro . . . is inaccurate and unmethodical; for it is acquired from books, the writers of which are not Negroes."[58] Because he was black, Merriman-Labor thought himself better qualified to write and lecture about his race than any person who approached the subject from a foreign point of view.

56. Merriman-Labor, *Negro Race,* pp. 13–14; J. A. Cole, "The Place of the Negro in the World's Evolution," *SLWN,* 30 October 1926; Horton, *West African Countries and Peoples,* pp. 67–68; also see Robert July, "Africanus Horton and the Idea of Independence in West Africa," *Sierra Leone Studies,* n.s. no. 18 (1966), pp. 2–17.

57. See *SLWN,* 29 March 1913, Letter to the Editor by Anoviphoee, for a similar view pronounced in the second decade of the twentieth century; also see D. L. Sumner, *Education in Sierra Leone* (Freetown, 1963), pp. 89–144.

58. Merriman-Labor, *Negro Race,* p. 7.

All too often, however, Creole intellectuals found themselves much more within the framework of European thought than they were willing to admit. This was both the benefit and the burden of their Europeanized upbringing. Having believed what their missionary teachers taught in the past—that European learning and technology were the keys to the kingdom of acceptance and modernity—they had readily absorbed European concepts and values and had become most adept at using materials from their Europeanized educational experience. For this reason, even what on the surface may have appeared as indigenous philosophy, like Blydenism, was in fact constructed from the intellectual bricks and mortar with which their Europeanized instruction had first acquainted them.

The Bible, for instance, was the book which the Creoles employed most frequently as a source of historical evidence. Blyden may have served to set the example. He relied heavily on the Old Testament to support his contentions about the black African past, and he did this in spite of the fact that he had urged African historians to collect "oral traditions" from among their own people so as not to be bound by the experiences and tools of a "foreign race."[59] Merriman-Labor interpreted the Bible as placing black Africans at the vanguard of civilization. Abayomi Cole used the Old Testament to prove that blacks were destined to retain possession of Africa until the end of time.[60]

For the Creoles, the Bible was a book whose revealed authority many in Europe recognized and which could, therefore, counter the new testament of racism:

> That Negroes we are, we are proud to maintain
> Ashamed of complexion! unless if insane . . .
> The Bible instructs us one man God did make,
> To whom He gave Eve of his joy to partake;
> The two marred their joys and caused sin to exist;
> The consequence suffered, their purity ceased;
> To these, after fall, Cain and Abel were born

59. E. W. Blyden, *Proceedings at the Inauguration of Liberia College at Monrovia, January 23, 1862* (Monrovia, 1862), p. 28. See also E. W. Blyden, Taylor Lewis, Theodore Dwight, et al., *The People of Africa*, pp. 3–29.

60. *Methodist Herald*, 27 April 1887.

But Cain slew his brother who'll no more return;
But God in His mercy the sad parents cheered
By giving another when Seth then appeared.
From Adam through Seth righteous Noah did descend
To whom were three sons on which sons we depend
Pure friends to instruct, to the right way them lead;
Remind them in earnest all sprang from one seed—
From Shem, Ham, and Japheth good Noah's three sons.
Strong weapons we've got, let's proceed on at once.
From these three the white and the black and all men
Descended we learn from God's book, why fear then?
(The children of brothers first-cousins are called)
Deny this you're godless, unfit for the world.
"Be fruitful and multiply" God's words to man,
Dispersion brought Ham to the African land;
The Bible tells this, but it never doth say
That Ham was become a baboon any way:
Some ignorant men of the proud-colour tribe
The notion that Negroes are monkeys imbibe;
A pity it is we are sorry to know
That some of our cousins themselves blind do show;
We only beg if *Anthropos* they are
To lift up their face and at us if they stare,
They surely will see we've the same upright form,
If Genesis read they will silent become.[61]

Even though Sierra Leoneans held an unshaken belief in the Bible as revealed truth, their use of it in historical analysis was approximately three-quarters of a century behind general trends in European historiography. In Europe, historical analysis had shifted throughout the nineteenth century from its reliance on Biblical and literary authority to take into account data from other disciplines. The works of physical anthropologists, ethnographers, classical economists, and biological scientists were increasingly employed in historical explanations.[62] Nevertheless, though seemingly aware of the directions that European historical studies had taken, Creole writers decisively rejected the new

61. Written by "S.A.C." from Fourah Bay College and printed in *SLWN,* 17 November 1888.
62. Curtin, *Image of Africa,* pp. 244, 388–89; Fritz Stern, *The Varieties of History* (New York, 1956), pp. 54–56.

approach. Merriman-Labor was quite explicit on this point. "Darwin," he said, "is undoubtedly an excellent philosopher; but what is human philosophy to Divine revelation? Human philosophy may err, has often erred; but Divine revelation—the Bible— never!"[63]

The faith which Creole intellectuals placed in the authority of the Bible was a result of their early Christian training. Religious instruction was an important part of the curriculum of the C.M.S. Grammar School, of the Wesleyan Boys' High School, and, of course, of Fourah Bay College, institutions which many of the most vocal Creoles had attended at one time or another. Before entering the Grammar School in 1892, A.B.C. Merriman-Labor had been raised and educated by his maternal grandfather, John Merriman of Hastings, a deeply religious man who was prevented from entering the ministry when he lost his eyesight, but who was nevertheless called "Father Merriman" out of respect for his piety.[64] Africanus Horton began his education under the Reverend James Beale, and, before being sent to England to be trained in medicine, he had attended Fourah Bay College intending to become a minister.[65]

More important still than the religious background of any individual writer was the character of the Christianity to which they all adhered and its all-pervading influence on the lives of the Creoles. The Christian faith, which had come to Freetown in the very beginning with the earliest settlers and the missionaries, became more to the parents and grandparents of the Creoles than "just another religion." Their understanding of Christian dogma was probably no greater nor less than that of the majority of their European contemporaries; the sincerity of their conversion to Christianity could only be measured on the basis of meaningless value-judgments. But, having been taught to identify Christianity with European civilization, they believed that an acceptance of that religion would reflect their own mastery of a way of life, presented to them as better than any they had known before. Church services, for this reason, were well attended and

63. Merriman-Labor, *Negro Race*, p. 13.

64. A. B. C. Merriman-Labor, *A Funeral Oration Delivered Over the Grave of the Late Father John Merriman* (Freetown, 1900); *SLWN*, 24 February and 15 March 1919; Fyfe, *History of Sierra Leone*, p. 526.

65. *Methodist Herald*, 26 October 1883

long; and the congregation was thoroughly acquainted with the ritual and orders of procedure. Hymns were sung with much spirit and they were seldom shortened by an omitted verse. The enthusiasm which had been characteristic of religion in the English evangelical movement merged with the predisposition for communal participation in worship, inherited from traditional African religion, and it remained characteristic of Creole Christianity. The Sabbath was kept holy, and special food and Sunday suits were reserved for its celebration. Sierra Leoneans had a general interest in questions of theology and a predilection for eternal debates on questions of eternity. If any book was to be found in a Creole home, it was certain to be the Bible; and the people took pride in being able to quote lengthy passages by heart. Like the missionaries who came to Sierra Leone in the early nineteenth century, even the most educated Creoles interpreted the Bible literally.

One other manifestation of the Creole tendency to stay within a European framework of thought is exemplified in their acceptance of the concept of the "true Negro." Merriman-Labor, for one, shared the belief then popular in Europe (and which is still retained in the 1957 edition of C. G. Seligman's *Races of Africa*) which held that West Africa alone was the home of the "true Negroes'" while other African peoples were mixtures of black and light-skinned invaders from outside the continent. Merriman-Labor defined "Negro Race" in narrow terms—as "the black descendants of a common ancestor"—and excluded "yellowish Copts . . . and Berbers," and "brown Kaffirs and Hottentots," because they were thought to lack the pure black skin color of the West Africans. Migration accounted for the settlement of Negroes in West Africa. Departing from Asia, the ancient Negroes traveled to Arabia and entered Africa over an isthmus now submerged. Some of the immigrants settled in Ethiopia while others "produced with the Egyptians the brown Kaffirs, Hottentots, and Hovaks [sic] of Madagascar." Still others—fishermen and hunters, captives and conquerors, seekers of congenial localities—emigrated from Ethiopia to other parts of the continent until they arrived in West Africa.[66]

In their reliance upon a framework of analysis learned from

66. Merriman-Labor, *Negro Race*, p. 13

Europe and acceptable to Europeans, Creole thinkers ran the danger of being trapped by concepts which racists used to point up the inferiority of Negroes. By endorsing the notion of the "true Negro," for instance, Merriman-Labor was dangerously close to the proposition used by racist European historians to explain how, in a continent where Negro capabilities were thought to be so low, those "higher" cultural traits which did exist had been introduced by light-skinned outsiders from the East. But, caught up as they were between their acquiescence in European models as the epitome of "civilization" and their psychological need to dignify the achievements of blacks in Africa, Creoles had few choices but to wrestle with these troublesome predicaments. Thus, in accepting the premise that the Bible was a revealed authority, and therefore infallible historical evidence, Merriman-Labor and other Creole intellectuals had worked themselves into a logical dilemma. If, according to the Bible, black Africans were considered to be the descendants of Ham, logic demanded that Negroes accept the implications of Noah's malediction on the sons of Ham.[67] Noah's curse was often quoted by European writers to support their argument for the perpetual subordination of the Negro race.[68] Creole thinkers, however, were unwilling to question the authority of the Bible, yet loath to accept the postulate of the divine malediction. They, therefore, played intellectual games with the Old Testament to disprove the curse on the sons of Ham while simultaneously destroying the assertion that blacks were destined to be "hewers of wood and drawers of water." They took their lead from Dr. Alexander Crummel, a citizen of the United States but frequent visitor to West Africa. In 1883, Dr. Crummel published "An Examination of Genesis 9:25" in which he concluded:

1. That the curse of Noah was pronounced upon Canaan, *not* upon Ham.

2. That it *fell* upon Canaan, and was designed to fall upon him only.

3. That neither Ham, nor any of his [other] three sons, was involved in this curse.

67. See Genesis 9:18–25.
68. Curtin, *Image of Africa*, pp. 36–37, 403.

4. That the Negro race did not descend from Canaan; was never involved in the curse pronounced upon him; and its peculiar sufferings, during the last three centuries, are not the result or evidences of any specific curse upon Ham.

5. That the fact of slavery in the Negro race is not peculiar to Negroes as a people. . . . In God's providence, the Negro family has bitterly been called to suffer greatly, and doubtless for some high and important ends.

6. That the geographical designations of Scriptures are to be taken in good faith; and that when the "land of Canaan" is mentioned in the Bible, it was not intended to include the Gold Coast, the Gaboon, Goree or Congo.[69]

A. B. C. Merriman-Labor spent nine out of the thirty-two pages of his *Epitome of a Series of Lectures on the Negro Race* rationalizing the Biblical malediction. Like Dr. Crummel, he contended that Canaan alone was cursed. For this reason the descendants of Canaan, the Canaanites and Phoenicians, were servants to the rest of the world, the former as attendants to the congregation of Israel, and the latter as "navigators whose business it was to promote commerce and navigation, then practically the support of the ancient world." On the other hand, history was full of examples showing nations that descended from the other sons of Ham to be in frequent political and cultural ascendancy. The Egyptians, for instance, were "a people appropriately called the fathers of learning, when the entire world was in a state of semibarbarism." The Ethiopians, descending from Ham's son Cush and direct ancestors of the West African blacks, had also once numbered among the favored nations of the earth. Negroes, for this reason, had no connection with Noah's malediction.[70]

Types of Response

Most Creoles, especially of the upper class, were at one time or

69. *West African Reporter*, 1 December 1883.
70. Merriman-Labor, *Negro Race*, pp. 21–23; James Bright Davies of the colonial treasury department wrote, "The Hamitic Race in Sacred History," another vindication of Negroes as the descendants of Ham. See *Independent*, Oct. 14, Nov. 11, Nov. 25, 1875.

another plagued by anxieties about their cultural identity. Blyden, the members of the Dress Reform Society, and the name reformers were neo-traditionalists. They rejected those aspects of westernization which they held unnecessary for progress in the modern world and sought instead to return to their idealized version of the traditions, values, and manners of black African society. Other Creole responses, however, ranged from indifference on the one end of the spectrum, through a more selective westernization, to an advocacy of total Europeanization and the complete destruction of even the most innocent vestiges of African culture.

"Europeanizers," Creoles advocating the total substitution of African cultural traits by European ones, sought to reject the past. They all fervently wished to be accepted by whites as successful products of British mission work, as black men and women who had indeed become "civilized." They were proud of their imported material possessions, of their literary achievements, and of their representation in the clergy, the law and medicine.[71] Many of the Europeanizers, believing that wars, kidnapping, slavery, and other calamities had destroyed their ancestors' powers of originality, justified assimilation to European ways as the only means to progress.[72] In every case, they were inexorably opposed to a withdrawal from Europeanization into a past whose validity they no longer accepted. "The circumstances under which the native manners and characteristic customs developed in the lands from whence our fathers came no longer obtain," stated an editorial in the *Sierra Leone Times* which well illustrated the position of the Europeanizers:

We have adopted the European's dress, his language, his social, moral, political, and domestic codes. We sail under the banner of England's potent and beneficient sovereign, and enjoy to the full as much freedom and advantage as any of her loyal subjects. Above all, we cling to those sacred truths which an army of sainted martyrs have, amidst innumerable difficulties, almost through a burning fiery climatic furnace, labored to plant in our midst. From, through, and

71. *SLWN,* 7 March 1885; Letter to the Editor by "Achilles," *SLWN,* 5 September 1885; T. B., "Our Mental Progress," *SLWN,* 2 November 1889.
72. Editorial, *The Watchman,* 28 February 1879.

by us, it may be, and is reasonably expected, that the aborigines still
groping in that abyss from which our progenitors were happily res-
cued, would be brought towards the same path trodden by ourselves. Why then, the substance having gone, cling to the shadow, by
the retention of those customs which land with no graceful effect
upon the armour of civilization and education which we pride ourselves upon wearing?[73]

Joseph Renner-Maxwell, in his book *The Negro Question, or
Hints for the Physical Improvement of the Negro Race, with
Special Reference to West Africa,* was an inordinate European-
izer, the most extreme example of this position. He was a Sierra
Leonean of Yoruba ancestry whose father had been chaplain at
Cape Coast. Attending Merton College, Oxford, where he took
Honors in Jurisprudence in 1879 and his Bachelor of Civil Law
degree in 1880, he was converted to Catholicism, a faith which
strongly appealed to him because of what he considered to be its
lack of racial prejudice.[74] After Oxford he first went to the Gold
Coast to practice law and then to the Gambia to enter government service. Eventually, he rose to the position of chief magis-
trate of the Gambia in 1887.[75]

Renner-Maxwell became convinced that selective westernization was folly and could not solve what he termed, the "Negro
Question." Instead, he became an impassioned advocate of mis-
cegenation and married an English wife, perhaps to offer proof
of the viability of such a union. The thesis of his book, *The Negro Question,* was simple and perversely unique. He claimed
that blacks were despised by Europeans not because they lacked
intellect, nor because they were immoral or inhuman, but for no
other reason than because they were ugly.

It is because he is ugly, because his woolly pate is not so becoming
as the flaxen hair of the Anglo-Saxon, because the flat nose of the

73. *SLT,* 23 June 1894; Letter to the Editor, by "Achilles," *SLWN,* 5
September 1885, expresses a similar sentiment.
74. Joseph Renner-Maxwell, *The Negro Question, or Hints for the
Physical Improvement of the Negro Race, with Special Reference to West
Africa* (London, 1892), pp. 134–47; Oxford University, *Oxford Honours,
1220–1894* (Oxford, 1894).
75. *SLWN,* 25 April 1891; Obituary, *West Africa,* 30 November 1901;
Fyfe, *History of Sierra Leone,* p. 406.

Negro is more like the nasal organ of the ape than is the aquiline nose of the Aryan races, because blubber lips are not as pretty as thin ones, because a black complexion is displeasing compared with a fair or olive one.[76]

Disagreeing with more orthodox Europeanizers, Renner-Maxwell believed that it was physically impossible for black Africans to pass themselves off as Europeans, an objective which could not "be brought about by anything short of a miracle." Influenced by the pseudoscientific racism which grew out of a misapplied Darwinism, he was persuaded that the Negro race would lose the struggle for survival. "The progress of civilization," he warned, "the struggle for existence, will not admit of the solution of questions of abstract right; if the white man wants room, the black, being the weaker and uglier, will have to make room for him."[77]

But, even though he was pessimistic, seeing little hope for blacks of his and his parents' generations, he was sure that the situation for future generations could begin to improve. "If a man finds his racial circumstances disadvantageous to his interests," he argued, "stunting to the development of his tone and manhood, and contemptible to his neighbors, he can at least ameliorate the condition of his progeny."[78] By marrying white women, black Africans would be instrumental in bringing forth a species of man that could be educated "to the highest pitch of perfection," while simultaneously eliminating Negroid features and skin color and the entire "Negro Question." Nor, he felt, should it be difficult to find white mates. England, Renner-Maxwell noted, had thousands of prostitutes and poor women who would be contributing to "the progress of civilization" if they married "civilized Negroes" instead of plying their wares or prolonging their poverty.[79]

Renner-Maxwell's influence on Sierra Leoneans was minimal. Neither he nor his work was well known in the colony. For the majority of Creole men racial intermarriage, if considered at all,

76. Renner-Maxwell, *The Negro Question*, p. 10.
77. Renner-Maxwell, *The Negro Question*, p. 54.
78. Renner-Maxwell, *The Negro Question*, pp. 65, 85–86.
79. Renner-Maxwell, *The Negro Question*, pp. 83–84, 104.

was certainly nothing more than an academic question. As a general rule no unattached European women came to Sierra Leone and only a handful of Creole men went to Europe with the specific intention of finding a wife. Although some Creole girls would on occasion form a liaison with a European male in Sierra Leone, the men were rarely willing to sanctify the union unless they had decided to make Africa their permanent home and were ready to bear social ostracism from the European community.

In sharp contrast to extremist Europeanizers like Renner-Maxwell, selective westernizers were pragmatists. Unlike Blyden, who viewed the westernization of black Africans as an aberration of a divine scheme for the separate development of the races, selective westernizers saw it as the only possible means to make headway in a world which was dominated by Europe. They agreed that not everything European was, by definition, good and that "civilization" in the European manner did not necessitate the total destruction of all traditional African cultural practices. "The African was aroused," commented an editorial in the *Sierra Leone Weekly News,* "as the European also had been roused, from his slumber of ages and in a state of half somnolence was asked to pledge himself to dazzling but vain institutions."[80] They realized that Sierra Leoneans had strayed far from the original moorings of their forefathers as a result of misdirected education. But they were also aware that the antidote for their situation also lay in education—education "in the right direction," enabling them to modify the character of the westernization they had received in order to suit their own particular exigencies. This education would give them an awareness of the incongruous elements in European culture which they could exclude, and would also guide them to keep those aspects of traditional African life which would enhance their development.

The position of the selective westernizers on the relationship of Christianity to traditional African life was expressed perhaps most cogently by the Reverend James Johnson, who was born in Sierra Leone, educated at the C.M.S. Grammar School and

80. Editorial, *SLWN,* 2 December 1905.

Fourah Bay College, and who later in life became assistant bishop of Western Equatorial Africa.[81] In an article entitled "The Relation of Mission Work to Native Customs" submitted to the Pan-Anglican Congress of 1908, Johnson emphasized that Christianity was not intended to be the religion of any one particular race of people, but of the entire world. In every continent it wore a slightly different garb so as to blend with indigenous beliefs. Johnson believed that, so far as Africa was concerned, Christianity could be spread without "denationalizing" and Europeanizing Africans. This did not mean that practices such as infanticide, ritual cannibalism, and witchcraft ordeals had to be tolerated. These were naturally repulsive, contrary to all justice, and were obviously legitimate objects of attack and suppression. Body and facial tatooing, domestic slavery, home sepulchres—customs which were unenlightened but not entirely abhorrent—were to be left to die naturally through quiet ameliorative influence. But, Johnson warned, Christian missionaries should not meddle in name-giving, dress, and marriage customs of African peoples. African names, he pointed out, were not necessarily heathen, and African dress was merely a matter of convenience and taste which should not at all be taken to reflect on the enlightenment or lack of enlightenment of a particular individual. Likewise, since Jesus Christ did not prescribe any one particular marriage custom or ceremony, Johnson saw nothing at all wrong with native marriage practices and felt that they could continue in the traditional African manner. Furthermore, while he believed that monogamy should be held up as an ultimate ideal, he was against excluding polygynists from the Church.[82]

81. *SLWN*, 18 May 1906; Jean Herskovits Kopytoff, *A Preface to Modern Nigeria* (Madison, 1965), p. 289; Fyfe, *History of Sierra Leone*, p. 351.

82. James Johnson, "The Relation of Mission Work to Native Customs," *Pan-Anglican Papers, Being Problems for Consideration at the Pan-Anglican Congress, 1908. Political and Social Conditions of Missionary Work*, vol. 2 (London, 1908). In 1888, Bishop T. J. Sawyerr, Bishop of the Diocese of the Native Pastorate, had also urged a new policy in respect to polygny if any progress was to be made toward evangelizing "heathens and Mohammedans" in Africa. The Bible, he

Johnson's views did not endear him to many of his fellow missionaries, nor to Creoles who viewed any apparent compromise in their Europeanization as a breach which would expose them to ridicule.[83] Nevertheless, his position toward selective westernization—toward a syncretism of African and European practices—was probably the one shared by the majority of Creole society. It is, of course, impossible to document this or to give a numerical estimate of the proportion of the Creole population which fell into the position between that of the extreme Europeanizers and that of the hardly touched, those Sierra Leoneans who by choice, location, or lack of educational opportunity, had escaped westernization in almost all its forms. But there can be little doubt that in their everyday life most Creoles retained and mixed elements from traditional African culture with the ways of the West.

---

stated, made no direct attack on this practice, but on the contrary, condoned it in many passages in the Old Testament. The C.M.S. Parent Committee, aghast at Sawyerr's statements, made him resign from the Church Finance Committee. See T. J. Sawyerr, *Sierra Leone Native Church (Two Papers read at the Church Conference held in Freetown, Sierra Leone, Jan. 24th, 25th, 26th, 1888)* (Freetown, 1888), pp. 17–31; Fyfe, *History of Sierra Leone*, pp. 508–9.

83. See J. F. Ade Ajayi, *Christian Missions in Nigeria, 1841–1891* (London, 1965), pp. 235–38; Kopytoff, *Preface to Modern Nigeria*, pp. 238–41.

Words Used by Creoles to Describe Europeans and Non-Creole Africans in Sierra Leone and its Hinterland[a]

I: CA. 1870 TO CA. 1885

Europeans

"Europeans," "Englishmen," "White Men," "Porto."[b] Divided into:
1) "Big Men," "Higher Class of English"; example: government officials, professional men, leading traders, and merchants.
2) "Lower Type of English"; example: any European insulting Creoles or demonstrating racial arrogance in writings or actions, e.g., Sir Richard Burton and Winwood Reade.

Foreign Africans

"Educated Africans": western-educated Creole and non-Creole Africans, usually West Indians, Afro-Americans, or Americo-Liberians, and, increasingly, from other areas of British Africa.
"Tribal Africans": tradesmen or laborers; these were often lumped with the up-countrymen and not differentiated as foreigners.

Foreign Europeans

No special term in this period.

Up-Countrymen

"Natives," "Tribal Africans," "Aborigines," "Native Traders."
1) Divided into traders like the Fullah and Mandingo—Muslim and of a "higher type"—and the rest. The adjectives used to describe the rest varied according to historical circumstance. For example, in the period of the so-called "tribal wars" in the hinterland (ca. 1870–1890), when influential Creole merchants felt that trade was being disrupted and Britain was urged to "pacify" and annex the interior, up-countrymen were frequently referred to as "vagabonds," "thieves," "cut-throats," "barbarous ruffians," "barbarous plunderers," "reckless tribesmen," "war-boys" bent on "rapine and bloodshed." The

---

[a] Based on Creole writings, particularly in the Freetown press, but also in essays and books.
[b] Krio, from "Portuguese." Also used by Timnes; *poto farar*, in Timne, referred to a "black white man," and *poto bi* to a white man, i.e., any European (see *SLWN*, 30 May 1885).

terms reflected the contrast felt by some Creoles between their own "civilization" and the "barbarity" of up-countrymen.

2) By the end of this period, however, with neo-traditionalists of the Blyden school reacting to increasing European racism and the Creole tendency to "ape the white man," up-countrymen were occasionally described in such terms as "simple and unspoiled," "virgin souls."

II: CA. 1885 TO CA. 1897

Europeans

"Europeans," "Englishmen," "White Men," "Porto." Divided into:
1) "Higher Class of English," "Benign Rulers."
2) "Lower Type of English," sometimes referred to as "foreign adventurers," "roving penny-a-liners," "brooding and irregular minds," "professional philanthropists."

Foreign Africans

No difference from earlier period.

Foreign Europeans

"Corals," a name given to Syrian traders.

Up-Countrymen

"Natives," "Tribal Africans," "Aborigines," "Country People."
1) As in the previous period, traders and wealthier up-countrymen maintained their higher status in Creole perceptions. Neo-traditionalists also continued to contrast their vision of "unspoiled" interior peoples with the "degeneracy" with which they characterized Creole society.
2) Within the Colony, the increasing influx of up-countrymen worried Creoles about being "overrun." With increasing frequency they began to refer to up-countrymen in terms like "unwashed aborigines," "army of burglars," "thieves." One Creole writer worried that the infusion of so many up-countrymen into the Colony would lead to the "degeneration of our race . . . by the accession of a large number of children, the descendants of the aborigines and daughters of the soil."

III: 1898

Europeans

Same as in the earlier periods, with perhaps more emphasis on the "Lower Type of English" perception as the effects of British discrimination against western-educated Africans became more apparent.

Foreign Africans

No difference from earlier period.

Foreign Europeans

Corals.[c]

Up-Countrymen

"Natives," "Tribal Africans," "Aborigines," "Country People."
The period of the Hut Tax War was crucial in shaping the Creole relationship to up-countrymen. Little or none of the neo-traditionalist romanticizing of interior Africans survived it. At the outbreak of the war in the northern part of the hinterland, a good deal of Creole sympathy for up-countrymen was reflected in the press. One article called interior people "bones of our bones, flesh of our flesh" (*SLWN*, 5 February 1898). Another complained of British-led troops "mowing down our brethren" in battle. These views were quickly and drastically modified, however, when Creole traders and missionaries, including women and children, were killed up-country in the Mende and Sherbro regions of the south. The following terms then appeared with frequency in reference to up-countrymen from the south: "horde of war-boys inspired by a spirit of rapine and murder," "marauders," "savages," "blood-thirsty tribes," "cruel tribes," "fighters and robbers of other peoples properties," people taking "unnatural delight in sanguinary enterprises," "uncivilized barbarians," "Mendi man no good."

---

[c] The Creole attitude towards Syrians turned increasingly hostile after 1910, a hostility reflected in epithets and name-calling.

THE SENEGALESE
URBAN ELITE, 1900–1945

G. Wesley Johnson, Jr.

In some respects Dakar, Saint Louis, Rufisque, and Gorée, the "four communes" of the Senegalese coast, were a French equivalent of Freetown. They had been legally and historically French through most of the nineteenth century—quite distinct from the shifting and uncertain boundaries of French authority over the rest of Senegal before the 1890s. In the twentieth century, they kept their special status, so that *originaires* born in one of the four communes were a politically privileged group of French citizens.

Though their political rights were greater than those of Creoles in Sierra Leone or Lagos, they were less western in culture. Most remained Muslim; all kept in contact with the vital African culture that surrounded them. A class of *créoles* existed in Senegal as well, but here the word meant people of mixed race, French and African. Such people were often culturally mixed as well, and they tended to be more French and less African than the ordinary French citizen of the communes.

In this setting, many responses to the West were imbedded in political struggles among the varying strata of a colonial society that was distinguished internally according to race, class, culture, and place of birth. In spite of the supposed French taste for theory rather than empiricism, the Sierra Leone response was often set in terms of theory, while the Senegalese responded with political maneuver.

G. Wesley Johnson has written *The Emergence of Black Politics in Senegal* (Stanford, 1971).

P.D.C.

Definition and Background of the Elite

To define the urban elite of Senegal for the period down to 1945 is easier than might be supposed because this group took its popular name, *les originaires,* from a historical tradition which eventually became sanctified by act of the French Parliament.[1] The inhabitants of the four communes of Senegal—Saint-Louis, Gorée, Dakar, and Rufisque—by 1900 were filled with a sense of historical association with the French presence in Africa since the early seventeenth century. By the mid-eighteenth century the assimilated Africans and *créoles* of Saint-Louis and Gorée already possessed an embryonic civic consciousness;[2] events of the nineteenth century so sharpened their identification with France, that many served voluntarily in the ranks of the French colonial forces which conquered West and Equatorial Africa, Madagascar, and Indochina;[3] by the twentieth century, *originaires* were demanding full French citizenship and the right to serve in the regular (not the colonial) French army, a request granted by the Chamber of Deputies in 1915.[4]

Tradition was ratified by law and the urban elite of the four

1. Much of the material used was drawn from interviews conducted in Senegal and is incorporated in the text unless otherwise cited. Following are the most important oral history sources (the date given is that of the first interview): 1. Raoul Diagne, son of Blaise Diagne, 19 August 1964; 2. Lamine Guèye, 10 June 1964; 3. Moustapha Diouf, son of Galandou Diouf, 19 April 1964; 4. Assane Seck, professor of geography, 17 June 1964; 5. Armand Angrand, lieutenant of Diagne, 28 February 1964; 6. Léopold Senghor, 28 September 1966; 7. Alpha Bâ, friend of Lamine Guèye, 4 June 1964; 8. Abdel Kader Diagne, 17 November 1963; 9. Amadou Assane N'Doye, 23 June 1964; 10. Ibrahima Seydou N'Daw, *originaire* politician, 26 June 1964; 11. Mme. François Baye Salzmann, 2 August 1964; 12. A. M. M'Bow, professor, 2 August 1964; 13. Mme. Marie Diop, family friend of Blaise Diagne, 5 February 1964.

2. See the discussion in Léonce Jore, "Les établissments français sur la côte occidentale d'Afrique de 1758 a 1809," *Revue française d'histoire d'outremer* 51, nos. 182–85 (1965), pp. 9–252, 255–476.

3. Shelby Cullom Davis, *Reservoirs of Men* (Chambéry, 1934), pp. 15–86.

4. See *La Démocratie* (Dakar), 28 July 1915.

communes became a privileged minority within the French African empire: *originaires* could vote in French elections, stand for public office, travel freely within the French empire and in France, but in matters of marriage, inheritance, and certain family arrangements they could, if they chose, follow customary law (which in practically all cases meant Koranic law as interpreted and applied in Senegal). They were in fact full French citizens (*citoyens français*), whereas relatives or friends born outside of the communes or living in the Protectorate (which included the rest of Senegal) were simply *sujets français*—subjects without status and with limited rights under the French colonial regime.

Despite the apparent precision of the legal definition, several qualifications should be made. First, all inhabitants of the four main urban centers were not necessarily *originaires*. Only those families who could show parents born in the communes, or long association with the cities, were eligible. This meant, increasingly after 1900 as Senegalese of various ethnic groupings flocked to the urban centers, especially Dakar, that the *originaires* were surrounded by people who were in point of legal fact *sujets français*. These persons could not vote, did not enjoy French citizenship, but they were an important element in city life and often diluted the influence of the *originaires*. In this essay, I intend to focus on the *originaires,* because, as a group, they were better educated and were easily identifiable by their participation in public life (politics, administration, newspapers), which was denied *sujets français*. Whether non-*originaire* urban dwellers should be called members of the urban elite is debatable, but the typical Senegalese who left his village for life in the city often became a privileged colonial subject in his associations and freedoms as compared with the family he left behind.[5]

Second, it is possible to discern several elites in Senegal's urban centers. One could distinguish the Catholics from the non-

5. Unfortunately before Abdoulaye Diop began his study of Tukolor migration to Dakar we have no reliable data on this process; my impressions are gained from interviews. The local press usually points out when someone is not an *originaire;* many of the people in the political crowds were in fact urban *sujets français*.

Catholics and argue for a small Christianized-assimilated elite as a well-defined historical entity. Or one could distinguish the Muslims from the non-Muslims and study a select Muslim elite which exerted more influence than the assimilated Catholic group. In the absence of statistics indicating the religious composition of the *originaires* from 1900 to 1945, I would estimate that about 5 percent were Catholics and the balance were Muslims. Toleration, however, was the hallmark of life in the communes, and despite the fact Catholics had advantages in gaining preference in school attendance, in certain jobs, and in having contact with Frenchmen on a personal basis, no great amount of prejudice towards the Muslims was exercised during this period. There were literally no more than several hundred Protestants, centered in Saint-Louis and Dakar, which reflected the fact that Protestant evangelization in Senegal had been less successful than that of the Catholics, who considered Senegal difficult terrain. Most Senegalese Catholics were converted in the Serer country to the south, which was outside of the communes.[6]

The Muslims were largely adherents of the Tidjaniyya brotherhood, whose most powerful *marabout,* Al Hajj Malik Sy, was resident in Tivouane until his death in 1922. Sy was apparently well disposed towards the French, urged his followers to cooperate with the colonial administration, even to serve in the French armed forces.[7] The Mouride brotherhood, founded by the Senegalese *marabout* Amadou Bamba M'Backé, were restricted to rural areas until the 1930s, when some *talibé* ("followers") began to move to the communes. But Bamba's emphasis was on rural development in Mouride-dominated villages in the interior, and his influence was not great in the urban areas. Many Senegalese Muslims owed personal allegiance to a local *marabout* rather than to a brotherhood; the variety of religious affiliations seems not to have affected one's status as an *originaire*. Religion was a distinguishing factor, but the difference between Christian

6. The Protestants operated a fairly successful mission in Sor near Saint-Louis. The history of their limited activity has yet to be written.
7. Archives de la République du Senégal [cited hereafter as ARS], 2-G-22-9.

or Muslim was of minimal importance and was not a criterion for membership in the elite.[8]

If religious differences were minimal for membership in the elite, ethnic differences were also minimal but with subtle shadings. The preponderant ethnic group was the Wolof, whose language and culture dominated the urban life of the communes, especially in Saint-Louis, the oldest and most important of the communes for development of *originaire* historical consciousness. Tukolor from the Senegal River Valley formed the second most populous group in Saint-Louis, and both Wolof and Tukolor began to migrate to Dakar after it was designated federal capital of French Africa in 1904. In total population of the communes, the second most numerous group during the period under discussion was the Lébou, who were the original inhabitants of Dakar and Rufisque.[9] Gorée, the fourth commune, had been a melting pot. Most of the leaders discussed in this paper were Wolof or highly Wolofized in their traditional cultural affiliations. It should also be noted that these ethnic groups were related in their language, social systems, and social practices, so that integration in the urban setting was relatively easy.[10]

Senegal has a highly developed caste system of long standing and data on its modification in the communes were difficult to obtain. In interviewing a number of political leaders active between 1900 and 1945, I learned that probably no more than a half dozen out of several hundred *originaires* who held public office were from the lower castes.[11] On the other hand, few important leaders had meaningful connections with important

8. See obituary in *L'Ouest Africain Français* (Dakar), 30 July 1927.

9. A number of works have touched on Lébou early history, but the most complete, although not entirely reliable, is Armand Angrand, *Les lébous de la presqu'île du Cap-Vert* (Dakar, 1950).

10. Migration to the communes was a gradual process before 1945 and although I cannot give specific data for the statement that integration was easy, this is the impression gained from reading reports and the local press. Post-1945 presented its own special problems, especially in Dakar.

11. Assane Seck, formerly professor of geography at the University of Dakar, now a member of Senghor's ministry, told me very few lower-caste members were politically active in the communes; many lived there because of the economic opportunities.

high-caste traditional families: Blaise Diagne was a self-made
man; Lamine Guèye's prestige grew from his grandfather, a
Saint-Louis politician; Galandou Diouf was also a member of
the old Saint-Louis elite; only Amadou Assane N'Doye of Dakar, the Lébou politician, had claim to immediate traditional
authority.[12] The leadership can properly be called achievement-
oriented, although Diagne (and Senghor years later) understood
the power wielded by such traditional leaders as the Mouride
marabout and solicited their favor.

Fortunately for the western observer, the Senegalese themselves perceived different interest groups, which is helpful in
classifying another important segment of the elite—the Senegalese *créoles,* or *métis* as they were often called. These *créoles*
were the descendants of French officials or traders and Senegalese women; during the period of the French Revolution the
créoles dominated Saint-Louis and Gorée and during the first
three quarters of the nineteenth century were the dominant force
in urban matters. Their leadership was challenged by new
French traders after the Franco-Prussian War, but such *créoles*
as Gaspard Devès, Louis Descemet, François Carpot, Louis
Huchard and others were more than a match for Frenchmen
who eventually returned to France. Competition from the
French traders caused the *créoles* to become even more assimilated to French culture, education, religion, and mores, so much
so that by 1900 the Africans considered them to be a separate
group.[13] The fact that the *créoles* had abandoned their intimate
relationship with the Africans was pointed up by Mody M'Baye,
a public letter writer and one of the most articulate of the *originaires:* "The *créoles* should have defended the natives, but they
didn't, because they became assimilated to the Europeans."[14]

12. He was the son of Assane N'Doye, Imam of the Great Mosque in
Dakar, who did not know French; he was one of Diagne's earliest supporters.
13. This statement is based upon interviews with *originaire* politicians
who were active during this period, upon articles in *La Démocratie* and
later *originaire* journals, and upon electoral campaign literature.
14. Rally for Blaise Diagne, 29 April 1914, Political report in Archives
de la Ministère de France d'Outre-Mer [cited hereafter as FOM], Senegal
VII-81.

In other words there was a difference between *créole* and *originaire* in Senegal, a difference perceived by both groups. Most *créoles* lived in the communes, especially Saint-Louis and Gorée, and were also part of the urban elite. But they were not *originaires,* did not favor or defend (with few exceptions) the *originaire* desire to become French citizens, and consequently were largely excluded from local politics by the triumph of Blaise Diagne's African party in 1919. For this paper the *créoles* are marginal because the bulk of their influence was in the nineteenth century; I consider them to be part of the larger urban elite but not *originaires.*

This gives us a triple-layered urban population in the communes: first, the *créoles,* second, the *originaires,* and third, the *sujets français* living in the cities. During this period the influence of the *créoles* diminished quickly and that of the *sujets français* began to rise; after the Lamine Guèye Law of 1946, which extended voting rights to all Africans in the French colonies, the *sujets* rapidly became the most important political group in Senegal. The period 1900–1945 was the time of *originaire* ascendancy and maximum influence.

Nothing has been said so far about economic indicators or educational criteria for membership in the urban elite. Meaningful statistics are difficult to obtain for this period; it would be impossible to fix a minimum annual income (as did Peter C. Lloyd and the Sixth International African Seminar on elites at Ibadan in 1964: $700 or Francs C.F.A. 150,000) in order to qualify for this elite.[15] Some *originaires* were poverty-striken urban dwellers, working as messengers or clerks, while some *sujets* were wealthy traders, with connections throughout the interior. But compared with most peasants of the interior, older inhabitants of the communes, such as the *originaires,* had a higher standard of living. By 1900 electric lights and telephones were in the four communes, paved streets for automobiles and trucks appeared after the First World War, and many substantial dwellings constructed by the French were inhabited by *originaires.* None of the other colonial cities of French West Africa rivalled either

15. P. C. Lloyd, ed., *The New Elites of Tropical Africa* (London, 1966), p. 2.

Saint-Louis or Dakar before 1945 and *originaires* who travelled the empire as traders were proud of this. Chambers of Commerce were organized in all communes before 1900. African traders and merchants were invited to join and became the largest group in the Chambers; a person was ranked, however, according to the volume of his business. Some Africans could match the Lebanese and small French traders but few were put in the same classification as the larger French traders who dominated the Chambers.[16] The *originaires* did have a sense of limited participation in the economic councils of the communes and by the 1930s placed several respected businessmen (such as Wagane Diouf) on the governing boards.

A more useful criterion for membership in the urban elite is education. Here statistics are also lacking but one can generalize from archival evidence and interviews. Practically all *créoles* were educated and were literate in French. The upper stratum of the *originaires* was exposed to some education, usually after Koranic school; the lower level was rarely schooled but its members often attended adult evening classes (which had a great vogue in Saint-Louis and Dakar) and were able to speak and comprehend rudimentary French. The *sujets* rarely knew French and few had attended school in the countryside; an occasional literate and ambitious *sujet* might arrange to become an *originaire* if he could persuade influential *originaire* friends to testify in court that he was in fact a member of the chosen few.[17]

An important related question is that of language. French was the official language of the colony and therefore the language aspired to by the *originaires* in their desire to enjoy full parity with

16. Robert Delmas, untitled manuscript on Bordeaux Families in Senegal; Delmas, one of the most important Bordeaux businessmen in Senegal, collected extensive material about the Chambers of Commerce and how many African members they admitted.

17. From 1915 to 1921 several thousand *jugements supplétifs* took place in the four communes which made *originaires* from people of varying backgrounds. The French finally made it very difficult for this process to take place; my impression is that there were not so many abuses as the French believed because after 1900 the French administration had disenfranchised many *originaires;* the vast majority of "new" *originaires* were Africans reclaiming their rights.

Frenchmen. But a basic ambiguity characterized this ambition since the vast majority of *originaires* spoke Wolof, the dominant language and lingua franca of Senegal. There was never any serious talk of replacing French with Wolof because Wolof was not written, at least not for public usage. Only a few books and documents were reduced to Roman or Arabic script and the idea of making Wolof the primary language of the elite was never seriously entertained.[18] Wolof was a convenient language precisely because few Frenchmen bothered to learn it; hence, political meetings and caucuses could be conducted with almost complete privacy from French intrusion.

Perhaps the best indication of the distinctiveness and self-awareness of the *originaire* group can be seen by examining the way they perceived other groups in the social order. A rough taxonomy of the *originaire* world can be constructed, drawn mainly from the newspapers edited by elite members and from oral history interviews. First there were the foreigners in Senegal. The Europeans, whether French or not, and the Lebanese were called *toubab*. This was a term reserved for white people, although occasionally a *créole* who was highly assimilated might be called a *toubab*. The *toubab* enjoyed prestige except for certain *petit-colons*, small French businessmen or employees, whose marginal existence caused them barely to survive.[19] *Originaires* had respect for a *toubab* who had style, position, or wealth and, in the context of the communes, *toubab* was rarely pejorative, as it often was in the countryside under authoritarian rule.

Other foreigners in Senegal were in several categories. There were the Cape Verdeans, who were often viewed as *créoles* and not distinguished from them; but Cape Verdeans rarely occupied

18. Many African languages owe their written history to some missionary who first translated the Bible into the vernacular; this never took place in Senegal, where in 1964 an English missionary was still laboring to put the Bible into Wolof.

19. The *petits-colons* became important before 1914 as the French empire grew and opportunities were created in Senegal for France's expansion; the First World War called most of them back to France and not until the later 1930s did significant numbers reappear in Senegal. Most of them came from southern French rural or seaside districts.

important positions in the communes. The opposite was true of the West Indians, mainly represented in the administration, men who seldom identified with the Africans and who were thought of as *créoles* by the *originaires*.[20] There were also Africans from other French colonies, each group having its own image with the *originaires:* the Soudanese or Bambara, thought to be rustics and former slaves; the Guineans, who by the 1930s began to replace Senegalese as domestics in many *toubab* households; the educated Dahomeyans, who were beginning to seek jobs in Senegal but were not yet a threat to educated *originaires;* and the Gambians (usually Wolof), who often worked for British steamship-line offices in Dakar. The Mauritanians were suspect and feared, since they had kept Negro slaves in the past, but the Moroccans were welcomed and often emulated in dress. The *originaire* could feel superior to any one of these groups, because none had the privileges of French citizenship, not even the Lebanese, who were forbidden to vote despite long residence in Senegal.[21]

The way in which the *originaires* viewed themselves as a distinct group from the old-line *créoles* of Saint-Louis and Gorée cannot be overemphasized. A person who was of mixed racial origin might fit in with the *originaires* provided he did not have close association with the former *créole* aristocrats. Public confessions were made by several old-line *créoles* in the 1919 election in which they admitted that their social group had neglected the welfare of "our African brothers."[22]

20. On the other hand, the West Indian Gratien Candace, deputy in the French Parliament, was widely admired in Senegal, at least until the 1920s. After that, he was considered to be as reactionary as Diagne.

21. The Lebanese were loathed by many *originaires* as well as the French for their success in the commercial world. They gained a great advantage during the First World War when French and Africans were liable for military service while the Lebanese were not. Governor Fernand Levecque of Senegal had the idea of enrolling them in an Oriental Legion, but no one in the central administration accepted the idea. See ARS, 2-G-17-5.

22. See the important article by Joseph Angrand de St. Jean, *L'Ouest Africain Français*, 29 November 1919: "I affirm that certain Senegalese mulattoes, during the past fifty years, by their egotistical attitude, their retrograde ideas about caste, and their prejudices are responsible for the

A different kind of relationship existed between the *originaires* and Christian Africans, mostly Catholics, since few Protestants were converted in Senegal. The Catholics had been called *gourmets* in the nineteenth century and were men who adopted European dress, manners, mores, and religion. On occasion, especially during political campaigns, *gourmets* were suspected by some rank and file; but the amiable toleration which characterized urban Senegal made it possible for most *gourmets* to be unnoticed members of the *originaires*. Diagne chose several important lieutenants from this group but never identified himself too closely with them for fear of isolating the Muslim majority.[23]

The sharpest perception of difference separated the *originaires* and the *sujets français*. Rural persons were often called *paysans*, but without a strong implication of inferior social status because most *originaires* had numerous relatives in the Protectorate area. Many *originaires* resided in the interior towns of Kaolack, Zinguinchor, Thiès, Louga, and Tivouane, where they were painstakingly careful to preserve their identities as *originaires* for obvious reasons. (For example, if one had a dispute with the local French administrator and one was a *sujet*, a summary trial by the administrator could put you in prison with no appeal; as an *originaire*, one was entitled to a French court hearing and trial.) By the 1930s it became popular among progressive *originaires* to support the idea of equal rights for *sujets;* indeed, twice in the 1920s Blaise Diagne had unsuccessfully sponsored legislation to extend the suffrage.[24]

Some members of the Senegal elite lived outside of Senegal. Those who remained home knew of two groups. One consisted of the *originaires* who emigrated to other French colonies in search of work, men who were usually well established and

---

misfortunes of our country." [All translations are mine, unless otherwise identified.]

23. Michel Sangué, Ambrose Mendy, and Pierre Chimère are examples of highly successful Catholic politicians during the Diagne period.

24. A poor substitute for Diagne's plans was enacted in 1925. It allowed a limited number of local notables in other French West African colonies to vote for local administrative councils. See ARS, 20-G-16-17.

found jobs in the French administration or with French companies, especially in Dahomey, Guinea, and the Ivory Coast.[25] The other group of expatriate elite were the few Senegalese who lived in France, but not all of these were *originaires*. After the First World War, a number of Francophone Africans had remained in France to work or study instead of returning to Africa. These men were not well known to the *originaires* in Senegal because their radical writings and papers were generally prohibited in the colonies.

Reactions of the Elite to the French Colonial Presence

The dominant characteristic of French colonial rule in Africa for the Senegalese urban elite was the emphasis on assimilation. A legacy from the French Revolution, assimilation was handed down imperfectly in a colonial policy which gave Senegal's urban dwellers much residual power over local political matters: a deputy, a colonial council, and municipal councils. The fact that metropolitan France fluctuated from empire to kingdom to republic during the nineteenth century meant little continuity of policy for colonial peoples. In Senegal, men could be slaves one month and electors the next, put on the voting rolls for municipal council elections and removed from them for the deputyship elections.[26] This assimilated group of Africans had grown up since the eighteenth century, identified with the French conquest, and remembered promises of assimilation when the home government did not. They were led by *créoles* and *gourmets* until 1900, when the larger mass awakened to the potential which the ballot box offered them. The urban elite was enfranchised in

25. Later the Dahomeyans were to fill the same function as the early *originaires*, when a surplus number of young educated elite members needed positions. The reverse kind of situation characterized Senegal after 1945, where Dahomeyans "colonized" Senegal and were bitterly resented by lower status elites in Senegal.

26. In 1848, when the franchise was first granted, complaints were made that some recent slaves were made electors. FOM, Senegal VII-44. After 1900, numerous changes were made in electoral lists by the French administration and by members of municipal councils.

the 1848 deputy elections and, despite attacks from visiting
French inspectors or governors during the intervening years, aspired to full French citizenship, which Diagne obtained in 1915.[27]

Blaise Diagne, who served as Senegal's first *originaire* deputy
to Paris from 1914 to 1934, was the archetype of the assimilated
Senegalese. He had been reared by *créole* foster parents in
Gorée, educated in Saint-Louis, entered the customs service of
the French colonial administration, and served for two decades
in various African colonies, in Madagascar, and in French Guiana. Diagne had married a Frenchwoman and took his leave
time in France, where he became intimately acquainted with
French culture and style of life. He became interested in politics
and met the most important politicians of the day during his
French sojourns; it fired his ambition and in 1914 he took leave
from his customs post in Guiana to contest successfully the post
of deputy in Senegal from the powerful *créole* lawyer, François
Carpot.[28] Diagne was an accomplished writer but his intellectual
interests were confined to political or current questions. He was
an effective orator, both in Senegal, where he handled large
crowds with ease, and in France, where he was feared in the
Chamber of Deputies for his wit and satire. Diagne vacationed
at the French seaside or in the mountains, kept an apartment in
a fashionable section of Paris, and visited Senegal with great for-
mality every year. On a European public speaking tour in 1922,
Diagne summed up his philosophy by telling his audience that
"an intellectual and material marriage is possible between European and African civilization."[29]

An alternative model, especially for younger elite members
after 1923, was Lamine Guèye, a Saint-Louisian Wolof who
was the first African to win a law degree in Paris. Guèye was
a young protege of Diagne's during the war, served on his staff

27. The criterion for voting rights in 1848 was five years' residence in
either Saint-Louis or Gorée (the only communes at that time); this was
the heart of the *originaires'* claim in later years that the administration
and not custom had given them the vote. FOM, AOF 534-2.

28. See G. Wesley Johnson, "The Ascendancy of Blaise Diagne and
the Beginning of African Politics in Senegal," *Africa* 36 (1966):235–53.

29. *L'Ouest Africain Français*, 15 January 1922.

briefly, but then broke with him in 1924 and served as an opposition leader until he was finally elected deputy in 1945. Guèye was a tall, serious man, a gifted speaker in Wolof and French, who was not so remote or aloof as Diagne but who also inspired admiration and confidence. At a banquet in his honor in 1924, given by the Young Senegalese, he was toasted in these terms: "Let us honor our young lawyer—he is the only one among us who possesses a higher education; despite this education, he still considers us to be his comrades."[30] Guèye was absent from Senegal for several years, serving in various posts of the French empire as an appeals judge. Unlike Diagne, who was nominally Catholic but in practice a Freemason, Guèye was a Muslim affiliated with the Tidjaniyya brotherhood of Tivouane. His interests were more firmly rooted in Senegal than were Diagne's.

In French political and colonial circles, Diagne (during the first half of the period) and Guèye (during the later years) were famed as products of France's assimilationist principles. Diagne's rhetoric and shrewd maneuver were responsible for a voice vote in the Chamber in 1915 to give citizenship; Guèye's diplomacy and parliamentary *savoir-faire* were responsible for the abolition of forced labor and the extension of citizenship during the constituent assembly of 1945–46. Diagne was viewed by some *originaires* as a demigod when he was received in 1918 by the Governor-General of West Africa *as an equal* and given a reception and quarters equal to those of a Minister of France; Guèye was received into the inner councils of the French Socialist Party in the 1930s and travelled between Paris and Dakar with ease, when discrimination in travel was still known.[31] Both Diagne and Guèye were admired and were represented to the Young Senegelese (before Léopold Senghor was known) as what one might become under the French policy of assimilation. But even to aspire to the heights reached by a Diagne or

30. ARS, 17-G-233-108.
31. Buell makes the reception of Diagne in Dakar during the recruitment trip seem unheard of and repeats the story of the European woman who supposedly dusted off his shoes. Raymond Leslie Buell, *The Native Problem in Africa*, 2 vols. (New York, 1928), 1:955.

a Guèye was not within the power of most elite members; Galandou Diouf, the personage in the Senegalese trinity of elite politicians less well known than Diagne or Guèye, was in practice a more realistic model and more typical of the *originaires*.

Galandou Diouf had not studied in France but served there as a lieutenant in the French army during the First World War. He had been active in commune politics since 1909 as a member of the General Council of the colony.[32] Diouf enjoyed the support of the young elite and probably would have become Senegal's first African deputy in the French Parliament if Diagne had not appeared on the scene in 1914. From then until 1928, when he broke with Diagne, Diouf stood in his shadow, as first lieutenant until 1925, and second lieutenant afterwards. Diouf was unlike Diagne or Guèye in many ways. He was Muslim, but unlike the monogamous Guèye, he had several wives. He was not sophisticated in his bearing, did not copy French mannerisms, did not savor Paris in the same way that Diagne or Guèye did. Robert Delavignette commented in later years that he could never forget visiting Diouf at his hotel —the deputy received the colonial official in undershirt with shoes off.[33] Diouf was intelligent but was not attracted to the formalities of French metropolitan life, which Diagne and Guèye enjoyed. Diouf was more at home with his companions of the war, the veterans organizations, and from this group he drew confidence, great praise, and steadfast devotion. Asked to describe these three men, the words most used by Senegalese and French informants were: for Diagne "intelligent, eloquent," for Guèye "shrewd, calculating," and for Diouf "sincere, human." One observer tried to separate Diouf from the other two by saying: "Diouf? He was the most African of the three."[34]

32. Diouf is a man who should be more closely studied. His greatest misfortune in politics was that Diagne returned to Senegal. His early writings show an original perspective but by 1919 his political philosophy had become a reflection of Diagne's.

33. Interview with Robert Delavignette, Paris, October 1964.

34. I realize that single words cannot possibly convey much about the complex personality of an individual, but in sorting my interviews my impression was very strong about the reoccurrence of certain words and concepts about these three men.

Diouf was more representative of the Senegalese elite (a group which in the main did not aspire to become "black Frenchmen") than either Diagne or Guèye. He kept in close touch with his constituents and despite certain scandals linked with his name—misappropriation of funds while Mayor of Rufisque, possible fraud in connection with the building of the Mouride mosque in Touba—he enjoyed the support of the Senegalese elite.[35] Diouf was a Wolof from Saint-Louis, had been a school teacher, businessman, clerk, and finally in 1909, was elected General Councillor from Rufisque, at that time a Lébou stronghold. He won the confidence of the Lébou and represented them for nearly thirty years. Diouf was as well educated as Diagne, but appeared less literate to the French; he was inferior to Diagne or Guèye in debate. But as a "stump" politician going from house to house to visit families for votes he was unequalled. His common touch, his sense of humor, his willingness to admit his errors and vices (in contrast to the pride of Diagne and the vanity of Guèye) endeared him to the urban elite.

Diouf was an example of limited or moderate assimilation. This is what the Senegalese elite aspired to before 1945. Only after the Second World War, when more scholarships sent hundreds of *originaires* to French universities for the first time, only after the *négritude* school arose, did some members of the elite aspire to become "black Frenchmen" with degrees from the Sorbonne. During the period 1900–1945, the quest of the elite was basically political rather than cultural. For example, the young men who in 1912 formed the Young Senegalese, the first political club in Senegal, did not want to become totally assimilated. They were proud of their African dress, proud of Wolof, proud to be Senegalese.[36] Their mentor was an old Saint-Louisian *no-*

35. The Rufisque scandal (coal ordered for the municipality was paid for but never delivered) undermined Diagne's confidence in Diouf. Moreover, the events surrounding the building of the Mouride mosque, in which a French administrator linked to Diouf was accused of making an immense profit, hastened the break between the two in 1928. FOM, Senegal VII-51bis.

36. See the debates reported in *La Démocratie*, the first newspaper fully open to the *originaires*, for 1913–1914.

table, Thiécouta Diop, who remained their leader from 1912 until 1919–1920, despite Diagne's great victory of 1914. It is instructive to see what kind of person Thiécouta Diop was.

An important fact about Diop as an urban leader was that he never spoke French in public. He apparently knew some French but proudly refused to speak with the *toubab* in anything except Wolof. His conversations with colonial officials were handled by an interpreter, his remonstrances to the Governor were written down in French and duly noted that they had been translated from Wolof. Uneducated in the French sense, Diop preferred traditional to European dress, and inspired young elite members because he dared to be African while demanding equal political rights with Frenchmen. At first he was not convinced Diagne could win the election of 1914—Diagne had been absent from the country twenty years, looked too sophisticated, had forgotten much of his Wolof (a political necessity), was married to a white woman, and professed to be a Catholic. Could such an anomaly, who represented himself as a Senegalese, actually win? Diop doubted this and for almost a month held out, giving initial support to a liberal Frenchman who was sympathetic to the elite.[37]

Thiécouta Diop and Galandou Diouf were important models for the Young Senegalese before Diagne arrived, Diop as the older adviser to the group, Diouf as the brash young man who had proved that a local African could succeed in politics. They were men of different generations: Diop unschooled, Diouf schooled by the Catholics despite the fact he was Muslim; Diop preferred African dress, Diouf wore European clothes when the occasion demanded; Diop proud to be a *notable,* an expression of older elite status, Diouf proud of his service to France as a soldier and of his membership in the Legion of Honor.

One important reason why Diop and Diouf were practical models for the younger men is the fact that these careers seemed obtainable in Senegal. Only exceptional persons such as Diagne and Guèye might travel the empire, socialize in France with the *toubab,* and enjoy an alien way of life. Diop's image was that of

37. Governor H. Cor to Governor-General William Ponty, 14 January 1914, in FOM, Senegal VII-81.

an older man bent on achieving political recognition by the French; indeed, some of his letters to the Governor-General reveal his tenacity of purpose, even going so far as to denounce Diagne to win recognition for his own efforts as *doyen* of the elite political community.[38] Diouf's image on the other hand was that of a practical, capable local politician who was overwhelmed by the dynamic and worldly Diagne, persuaded to play second fiddle for twelve years, and who finally broke with his senior friend only after concluding Diagne was blocking the expression of his own ideas.[39]

Both Diop and Diouf were studies in frustration, and in this they were typical of the elite both before and after the 1915 law which conveyed citizenship—before because the elite were stymied in their goal of political parity with the French; after because they realized that this political parity (as citizens) still did not end the colonial regime with its authoritarian nature, its ultimate control of local politics, and its basic assumption that Africans were inferior, without history, without adequate language, who were malleable and educable only as full-fledged *assimilés.* The local administrator might now shake hands with the *originaire* politician, might give him warm welcome in his office to discuss business, but was cold and reserved in the evening at the cafe terrace where blacks and whites remained separated. He would rarely receive the *originaire* in his home. A Diagne might bask in the acclaim of his collegues in the Chamber, a Guèye might receive commendation from the bench for his legal opinions, but a Diop was ignored by the official colonial mind and a Diouf (until he was deputy) was noticed mainly because of his several political scandals.

Assimilation, then, was not an ultimate goal for most *originaires,* despite a small group of colonial officials who thought that it was and who delighted in the notion that France had spawned a black aristocracy. Such a person was Governor-Gen-

38. Letter from Thiécouta Diop to d'Iriart d'Etchepare, President of the Commission on Colonies, 9 August 1921, in ARS, 17-G-234-108.

39. After 1928, during the next six years of opposition to Diagne, Diouf never really fundamentally challenged his political philosophy. His political program was different only in detail.

eral William Ponty of French West Africa, who devoted much time trying to understand the elite, was deferential to it, and took with good humor the barbs directed at him in the *originaire* press.[40] Ponty believed in assimilation and protected the rights of the elite; he was one of the few colonial officials who was not shocked by Blaise Diagne's election in 1914.[41] On the other hand, Maurice Delafosse, France's first serious administrator-scholar, was opposed to the elite and considered its special privilege over rural Africans to be immoral. Delafosse became the *bête-noire* of the elite and was roundly denounced in *La Démocratie* and other *originaire* publications for his hostility to assimilation.[42]

An example of the reluctance of the elite to pursue assimilation to its logical conclusion was the *originaire* reaction to the 1915 law which made them citizens. They had demanded citizenship, had backed Diagne's efforts in Paris, but the victory meant they no longer could avoid serving in the French army (they steadfastly had refused to be called to the *tirailleurs séné-galais,* the French colonial forces composed of various West African ethnic groups). In short, they were now liable for military service in wartime. Only through the urging of Diagne, fresh from Paris, could the *originaires* be persuaded to put their lives on the line for the preservation of French culture and glory. For the conscript, assimilation now seemed a poor reward for being shipped off to the trenches of northern France.[43]

Although assimilation was the most distinctive aspect of French policy which affected the urban elite, other facets of colonial rule should be considered. How did the *originaires* react to such representative institutions as the General Council and

40. *La Démocratie* in 1914 referred to Ponty as Seigneur Guillaume I, El Reverendendissimo Guglielmo, and Guglielmo Ponty Africano.

41. Ponty refused to accept the idea that Diagne's election spelled disaster for the French regime; he worked actively after war was declared in 1914 to get the *originaires* into the French army. Ponty's death in 1915 was genuinely regretted in the *originaire* press.

42. See the attack on Delafosse by Armand Cathy, "An Insult to Senegal," *La Démocratie,* 5 September 1915.

43. Lt. Governor of Senegal to Governor-General, 2 January 1916, FOM, AOF 534-18.

the municipal governments of which they took charge in 1919? These western institutions were never seriously questioned; they seemed to be convenient centers of power to be controlled, since many jobs and other patronage could be dispensed. In 1921 the composition of the General Council was changed and regional chiefs were brought in to give representation to rural areas and to provide the French colonial administration with "safe men." The elite reacted violently, perceiving the new arrangement (called the Colonial Council) as a way of reducing their power, especially over the budget of Senegal. The number of chiefs was eventually reduced and the *originaires* retained control, but the important days of the Council, during the *créole* period of domination, were over and the party politics controlled by the deputy became more important.[44] To make sure the Council functioned to his liking, Diagne put his second lieutenant after Diouf in charge—Amadou N'Diaye Duguay-Clédor, a colorful and controversial member of the Diagne entourage.

Duguay-Clédor was a Saint-Louisian who had taught school and gained recognition as one of the first *originaire* journalists. Even before the war he had sung the praises of old Senegal in one of the first histories written by a full African; after the war he was put in charge of Diagne's new journal, *La France Coloniale,* which replaced the earlier radical *La Démocratie.*[45] Duguay-Clédor was an immense man, in size and in interests, and his preferences ran to wine and polemics; these indulgences alienated many colleagues and removed him as a claimant for the mantle of Diagne after the deputy's death in 1934. He stood

44. Diagne originally favored the idea of expanding the Council, because he felt more representation would be desirable; but after his political foe Governor-General Martial Merlin revealed that he conceived of it as a means of diluting the local political influence of the communes, Diagne favored revision of the number of chiefs in the Council's composition.

45. *La Démocratie* was founded in 1913 by d'Oxoby, came under Diagne's influence in 1914, was replaced in 1919 by *L'Ouest Africain Français.* D'Oxoby broke with Diagne in 1925–1926 and in 1927 Diagne finally founded his own journal, *La France Coloniale* (Dakar), with Duguay-Clédor as editor.

by Diagne as others changed to the opposition to support Diouf or Guèye; he more than any other *originaire* popularized an assimilationist line in his newspaper. His reward from Diagne was the Presidency of the Colonial Council, which he discharged with much verve and show but with minimal political influence.[46] The mind of Duguay-Clédor was printed in the pages of *La France Coloniale* and in his prose the ideals of assimalitionist *originaires* were often articulated. Duguay-Clédor relished pomp, European clothes, and festivity: he popularized the *vin d'honneur* for African political gatherings in a land where many Muslims were nondrinkers.

Duguay-Clédor is also interesting for his attitude towards political parties. Diagne had pioneered the modern political party in Senegal with his Republican Socialist party in the 1919 election.[47] Previously, political clubs (such as the Young Senegalese) and interest groups (such as the inhabitants of Guet N'Dar near Saint-Louis) were loosely knit associations of convenience, but Diagne welded together veterans, Young Senegalese, Lébou, traders, dock workers, and others into a political party. Duguay-Clédor was given the responsibility of party secretary and until the end of *diagnisme* in 1934 exercised these functions. Diagne knew the rough and tumble world of metropolitan politics but never fully translated the techniques of French politics to Senegal; he understood that his lively oratory and great prestige were more important than ideological programs. Duguay-Clédor on the other hand labored to build a coherent political organization from the diverse elements attracted to Diagne, but never fully succeeded, since his contact with ideo-

46. Duguay-Clédor was accused of being decended from Bambara slaves (there was a small Bambara community in Saint-Louis). I have never verified this but it might have something to do with the low personal esteem in which he was held by many elite members. His political power vanished completely with Diagne's death; neither Diouf nor Guèye took him seriously in their courting of support from former Diagne lieutenants.

47. G. Wesley Johnson, "The Development of Political Parties in Senegal, 1900–1945" (Paper delivered to the African Studies Association meetings, Philadelphia, November 1965).

logical politics of France was limited.[48] Only Lamine Guèye, after the death of Diagne, began to effect a more structured and
sustained party organization with his version of French socialism
in Senegal, but Lamine Guèye had lived in Paris for many years.[49]
If Duguay-Clédor failed to understand fully European-style
political parties, so did his *originaire* friends, who shied away
from ideology even during Popular Front days. The issues preferred by *originaires* were personal ones which concerned local
candidates and their factional relationships, not metropolitan
questions.

Interest in domestic French affairs was negligible. Occasionally, a demonstration that the average *originaire* cared about life
in France did occur, as in 1926, when a beleaguered France sent
out appeals for financial aid from the colonies to help restore the
value of the franc. The colony of Senegal responded by diverting
certain local funds to France; the *originaires* seemed proud of
helping the metropole. On the other hand, the pages of the *originaire* press reveal that African intellectuals were well informed
about France; Galandou Diouf wrote in *La Démocratie* in 1914
that the elite had excellent models to use in establishing an opposition newspaper; he himself read *L'Homme Libre* of Clemen-
ceau, *L'Humanité* of Jaurès, and *La Guerre Sociale* of Hervé.[50]
But at the same time he lamented the fact that, before the establishment of *La Démocratie,* Senegal did not have an authentic
African press to sit in judgment and comment on the colonial
administration in the same way the French press in Paris scruti-
nized the French parliament.[51]

The newspaper was an institution imported from France
which the elite found useful for politics. *Créoles* had edited

48. Diagne had great confidence in Duguay-Clédor but rarely allowed
him to visit France. Both Lamine Guèye and Galandou Diouf were more
in touch with French politics.

49. Upon his return to Senegal after Diagne's death in 1934, Lamine
Guèye helped organize the Parti Socialiste Sénégalais. The party chose a
green and red flag which later became part of the flag of independent
Senegal. See *Clarté* (Dakar), 25 April 1935.

50. *La Démocratie,* 20 January 1914.

51. Conseil Général, minutes of *séance* of 6 November 1912.

newspapers since the 1880s, but the first newspaper which regularly printed predominantly African writers was *La Démocratie,* founded by the *petit colon* Jean Daramy d'Oxoby and quickly patronized by Blaise Diagne, who became *directeur politique* of the journal in classic French political fashion. Mody M'Baye, Thiécouta Diop, Amadou N'Diaye Duguay-Clédor, Galandou Diouf, and other *originaires* contributed to its columns, which made the liveliest reading in Senegal from 1913 to 1919.[52] After the reactionary Martial Merlin became Governor-General in 1919, newspapers lost the freedom they had enjoyed under William Ponty; the stinging satire and forthright candor of *La Démocratie* became the standard for the next several decades and was rarely equalled. The Diagne official line was propounded in a new journal, *La France Coloniale,* founded for his party and edited by Duguay-Clédor after d'Oxoby left to start a new journal more in harmony with *petit-colon* interests; nevertheless, it is remarkable that for almost a decade the most effective mouthpiece for the elite party was the volatile Frenchman d'Oxoby.

Mody M'Baye was a pioneer journalist and prime awakener of the political consciousness of *originaires* before 1914, who conveyed the ambiguity which most of the elite felt towards Frenchmen. In a column in *La Démocratie,* M'Baye wrote that two kinds of Frenchmen lived in the colonies, those who served France loyally, "inculcating the principles of 1789," and those who were free agents "dedicated to making the greatest possible profit before returning to France." M'Baye claimed the Senegalese knew how to distinguish between the two types, how to react towards them—with respect or defiance.[53] He then wrote a long description of the enlightened Frenchman, who swore an oath to bring civilization and freedom to the peoples under his charge, contrasted to the self-seeking Frenchman, who found himself in a position of power in the colonies from which he could exploit his charges forever.

This simple dualistic image of Frenchmen recurred in the *origi-*

52. *La Démocratie* gained a reputation in France as a journal "which is inciting the black population to revolution." 24 June 1914.
53. *La Démocratie,* 25 December 1913.

naire press during the next several decades because it provided a means for attacking the attitude of many administrators without incurring real official displeasure. But the message was clear, whether written by M'Baye, Télémaque Sow, or Galandou Diouf, that the elite knew of Frenchmen in France who treated them as equals, representatives of the republican France who practiced the ideals of the Revolution, and therefore they would not be bullied by crass official agents, jealous *petit-colons,* or egocentric self-proclaimed experts on native culture. This latter category was reserved for Maurice Delafosse, who wrote many columns questioning the *raison d'être* of the Senegalese elite and its special privileges; in return, the *originaires* delighted in waging polemical battles with Delafosse, whom Galandou Diouf labelled the *griot* or praise singer of the *créoles* (who were also opposed to ratifying elite status for the *originaires*). Delafosse, who served in Senegal several times during his long career, but most notably as Director of Native Affairs under Joost Van Vollenhoven in 1917, had little sympathy for urbanized Africans, who seemed a sort of aberration to him; indeed, Delafosse was accused of adopting a Rousseau-like stance of wanting to keep all Africans like noble savages—in the bush and unassimilated.[54]

The attitude of *originaires* towards other Europeans, as expressed in their newspapers, is instructive. In the 1902 election for deputy, a definite anti-Semitic tinge to the election was revealed when the African electors accused Robert Dreyfus, a Parisian lawyer who was seeking office as an absentee candidate, of being linked with the "vile Jew Dreyfus." Mobs ran amok through the streets of Dakar and Saint-Louis shouting "down with the Jew."[55] Whether this anti-Semitism was the work of a particular political group in the communes, whether it was learned at the Catholic schools which had trained most of the elite in that day, or whether it was simply picked up as a kind of supposed sophistication is difficult to say. Much the same thing occurred during the opening days of the First World War, when

54. *La Démocratie,* 5 September 1915.
55. Report on election, ARS 20-G-12.

the elite news columns were filled with anti-German stories. The imagination of the *originaires* was captured by the image of "tribal Teutonic hordes invading France" and the argument that they, as members of France's elite, should be called upon to help save the "light of civilization."[56] Also in 1914, another French candidate for deputy, Henri Heimburger from Alsace, was constantly referred to as "that Jew," with a pejorative adjective often placed in front. Some well-educated elite members became Freemasons and one issue of *La Démocratie* featured a letter signed by several of these *originaires* denouncing Heimburger.[57]

The elite had learned its history well in the French classrooms. The identification of its origin and evolution as a social group with that of France, and France's efforts in West Africa, were inseparable. Rather than have Marshal Philippe Pétain received by a notable chief, the elite rushed Duguay-Clédor to meet the visiting soldier in 1925. Diagne's lieutenant gave a flowery oration of welcome and compared Pétain to Turenne and Condé. It was also Duguay-Clédor who reprinted speeches of Faidherbe from the 1850s in many issues of *La France Coloniale:* Faidherbe dedicating a bridge, Faidherbe describing victory in battle, Faidherbe distributing prizes to the pupils of the Ecole des Otages. Duguay-Clédor constantly invoked images of the French past to describe its relevance for the present: "We work to save the old capital of Senegal [Saint-Louis], the glorious city of André Bruë, of Blanchot, and of Faidherbe."[58] Earlier in his career, before the war, Duguay-Clédor had written two brief historical essays which glorified Senegalese participation in the French conquest: "La Bataille de Guile" and "De Faidherbe à Coppolani." Duguay-Clédor, arguing for greater status for indigenous members of the administration, wanted to show the loyal devotion of the elite to the French cause and: "the many bloody sacrifices and loyalty to France consented to by our fathers from the stormy days of the French Revolution,

56. *La Démocratie*, 14 August 1914.
57. *La Démocratie*, 22 July 1914.
58. *La France Coloniale*, 8 May 1930.

the Consulate and the Empire and by their descendants of the Senegalese epic under Faidherbe, Pinet-Laprade, Brière de l'Ile and Canard."[59]

The same historical perspective was voiced by Galandou Diouf at a time when debate raged in Senegal over whether the *originaires* were citizens or should be made citizens. Diouf acidly described their opponents: "Forgetting the past of their ancestors and their own past, these undesirables from the metropole want to keep us under the yoke of slavery despite the liberties which the great French Revolution generously gave us. Gentlemen, the French Republic freed us as well as you; if we are the serfs of the last hour, remember you were those of the first hour."[60] The appeals to the Revolution, to the principles of republicanism, and to the promises made in earlier times about the rewards of assimilation characterized the rhetoric and informed the historical consciousness of the *originaires*. The French attack on the privileges of the elite after 1900 drew them together and was a fundamental reason for the groundswell for Diagne in 1914.

By 1934 two decades of elite self-consciousness brought forward a classic statement of how the *originaires* viewed themselves in relation to other peoples of Africa and the French. François Baye Salzmann was one of the young radicals who detested Diagne and his later "politics of collaboration"; he joined the opposition in 1928 and helped publish several newsletters and journals. Salzmann was an anomaly because he was a *métis* who grew up among the *originaires* and did not have the old-line connections of most *créoles*. He became a passionate and articulate defender of the African elite. In his journal *Clarté* he explained his postion:

. . . I can say that the growing aspirations of our young native generation can be made very precise. Regardless of the level of our civilization at the beginning of colonization, it is incontestable that our indigenous society is divided into minority and leading elites and

59. Cited by Claude Wauthier, *L'Afrique des Africains* (Paris, 1964), p. 208.
60. *La Démocratie*, 18 July 1915.

into multitudes of masses to be led. This postulated, we can then demand the following:

1. A solid education and social instruction for those who can immediately benefit from its advantages. For we believe that colonization rationally viewed calls for the participation of native elites in directing the affairs of the country.
2. Progressive intellectual and social cleansing of the masses, if I can express myself in that way. The masses should learn various trades as they do in France, and one day they might enter the ranks of the elite.[61]

Salzmann and his older brother, Pierre, formed a journalistic duo which remained a constant source of irritation for the established political regime and the administration. Pierre had spent time in Paris and was the more learned of the two; he founded a short-lived newspaper called *La Renaissance Coloniale* in Dakar and, unlike other members of the elite, was often preoccupied with cultural matters. For the intelligentsia of the urban elite were basically preoccupied with political matters prior to 1945, even though citizenship was conferred in 1915. It was as though the battle had been won too easily and there was a surplus of energy to be expended to convince the French (and themselves) that their privileged position was justified. Several attempts were made to disenfranchise the *originaires,* but Blaise Diagne, serving first as High Commissioner of colonial troops, then Chairman of the Chamber's Commission on Colonies, and later as Undersecretary of State for Colonies, would not have allowed the crowning act of his career to be undone.[62] By the 1930s the defense of the elite had been supplanted by a new question: How should the elite be trained and what should they do?

61. *Clarté,* 7 November 1934.
62. Diagne gained in stature during the 1920s in France as his stature in Senegal diminished. Not only his key position as Chairman of the Commission on Colonies, but also his position as second in command of the Freemasons in Paris (many important colonial administration leaders were Freemasons) helped insure that the privileges of his constituents would be safeguarded. But his connections were not strong enough to spread the privilege of being an elector to the interior or to other colonies.

This shifts us from historical consciousness to the closely related subject of education under the colonial regime. How did
the elite react to the French system? Before separation of church
and state in 1905, practically all schools in Senegal were Catholic. This meant that the generation of Galandou Diouf was
trained in Catholic schools. It was significant that Diouf and his
colleagues, who were predominantly Muslims, were allowed by
their families to attend the Catholic schools.[63] The fear that children would be enticed to mass and sacraments kept many parents indifferent to the advantages of a western education. The
state schools, chartered in 1904 for all of French West Africa,
provided a different climate. Here students did not learn Catholic philosophy or Biblical parables, but rather the catechisms of
the Republic and the principles of the Revolution. Instruction
was allowed only in French, since Senegal had not received a
great influx of missionaries to render the Bible into Wolof and to
create a written vernacular. The replacing of Catholic school-
books was seen as a necessity by anti-clerical administrators,
who wanted to eradicate certain religious dogmas by using texts
"truly republican and not hostile to democracy."[64]

Another problem was the Koranic schools. Since most *originaires* attended them, it meant starting French school three to
six years later in life than the French desired. Rather than attacking the Islamic *medersa,* the French had sponsored several
in the communes; they also gained the cooperation of individual
marabout who often instructed several children in order to support themselves. Maintaining a policy of toleration, the French
persuaded many students to attend both French school and *medersa,* or to defer Koranic studies until later.

The French found it hard to recruit devoted teachers to equal
those in Catholic or Muslim schools; by 1915 the *originaires*
claimed that after a decade of reform, secular classes were inferior to those run by the clergy. Rather than eliminating racial
criteria (that is, giving preference to *créole* children), the public
schools were accused of maintaining prejudicial admissions poli-

63. See Diouf's remarks in ARS, 4-E-13.
64. Colonie du Sénégal, *Rapport d'Ensemble,* 1903.

cies, especially in the urban areas, leaving African children to attend the regional schools. The elite considered this an affront, since the urban schools followed the same program as in France but the regional schools followed a simplified curriculum. This concern for equivalence of education was already manifest in 1900; by 1919 the elite was demanding secondary school instruction identical to that given in France.[65] Jean Daramy d'Oxoby put the blame for lack of progress on the Bordeaux merchants, who he claimed were afraid of the challenge posed by a developing elite. D'Oxoby cited a brochure in which the Union Coloniale, a group of overseas businessmen in France, advocated restricting education in the African colonies to simple agricultural and mechanical instruction. By 1922 the *originaires* were fighting to win more places in the new Lycée Faidherbe, which did give identical instruction. The number of places in the Lycée occupied by different groups was:

European students from France	33
Métis from four communes	24
Africans from four communes (*originaires*)	79
Africans from Protectorate (*sujets*)	19
Lebanese and Syrians	9

total students 164[66]

The long-awaited expansion of education for the elite was held in abeyance by an administration perplexed by its own creation, unsure of what to do. By 1932, the editors of the opposition paper *l'Action Sénégalaise* could point accusingly to Diagne's unfulfilled promises to make more educational opportunities available: "For eighteen years Diagne has represented us, but how many doctors have we trained? How many engineers? How many professors? How many lawyers? The answer is zero for the first three, and one for the last—and he got there by his own means."[67] The *originaires* had not found the key to advancement in higher education, which was practically nonexis-

65. *L'Ouest Africain Français,* 12 July 1919.
66. ARS, 17-G-241-108.
67. *L'Action Sénégalaise* (Dakar), 6 August 1932.

tent for them. There were exceptions, men who managed to get to France and study. Léopold Senghor, graduate of the Catholic mission schools, won a fellowship to study in the metropolis, but Birago Diop and Ousmane Socé Diop, also gifted literary men, were forced to become veterinarians because no other opportunities for a European education were open. In fact, when Diagne died in 1934 a manifesto was issued by the young men who had gone to France which was a roster of those who had broken the "education barrier" in Senegal. Led by Birago Diop and Léopold Senghor, the thirteen young men pleaded with Lamine Guèye, their idol, to return to Senegal from his magistracy in Réunion and contest the succession of Diagne with Galandou Diouf.[68] The failure of participation in politics after 1914 to bring an educational policy commensurate with their ambitions was the major source of elite grievances during the 1930s and set the stage for the vigorous demands in 1945–1946, which resulted in hundreds of new scholarships for African students to attend French *lycées* and universities in all subjects, not just veterinary medicine.

The lack of opportunities in higher education meant that the African *originaires* during the interwar period produced only a limited number of candidates for a Senegalese intelligentsia. If one were to consider the *créoles*, then one would find a small intelligentsia dating from the mid-nineteenth century. But such twentieth-century *créoles* as Louis Guillabert, François Carpot, and the Angrand brothers, while active and well educated, were certainly no match for such assimilated persons in the British areas as Casely Hayford or Mensah Sarbah with their wide range of intellectual interests.[69] Who would qualify among the *originaires* as members of an intelligentsia (defined here as the articulate part of the elite interested in intellectual questions) if the Senegalese *créoles* are left aside? One must look to the most assimilated politicians—Diagne, Guèye—and to those who manned the newsletters and journals—Duguay-Clédor, Mody

68. FOM, AOF, 7-VII-34.

69. The main example of an intellectual looking at African origins during this period was Armand, *Les lébous de la presqu'île du Cap-Vert.*

M'Baye, Télémaque Sow, the Salzmann brothers, and perhaps three dozen others, counting the young university men, individuals who entered public life in the 1930s.

One has the impression that these members of the upper stratum did consider themselves members of an African intelligentsia. The level of discussion tended to degenerate into polemics as an election approached, but Duguay-Clédor, Télémaque Sow, F. Baye Salzmann, Pierre Salzmann, Sarr Papa Guèye, and others filled the columns of their publications with observations on the world which reflected a certain sophistication and urbanity. Because the publications were usually badly printed and because the French used was colloquial rather than literary, Frenchmen tended to ignore these publications. But if the combined holdings of Institut Fondamental d'Afrique Noire in Dakar and the Bibliothèque Nationale in Paris of journals published in the four communes, 1900–1945, are ever microfilmed and made generally available, a picture of a political intelligentsia with a wide range of other interests would emerge. The lack of any single commanding intellectual figure such as Edward Blyden would, however, be noticeable.[70]

If one were to do a content analysis of the writings which this intelligentsia has left, one would find few topics discussed in depth which did not relate to politics. In fact one would probably be justified in calling this a political intelligentsia. Only the young men of the 1930s, the university expatriates to France, hint of the cultural renaissance of the Senegalese elite after the Second World War. Preoccupation with political privileges (which they gained earlier than most other African elites) directed their attention to the political realm with such energy that educational and cultural matters had to wait for another generation.

70. Adrien Edgar Allègre, a Joal créole, made a bid for intellectual note in his Aperçu sur la situation politique au Sénégal (Nice, 1923), but Allègre never gained attention in Senegal. He was really analogous to the Parisian emigrés; hence, the intelligentsia of Senegal was really two distinct groups: those in France, who were catholic in their interests and without influence on the elite in Senegal; and those in Senegal, who were narrow in their interests and did have influence on the elite.

The uncritical acceptance of the basic premise of assimilation —European superiority—gave way towards the end of the period. The new posture of the *originaires* was put forward in 1942 by young Mamadou Dia, who had come under the influence of Senghor, then still largely unknown to the urban milieu. Dia wrote an article in *Dakar Jeunes* in which he posed the question, "Should we be for or against an African culture?" He elaborated:

What orientation should be given to African youth? Should we stay with the assimilation method of the colonial administration or would it be better to build our kind of *cité universitaire* on the ruins and with the relics of the empires of Sundiata and Askia Mohammed?

If we turn ourselves away from natural sources of inspiration, fascinated by the brilliance of another culture, we will stifle the genius of our race, we will kill the African man who also wants to take his place under the sun.[71]

Such a formulation would have seemed strange to Diagne, and it proved strange for Lamine Guèye, who was eventually eclipsed by Senghor in the post-Second World War era.

It pointed the way, however, for another young man, Cheikh Anta Diop, who would emerge in the 1950s as a new kind of historian for the elite, a man who would fashion historical consciousness from the African tradition rather than the French tradition. Diop, like Duguay-Clédor, was also trained in French schools, but the distance between them would seem much more than one generation. This is not to say that the elite of Duguay-Clédor's day fully believed his assimilated view of their past, for most *originaires* undoubtedly gained more meaning and identification from stories of Al-Hajj Umar and Lat-Dior than from Africans serving with Faidherbe and Brière de l'Ile. Traditional history was certainly not accessible in the French schools, but, in the setting of the African family, with special occasions for *griots* to sing the praises of African heroes of yesteryear, there was ample opportunity for the young *originaire* to learn of his African past. Only the hyper-assimilated or the early university

71. *Dakar Jeunes,* 12 March 1942.

graduates took seriously the notion that African history was an unimportant part of their past.

This commentary may imply there was a dichotomy between African- and French-oriented history in urban Senegal. The opposite was true. The history of the *originaires* was a blending of African reaction to French activities over several centuries. The historical and social consciousness of the larger elite, whether *créole, originaire,* or urbanized *sujet,* was fashioned by the Franco-Senegalese interaction in the communes. The best proof of this is the fact that by 1900 urban Africans called themselves "Senegalese," verified by newspaper accounts, archival reports, and interviews.[72] The elite had a special conception of their history, their evolution in the communes, which was popularly articulated in the *originaire* press, but which was never examined by a local historian. French historians were interested in the larger conquest and the first Africans trained in western historical methods became interested first in French colonial history and secondly in African traditional history. Consequently history of the urban Senegalese has been written exclusively by non-Senegalese, although this urban historical tradition still exists among the older *originaires* and *créoles.*[73] This historical tradition stayed alive longest in Saint-Louis, where in 1959, on the eve of independence, many urban citizens voted to have Senegal incorporated into France as several full-fledged *dèpartements* rather than become an independent nation. Thus the highest point for political assimilation was reached just as the French flag was lowered after three centuries in Senegal.

72. The usage of the term Senegalese spread to France in the eighteenth century and until after the First World War was often interchangeable with the notion of any black African. Again, the pages of *La Démocratie* and its rival anti-*originaire* paper, *L'A.O.F.,* give ample proof of this before the First World War.

73. Alioune Diop, editor of *Présence Africaine,* told me he has long wished that an African would become interested in writing on the historical traditions of urban Senegal. The best work to date has been done by the Nigerian scholar, H. O. Idowu, in several articles and a dissertation for Ibadan. Idowu has emphasized *créole* participation in politics. See his "Assimilation in Nineteenth Century Senegal," *Bulletin de l'IFAN,* series B (1968), pp. 1422–47.

Reactions to Issues Raised During the French Presence

Certain widely discussed issues and events (treated very briefly here) may help to pinpoint elite reactions toward the West: the First World War, Pan-Africanism and Garveyism, Senegalese expatriates, the Lébou political question, non-*originaires*, the Popular Front, and the Second World War.

The First World War had a momentous impact on Senegal, for the French had determined as early as 1910 to use African troops to expand their armies; the elite, however, were not among the thousands of Senegalese and other West Africans who marched off in 1914 and 1915. They refused service in the colonial troops, demanding to serve in the regular French army; Diagne's 1915 law made this possible, and after a period of hesitation, thousands of *originaires* were called to the colors in the French army, where they ate French food instead of African food, were paid French wages instead of colonial troop wages, and were eligible to become noncommissioned and commissioned officers.

The impact of serving in France in the regular army can be seen in several ways. First, the *originaires* had a feeling of direct access to the French Parliament through Diagne. When they complained of the cold winter in the northern sector, Diagne's colleagues voted to have the Senegalese spend the winter in Cannes and fight only during the temperate season. Second, many had their feelings of identification reinforced by the warm welcome given them by the French people, in contrast to the aloof stance of the colonial administrators. In later years the horror of the war and of the casualties suffered was softened in the memories of many *anciens combattants* by the personal contact they had made with the metropolitan French; in fact, it was from this period that the myth of a French society free of race prejudice gained greatest currency. *Originaires* in later years recalled being invited to dine in French homes, marching in parades and receiving great ovations, and wintering in the sun on the Riviera. Third, when the war was over the *originaires* formed the strongest segment of Diagne's political machine; even before men returned to Senegal they visited his Paris office and lobbied for patronage.

The war heightened the sense of identification of the elite with France. Even in the darkest days of the conflict, the *originaires* maintained a strong belief in French invincibility. One Lébou notable, seeing French troops parade, observed: "France is too strong—nothing, absolutely nothing, could convince me there is a nation strong enough to resist her."[74] An old chief of N'Dande was quoted in the same context: "Having fought with Lat-Dior against the French, I know by experience that God has given them strength. I don't know these Germans, but it is impossible for them to beat the French."[75] These observations were published in early 1918 by Télémaque Sow, young Senegalese journalist, and were not part of French propaganda. Sow investigated how people in the communes were faring during the war and came up with these conclusions: "All of the sacrifices demanded by the Motherland have been freely consented to without recrimination. . . . The blacks know perfectly well that their sacrifices will not be in vain and that the combined efforts of France and her powerful allies will win in the end."[76] After the war, however, the troops returning to the communes found a mixed welcome from the French in Senegal. The anti-*originaire* press of Dakar acidly commented on the experience of the black troops in France: "To have fought for the whites, at the side of the whites, against the whites; to have lived the life of the camps, to have frequented white women—they have contracted bad habits and now believe they have every conceivable right. Moreover, they even call the other Africans dirty niggers."[77] There appears to be little evidence that contact with France during the war heightened ambitions for cultural assimilation; political ambitions, on the other hand, were obviously increased, and it is significant that 1919–1921 was the period when the French administration was most alarmed about talk of separatism among the *originaires*.

74. *La Presse Coloniale* (Paris), 10 April 1918.
75. *La Presse Coloniale*, 10 April 1918.
76. *La Presse Coloniale*, 10 April 1918.
77. *La Dépèche Coloniale* (Dakar), 30 August 1918.

The end of the war saw the appearance of two related movements which had little impact on the *originaires:* Pan-Africanism and Garveyism. It is instructive to examine briefly why these two Negro-inspired western ideologies were not well received by an African elite, especially since Blaise Diagne presided over the first two Pan-African congresses held on the Continent. Diagne was responsible for the 1919 conference at the Grand Hôtel in Paris after W. E. B. Du Bois' plans for a meeting were blocked by American diplomats. The final declaration of the meeting was a strong call for greater participation for Africans in colonial areas. (In the context of today's world, it reads as a rather pious declaration, but given the hostile climate in Paris, it was a brave stand.) The Paris press covered the event largely because Diagne was involved; the *originaire* press of Senegal covered it, and applauded the demands for greater participation. The anti-*originaire* press in Senegal noted the conference and reminded the elite that France had given them a favored position, for which they should be grateful. Diagne was interested in the idea of the moral union of Negro peoples, but from the first was suspicious of Marcus Garvey's influence, and agreed to arrange the conference only after being convinced Du Bois was independent of Garvey. But the 1921 congress was different, because Diagne was under the impression that Du Bois had Bolshevist leanings; he determined to leave the Pan-African movement after the American delegation attempted to issue stronger statements than he was prepared to accept.[78]

Diagne's attitudes about Garvey and his movement and Du Bois' Pan-African congresses were transmitted to his affiliated newspapers in Senegal and became the official view of the elite; hence his disenchantment was picked up by his constituents. Although Diagne had started in the Chamber as a Socialist in 1914, he moved toward the center during the war and after the Russian Revolution developed a fear of Bolshevism and preferred not to associate with Socialists. One reason for his attitude was the French lack of understanding of the Garvey movement —for several years the French believed Garvey was an agent of

78. *L'A.O.F.*, 24 July 1919.

Moscow at work in the United States to help plan a Negro revolution and to foment black American imperialism in the African colonies, which would possibly turn into a war of liberation.[79]

Moreover, after 1920, a comparatively free and open press was no longer the rule in Senegal. Censorship was not established by the administration, but journalists were prevented from receiving materials from outside the French orbit and mail was often opened and screened. This meant that Pan-African broadsides and Garvey newspapers rarely penetrated Senegal, in contrast to Gold Coast and Nigeria.

Through a mistranslation, the French thought a Garvey subsidiary organization was the African Communists League instead of the African Communities League. A witch hunt for Garvey agents, believed to be Bolshevists, was carried on for the next two years in French West Africa—Niger was searched, Ivory Coast and Dahomey borders were checked for possible agents from Gold Coast or Nigeria; finally, in 1922 a Garvey cell organization was uncovered a few miles from the palace of the Governor-General in Dakar. A group of clandestine Garveyists, mostly Gambians, was taken in hand and the movement stopped.[80] Despite the final clarification that Garveyists were non-Bolshevists, the association with the Soviets lingered in the mind of many Senegalese and helped to color their impressions of the Pan-Africanists. Diagne's claim that France had done more for men of color (at least in the West Indies and four communes) was rarely doubted by the *originaires*.

A number of Senegalese who lived outside of Senegal during the interwar years had varying reactions to western culture, different from those who stayed home. *Originaires* who settled in other French colonies, mostly to work in the administration, kept their attitudes and identity intact, as this observation from Mademba Guèye, President of the Senegalese Union of the Ivory

79. The French mistranslated the organization's name in its first appearance in the French records; the conservative colonial administration was in the midst of a Bolshevist scare anyway and simply reasoned that Garvey must be a Bolshevist.

80. The Dakar archives contains unclassified materials captured from the Garveyists.

Coast, in support of a new newspaper, *L'Indépendant Colonial,*
makes clear: "It is in the interest of all, whites and blacks, come
from afar to bring the light of civilization to this country. [We
have been] faithful and constant auxiliaries of Greater France in
grand and noble causes of which she has been the champion
since her penetration into West Africa."[81]

Originaire expatriate communities in Africa were reinforced by
the experience of living among Africans who were not citizens.
The role of the *originaire* as partner in civilizing Africa was
firmly believed in; this great identification with the French was
well understood by other African peoples who resented these
men of special privilege.

It was in France during the interwar years that a small number of Senegalese had a vastly different experience from those
who stayed in Senegal or Ivory Coast. Expatriate communities
of Senegalese workers, including many *originaires,* flourished in
the port cities of Marseilles, Le Havre, Dunkerque, and Bordeaux during the 1920s, where they came in contact with French
labor unions and attempts by more radical Africans such as Ma-
gatte N'Diaye to organize minority group unions.[82] A small
number of expatriates were also active in Paris, some workers
(usually veterans of the war) and a few students. The activities
of these two groups can be conveniently studied in brief sketches
of two cousins—Lamine Senghor and Léopold Senghor.

Both Senghors were born in Joal in southern Senegal but their
similarity ends there. Lamine was older; he fought in the First
World War, remained in France as student and postman, joined
the Communist party, found himself unwelcome in Senegal because of his new politicization, and returned to France to participate with the Dahomeyan radical Kojo Tovalou Quénum in his
recently organized Ligue Universelle pour la Défense de la Race
Noire. Tovalou ran into trouble with the French police and left
for Senegal, where he was later an important aid to Diouf and
the Diagne opposition forces.[83] In 1926 Lamine Senghor helped
take over the remnants of Tovalou's Ligue and organized the

81. *L'Indépendant Colonial* (Paris), 15 August 1931.
82. ARS, 21-G-127-108.
83. *La France Coloniale,* 22 March 1928; ARS, 20-G-83-23.

Comité de Défense de la Race Nègre, which attracted many Negroes living in Paris. A statement of purpose, reprinted in *L'Humanité*, indicated a much wider perspective than that of any *originaire* we have discussed so far:

We want the Negro to be treated with much more humanity all around the world. . . . We want to offer to each Negro, members of our Committee, intellectual, moral, and material advantages. We want to make available for each of our members a museum consecrated to Negro art, a library with books, colonial studies, novels, periodical publications, political journals, literary reviews and diverse collections.

The Negro race has something to bring to the world. It can not remain eternally struck by ostracism. The Negro race when cultivated will reveal to the world universal geniuses.[84]

The Comité had close connections with the French Communist party, was anti-Blaise Diagne, pro-Garvey, and was concerned about developing the "Negro personality."[85] Lamine Senghor was convinced that Diagne and West Indian black deputies in the Chamber of Deputies were the greatest obstacle to their eventual success. In 1927 Senghor represented the Comité at the League Against Imperialism conference in Brussels, where he called for Negroes to awaken, and condemned French colonialism. Stricken with tuberculosis, he died in France in 1927, feared by Diagne and watched by the French police.

The other Senghor was Léopold, who went to France soon after Lamine's death. Léopold Senghor became a protegé of Blaise Diagne, dined at his table, and had his first lessons in politics "at the school of Diagne."[86] Léopold did not join the militant Comité or subsequent organizations led by Garan Kouyaté, the successor to Lamine Senghor. But the anti-colonial stance, the connection with Garveyism, the discussion of the cultural

84. Quoted in *L'Humanité,* 25 July 1926.
85. J. Ayo Langley, "Pan-Africanism in Paris, 1924–36," *Journal of Modern African Studies* 7 (1969):69–94. The forthcoming revision of James Spiegler's Oxford D.Phil. dissertation on African expatriates in France will shed much light on these obscure but important persons.
86. Personal communication from Léopold Senghor.

potentials of the Negro were part of the intellectual climate in which African and West Indian students lived in Paris in the early 1930s. The West Indians Aimé Césaire and Jean Price-Mars greatly influenced Senghor; the development of his theories and expression of *négritude* (in its early phase at least) can be understood only in relation to the work of Price-Mars and Césaire. Senghor's activities in Paris have been described by Lilyan Kesteloot and need not be repeated here; he gained his *agrégé*, the first African to do so, and stayed in France as a *lycée* professor rather than returning to Senegal. Intellectually, however, Senghor made a *retour aux sources* in his writings and this new concern for the essence of African civilization and the African personality changed his perspective. He was still better known in France than in Senegal when he became the grammarian of the French Constituent Assembly in 1945–1946, after his election as deputy which launched him upon his successful career of politics in Senegal.[87]

Other Senegalese who were students in France could also be mentioned: Birago Diop, later to become known for his telling of traditional tales, and Ousmane Socé Diop, author of *Karim*, one of the first published Senegalese novels, which anticipated the classic Senegalese novel of cultural conflict, Cheikh Hamidou Kane's *Ambiguous Adventure*. Both Diops were *originaires* who managed to study in France by accepting scholarships to veterinary school—one of the few subjects open to Africans in the 1930s. In summary, then, the Senghors and the Diops were part of the expatriate community which enriched the perspective of some *originaires* and gave them a viewpoint unobtainable in the restricted and isolated world of the four communes during the interwar years. But contact with European post-war ideology through the influence of these expatriates remained minimal until late in the period, after the Second World War, when French colonialism was liberalized.

The Lébou were the original inhabitants of the Cape Verde peninsula in Senegal. They broke away from the Damel of Ca-

87. Ironically it was Lamine Guèye who introduced him to the public as his new protegé; within several years, Senghor's politics put Guèye into semi-retirement.

yor in the late eighteenth century and formed an independent state which was conquered by the French after the establishment of Dakar in 1857. By 1900 two of the communes (Dakar and Rufisque) had predominantly Lébou populations and these formed the largest block of nonliterate, nonwestern-educated Africans among the *originaires*. The Lébou resisted attending French schools first because they were Catholic, later because they were European. The Lébou found themselves inundated by Frenchmen, Cape Verdeans, Lebanese, and other Africans (mainly Wolof and Tukolor) migrating to the cities and bitterly resented the loss of their land. The French paid for land they used, but every generation of Lébou after 1857 argued that the French had not really settled matters with the new generation, which again demanded reparations. One area of Dakar was called the *tound,* and the reluctance of France to settle succeeding Lébou claims caused the *tound* land question to become the most persistent local political issue in Dakar.[88]

Amadou Assane N'Doye is a good example of how the Lébou eventually (and reluctantly) reacted favorably to western influences in Dakar and Rufisque. N'Doye's father was a powerful Lébou *marabout* and an important early backer of Blaise Diagne. Young Amadou was one of the first Lébou to attend school in Saint-Louis; after the war he decided to enter politics with Blaise Diagne, since most of Diagne's lieutenants in Dakar and Rufisque were Wolof. But N'Doye, like Lamine Guèye, was something of a maverick and soon defected to the formal opposition Galandou Diouf launched against Diagne in 1928. N'Doye was determined to raise the tone of local politics; he began corresponding with the S.F.I.O. (French Socialist party) in 1930 (not because of socialist ideology, but because the socialists were the only party with much interest in colonials at the time). N'Doye became the primary political leader of the Lébou community after 1930, inherited claims to important Dakar real estate, and, as an affluent African, put his energy into advancing Lébou claims and getting more young Lébou into schools and participating in politics. He helped to form a Lébou youth orga-

88. See memorandum on *Terrains de Tound,* ARS, 2-G-25-11.

nization, to modernize the traditional Lébou political organization, which had stayed intact in a clandestine manner during the
French occupation, and to arrange leaseholds of Lébou lands
for Lebanese merchants now concentrating their economic activities in Dakar. Anxious for Lebanese money, some Lébou sold
their lands outright, but regretted it after their cash was spent,
thus adding fuel to the fire of the *tound* question.[89]

N'Doye continued to dress in African clothes, maintained several wives and luxurious households, and was the political mentor of new Lébou politicians during the 1930s, much as Thiécouta Diop had been the mentor of the Young Senegalese two
decades earlier. But his activity was an exception to the Lébou
position of noncooperation with the French, a position that still
had many adherents long after 1945. Even N'Doye could not
cope with the electors of Bargny, a small village south of Rufisque which the French administration claimed was under the
administrative jurisdiction of the town of Thiès. But the Lébou
of Bargny considered themselves allied with the Lébou of Rufisque and claimed to be their equals; hence, if the Rufisque Lébou were *originaires,* then they must also be members of the
elite. This was contested until Blaise Diagne perceived more vot-
ers among the people of Bargny, and interceded on their behalf.
But the inhabitants of the fishing village appeared to change little after the 1929 settlement in their favor: as freshly created
originaires, they delighted in being more recalcitrant to French
acculturation than other Lébou communities. For French administrative officials, Bargny was synonymous with rotten-bor-
ough politics and was referred to when making the point that
originaires were really not assimilated. For the French it was a
caricature of elite aspiration to political but not cultural assimilation during the interwar period.[90]

To provide some contrast, it is useful to look briefly at two
non-*originaires* from Senegal's traditional sector who had different reactions to western culture and the urban elite: Bouna
N'Diaye and Amadou Bamba M'Backé. N'Diaye, a traditional

89. Personal communication from A. A. N'Doye.
90. Politicians feared to speak in Bargny because of the excitable populace.

chief who had been educated by the French, was a claimant to Senegal's most prestigious traditional political position, the Bourba of Djolof. Several centuries earlier, when the Wolof had ruled most of what is present-day Senegal, the Bourba had been supreme lord in the land. Bouna N'Diaye decided to collaborate with the French as the best hope of eventually receiving recognition as Bourba (which for practical purposes had vanished as an effective political office with the French conquest). He served in the French colonial forces, where he gained a healthy disrespect for the *originaires* who served in the regular French army. N'Diaye was contemptuous of the elite, sharply criticized the assimilation policy, and was one of Diagne's most vociferous critics when he recruited 80,000 men in West Africa in 1918. N'Diaye's life was one of increasing accommodation and frustration and he was finally persuaded to serve in the new Colonial Council after 1920 as one of the colonial administration's chiefs.[91]

Amadou Bamba refused to come to terms with the French, early in his career as a *marabout*. He was suspect because he had been an intimate of the resistance leader, Lat-Dior, and because his new Islamic order, the Mouride, appeared to be anti-French. Bamba attracted tens of thousands of pilgrims to his home in Diourbel; the French accused him of erecting a theocratic state within the new colony of Senegal and exiled him first to Gabon and later to Mauritania. Amadou Bamba was allowed to return on condition that he accept house arrest, and his influence was heightened rather than diminished by his living martyrdom. His followers obediently created new villages in the interior of Senegal, where they became accomplished peanut cultivators known for their labor and discipline. Bamba was forced to seek an accommodation with the French and publicly gave his approval to young Mouride who served in the French colonial troops. Bamba had few followers in the communes during his lifetime (he died in 1927), but he maintained an interest in the political life of the elite, recognizing the fact that the *originaires* did have real political power in local matters. He was an important financial contributor to Blaise Diagne's campaign in 1914.

91. See letter of 20 August 1921 from Bouna N'Diaye to Governor-General Merlin, ARS, 3-G3-3-108.

His understanding of the importance of elite politics and his con-
cession to the French on the war were rewarded with the promise by the French administration and Diagne to build a mosque
in his honor at Touba. After realizing that Bamba's Mouride villages were among the most efficient producers of peanuts, the
French became more tolerant of his innovations, which were re-
inforcing traditional values but creating new institutions in rural
Senegal. Bamba's career was dedicated to harmonizing Islam
with the needs of the Senegalese peasant and he stands much
less affected in history by the encroachments of westernization
than his contemporary, Bouna N'Diaye.[92]

The advent of the Popular Front in Senegal in 1936 brought
new Frenchmen to the colonies—men of socialist and communist persuasions, formerly banned by an ultra-conservative administration, but now placed in administrative, teaching, and
leadership positions. At first the climate was one of invigoration,
since Léon Blum had promised colonial reforms and his minister of colonies, Marius Moutet, a veteran Socialist, had shown
interest in colonial peoples for two decades. But this infusion of
new political perspectives also brought to Senegal highly politi-
cized Frenchmen who were not impressed by the insular character of local politics, which they saw as provincial rather than Af-
rican-oriented. The Socialists especially influenced the local
newspapers and their message was clear: the Senegalese elite
would henceforth be schooled politically.[93]

To add to the confusion, a Frenchman profited from the disruption of local politics and replaced an *originaire* as Mayor of
Dakar. He was Alfred Goux, Dakar businessman and amateur
ethnologist. Goux rapidly became chief advisor to deputy Galandou Diouf, editor of Diouf's party newspaper for Senegal, dis-
penser of patronage for the Diouf party, and anathema to the
younger elite. The defeat of Lamine Guèye in 1934 and again in
1936 discouraged the younger elite members, who correctly saw

92. There are a number of special dossiers on Bamba in the Dakar
archives.
93. The S.F.I.O. was accused of letting only a few Africans in its Dakar
chapter even after the Popular Front came to power; most Senegalese
elite members who were interested in socialism joined the P.S.S. (Senegalese Socialist party) of Lamine Guèye.

that Diouf would eventually follow in Diagne's footsteps and establish a policy of collaboration with the French regime. Diouf struggled to give an appearance of independence. He boasted that if he raised his little finger, 200,000 Africans would be ready to join the French army to help France. His politics were ambiguous, however. He supported the Popular Front for a time in France while his lieutenant, Goux, was editorializing against it in Diouf's paper in Dakar, *Le Sénégal*.[94]

The youthful elite still placed hope in the success of the Popular Front in France, despite checks in the four communes, and the announcement that the defeated Lamine Guèye was invited to a special blue ribbon commission (appointed by Moutet as Minister of Colonies) raised the hope of reform, especially in scholarships and access to higher education. But before the commission could accomplish its goals, the Popular Front had fallen from power, and by 1938 the spectre of war hung over Europe. Colonial questions were shelved.

The impact of the Second World War on the *originaires* was not so great as that of the 1914–1918 war. Vichy France's Governor-General, Pierre Boisson, suspended all local political institutions in the four communes and for the first time since the 1790s, the local populace was cut off from political participation. Some Senegalese, such as Léopold Senghor, were in France, fought for the Paris government and were taken prisoner of war; others resisted the Vichy regime in Senegal by clandestine methods.

An important wartime resistance leader was Abdel Kader Diagne, who had been a Dakar municipal councilman during the 1930s. Kader Diagne was a fervent Muslim who often took an anti-administration line and worked for the use of Arabic in schools and in publications in Senegal. He was more imaginative and fervent than well schooled, and his Pan-Islamic point of view was attractive to some *originaires* who felt Arabic should not be allowed to disappear from Senegal in the face of growing

94. See *Le Sénégal's* editorial columns for 1936–1937. Diouf did not have the same influence on his printed outlet in the colony that Diagne did; when d'Oxoby refused to follow Diagne, the deputy sacked him and put in Duguay-Clédor; Diouf on the other hand became dependent on Goux.

French usage.[95] With the advent of Vichy, Kader Diagne became enraged with Boisson's politics and shifted ground; he became the leader of an underground network to smuggle suspected individuals to the Gambia and to bring in supplies and
money for the resistance to Vichy. It is difficult to estimate how
effective the harassment of Vichy officials by Kader Diagne and
his colleagues was, but the Senegalese recognized the valor of his
endeavors and after the war he was decorated as though he had
fought on the field of battle. Kader Diagne's loyalty to the Free
French was shared by many *originaires,* who were well aware of
Vichy's alliance with racist Nazi Germany; but the majority of
originaires could do little against the regime, except to hope for
the arrival of de Gaulle.

Kader Diagne is an interesting case of a man who had utopian
leanings—converting all Senegal to Islam and making Arabic
the official language—who was antipathetic to the regime until
the war changed him into an ardent defender of the old France
the *originaires* knew. Many *originaires* took a more realistic appraisal of France's defeat in 1940 and realized that after the war
the colonial situation would change since France was no longer
the invincible nation the elite had helped defend in 1916–1918.[96]

Conclusion

In conclusion then, the *originaires* had a remarkably unified reaction to French (western) culture. This study has attempted to
explain why an elite, famous in France and generally well known
in the literature as the epitome of assimilated Africans, was not
in fact totally assimilated and did not desire to be. The *originaires'* reactions were conditioned by a number of factors which
limited their desire for full assimilation:

First was Wolofization; the facts that Wolof was the language
of the four communes, and that Senegal had a long history of
Wolof domination, both politically and culturally, meant that
there never existed an unstable urban situation with no clear

95. Personal communication from A. Kader Diane, Dakar.
96. Newspapers were suppressed as well as political offices; little evidence remains for this period except in the minds of the *originaires.*

dominant ethnic language or culture. Stability here meant effective resistance to total acculturation.

Second, the factor of Islam cannot be overestimated. Islam, whether Lébou particularism, Mouridism, the Tidjaniyya of Al Hajj Malick Sy or the Falls, stiffened the African consciousness of the commune citizens. New arrivals in the cities who were not Muslim were actively proselytized.

Third, the lack of Christian missions. This meant that the Muslims did not come under constant religious attack for the inferiority of their culture, while the combination of Wolof language and culture and Islam gave the elite a sub-culture which resisted the few Catholic and Protestant missionaries who did operate in Senegal during this period. The lack of missionaries was also crucial in reducing the number of more educated elite members, and it is significant that many elite figures, even though not Catholic, were educated in Catholic schools but were little influenced religiously (such as Galandou Diouf).

Fourth, the lack of educational opportunities provided by the French, which led to a low level of education in the elite, compared to the *créole* community in Senegal, or the elite communities in Sierra Leone or the Gold Coast. The French government consciously pursued a policy of restricted access to higher education, schools were limited, and few fellowships available. The fact that only French was used in the schools meant that a large number of *originaires* could in fact speak fair French but the number who could read and write it at an adult level was more restricted. Also, the lack of desire for educational opportunities by the majority of the elite during this period should be mentioned. A small number did demand more schools in 1919, again in 1928 when the opposition to Diagne became formalized, and sporadically during the 1930s, but the satisfaction with the status quo on the part of the majority until 1945 meant few opportunities and little real pressure on the French for educational change.

Fifth, preoccupation with intrigues of local politics, client-patron factional relationships, identification with individuals rather than concentration on issues, and the dispensing of patronage positions helped reduce the aspirations of the *originaires* for fundamental colonial reform. Only a few radicals in the communes of the early 1930s seriously suggested doing something about the inadequacies of the French colonial system; the majority seemed content with their limited political privileges and were caught up in a well-established system of local politics which they had known for almost a century and which the elections of 1914 and 1919 and the prerogatives granted by the 1915 and 1916 laws confirmed to them.

Sixth, the historical perspective of serving as loyal auxiliaries to the French (translated by the 1920s and 1930s as "loyal partners with the French") militated against the idea of full assimilation. The leadership of the *originaires* (Diouf, Guèye, and others) was imbued with this perspective and communicated it to the body of the elite, even though the majority, especially the Lébou, had not in fact served as loyal auxiliaries.

This middle period of activity of the Senegalese urban elite, as opposed to the nineteenth-century, *créole* period and post-1945 period of Senghor, did not produce a group of highly acculturated intellectuals interested in larger cultural questions. It was dominated by political men who were highly assimilated—Carpot, Diagne, and Guèye—and who created an image in France of the assimilated Senegalese elite. The evidence reviewed here, however, suggests that in reality the moderate assimilation of a Galandou Diouf was far more representative of the elite. Significantly, the post-1945 generation of university-trained elite members relegated Diouf to oblivion while paying homage to Diagne and Guèye, models in whom they could take pride. The opportunity to participate in limited politics gave the urban elite a practical diversion which set the tone of discussion for the period.

Finally, it should be noted that the gap between political participation and educational opportunities created a unique situation in the general evolution of Senegal's acculturated sector. The chart below demonstrates this variance between political and cultural assimilation in Senegal between 1900 and 1945 and indicates the special character of the period of *originaire* ascendancy.

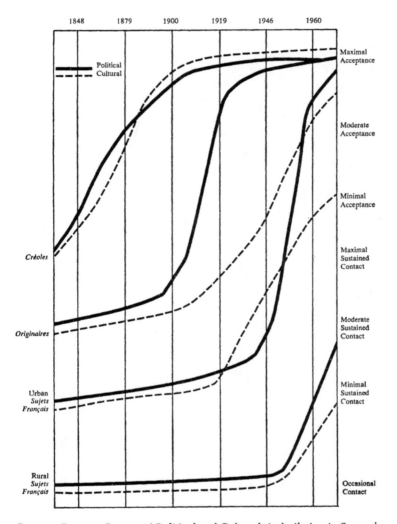

Contrast Between Degree of Political and Cultural Assimilation in Senegal,
1848–1960. 1848: vote given to urban elite; 1879: establishment of the
Conseil Général; 1900: awakening of the *originaires;* 1919: Diagne's party
is victorious; 1946: Lamine Guèye laws—extension of suffrage to *sujets*
and end of *originaire* privileges; 1960: independence.

SOUKEÎNA AND ISABELLE—
SENGHOR AND THE WEST

Harold Scheub

This contribution differs from its predecessors in focusing on a single individual. In this sense, it completes a sequence that began with popular beliefs and mass reactions, passed through a phase of discussing smaller groups of named individuals, and now finishes with one person. This article completes other sequences as well. The disciplinary character of the discussion began with anthropologists, moved on to historians, and now ends with a literary critic. This variety should illustrate the value of coming at a common problem from several points of view. Finally, this chapter completes the sequence through time and brings the discussion down to the present and recent past.

There is no intention of holding up Léopold Sédar Senghor as typical. No one who was simultaneously a great poet in the French language and President of Senegal could belong anywhere but in a class by himself. As the leader who brought his country to independence, however, he has had to struggle with the problem of the proper role of western culture in modern Africa. This experience may merely have highlighted a problem that was no less serious to other Africans of his generation, but he expressed his views with unusual sensitivity.

Professor Scheub is a member of the Department of African Languages and Literature at the University of Wisconsin, author of *African Images* (New York, 1971), and of the forthcoming *The Xhosa Ntsomi*.

P.D.C.

Snow Upon Paris

LORD, you have visited Paris on this day of your birth
Because it was becoming mean and wicked
You have purified it by incorruptible cold
By white death.
This morning, even the factory chimneys that sing in unison
Flying white flags
—'Peace to Men of goodwill'.

Lord, the snow of your Peace is your proposal to a divided world to a
        divided Europe
To Spain torn apart
And the Rebel, both Jew and Catholic, has fired his 1,400 guns
        against the mountains of your Peace.
Lord, I have accepted your white cold more burning than salt.
See my heart melts like snow beneath the sun.
And I forget
White hands that fired the shots which brought the empires crumbling
Hands that flogged the slaves, that flogged You
Chalk-white hands that buffeted You, powdered painted hands that
        buffeted me
Confident hands that delivered me to solitude to hatred
White hands that felled the forest of palm trees once commanding
        Africa, in the heart of Africa
Straight and stout, the Saras handsome as the first men who issued
        from Your brown hands.
They cut down the dark forest for railway sleepers
They cut down the forests of Africa to save Civilization, for there
        was a shortage of human raw-material.

Lord, I know I will not bring out my store of hatred against the
        diplomats who flash their long teeth
And tomorrow will barter black flesh.
My heart, Lord, is melted like the snow on the roofs of Paris
Under the sun of Your gentleness.

It is gentle to my enemies, to my brothers with white hands without
    snow
And because of the hands like dew, at evening, over my burning
    cheeks.

For Koras and Balafong

A lament for three koras and a balafong
To René Maran

I

By the bend in the road the river, blue among the fields fresh with
    September.
A Paradise where guard is kept against fevers by a child with eyes
    bright as two swords
Paradise my African childhood, that kept guard over the innocence
    of Europe.
What were the months? What was the year? I remember its fleeting
    softness at twilight
That men died far off as they still do, and the shadow of the *dakhars*
    was as fresh as a lime.
Facing altars by the side of the hard salt plain, by the side of the
    broad glittering road of the Spirits
Midway enclosure on the way to the tombs.
And you, Fountain of Kam-Dyamé, when at noon among my naked
    sleek companions decked in bush flowers
I drank your mystical waters out of my cupped hands.
The herdsman's flute piped to the slow movements of the cattle
And when in its shadow it fell silent, the drums sounded from the
    insistent *tanns*
Beating a rhythm for the line of dancers at the feast of the Dead.
The *tirailleurs* threw down their caps in the circle with aphonic shouts
    and my sisters danced like leaping flames
Tening-Ndyaré and Tyagum-Ndyaré, brighter now than copper from
    across the sea.

II

Later there were fountains, in the narrow shade of the Latin Muses
    proclaimed as my guardian angels

Stone wells, *Ngas-o-bil!* you did not quench my thirsts.
But after the grilled and salted pistachios, after the intoxication of
    Vespers and noon
I turned to you for refuge, Fountain-of-Elephants, where the stam-
    mering water is good
To you, Forefathers, with solemn eyes seeing to the bottom of all
    things.
And I was guided through thorns and signs by Verdun, yes Verdun
    the dog that kept guard over the innocence of Europe.
Of your laughter and games and songs, of your stories that fall in my
    memory like flowers
Nothing remains but the black priest dancing
Leaping like David before the Ark of God, like the shrewd-headed
    Ancestor
To the rhythm of our hands: 'Ndyaga-bass! Ndyaga-riti!'

III

Drum, drum, hear the drum
Hear my mammy yell!
She said I was a white man
Kissing the prettiest girl.

She said to me 'Lord'!
To have to choose! deliciously torn between these two friendly hands
—A kiss from you Soukeîna! . . . these two antagonistic worlds
When the pain . . . ah! I cannot tell now which is my sister and which
    is my foster-sister
Of the two who cradled my nights with their dreamt-of-tenderness,
    with their mingled hands
When the pain—a kiss from you Isabella!—between those two hands
That I want to make one again in my own warm hand.
But if I must choose at the hour of testing
I have chosen the verset of streams and of winds and of forests
The assonance of plains and rivers, chosen the rhythm of blood in my
    naked body
Chosen the tremulsion of *balafongs*, the harmony of strings and brass
    that seem to clash, chosen the
Swing swing yes chosen the swing
And the far-off muted trumpet, like the plaint of a nebulous star
    adrift across the night
Like the summons to Judgement, the burst of the trumpet over the
    snowy graveyards of Europe.

I have chosen my toiling black people, my peasant people, the peasant
     race through all the world.
'And thy brothers are wrath against thee, they have set thee to till the
     earth.'
To be your trumpet!

IV

You, my lambs, my delight with eyes that shall not look upon my age
I was not always a shepherd of fair heads on the arid plains of your
     books
Not always the good official, deferring to his superiors
The good colleague, polite, elegant—with gloves?—smiling but rarely
     laughing
Old France, old University, all the old routine.
My lambs, my childhood is as old as the world and I am as young as
     the everlasting youth of the world's dawn.
The poetesses of the sanctuary have given me suck
The king's *griots* have sung me the authentic legend of my race to the
     sounds of the high *koras*.

V

What were the months? What was the year?
Kumba Ndofene Dyouf reigned at Dyakhaw, a proud vassal
And governed the administrator of Sine-Salum.
The noise of his forefathers and of the *dyoung-dyoungs* went before
     him.
The royal pilgrim went about his provinces, gave ear in the wood to
     murmured grievance
To the prattle of birds; the sun was magnificent upon their plumage
Gave ear to the conch eloquent among the prophetic tombs.
He called my father *Tokor*. They exchanged riddles carried by grey-
     hounds with golden bells,
Cousins in peace, they exchanged gifts on the banks of the Salum
Precious pelts bars of salt and of gold from Bouré, of gold from
     Boundou
And high council like horses of the River.
The man wept at evening, and in the violet shadow there was lamen-
     tation of the *khalams*.

VI

I was myself the grandfather of my grandfather

I was his soul and his ascendancy, head of the house of Elissa of Gabu
Erect. Opposite, Fouta-Djallong and the Almamy of Fouta.
'We are killed, Almamy, but not dishonoured.'
The mountains could not subdue us, nor his horsemen encircle us
        nor his bright skin lead us astray
Nor his prophets make bastards of us.
My pagan sap is a well-aged unsouring wine, not the palm wine of a
        single day.
Sixteen years of war! sixteen years the beating of the *tabalas* of war
        the *tabalas* of bullets!
Sixteen years the clouds of powder! sixteen years of storm without a
        single clear day
—And sing towards the fountains, young women in procession with
        breasts triumphant as towers in the sun
Sixteen years of twilight—women laying out the red cloths around
        the springs
Sixteen years among the marshes of Elissa where the flowers are rust-
        ing spears
'We are killed, Almamy!' On the high pyre I have thrown
All my dusty riches: treasures of ambergris and cowries
Prisoners pillars of my house, the wives who have mothered my sons
Furniture of the sanctuary, solemn masks, ritual garments
My parasol, my staff of authority which is of three *kintars* of ivory
And my ancient pelt.
Sleep, heroes, in this evening which brings new life to birth, in this
        night heavy with grandeur.
But saved is the Singer, my pagan sap that rises, struts and dances
My two daughters with delicate ankles, princesses ringed with heavy
        bracelets of grief
Like peasants. Peasants escort them to be their lords and their subjects
And among them, the mother of Sira-Badral, foundress of kingdoms
Who is to be the salt of the Serers who are to be the salt of the salt
        peoples.

VII

Ele-yaye! Again I sing a noble subject: *koras* and *balafong* accom-
        pany me!
Princess, this song of gold is for you, louder than the baying of
        pedants!
You are no parasitic plant on the branchy fulness of your people.
They lie; you are no tyrant fed upon their fat.
You are the member storing plenty, the barns full to bursting against

the days of trial
—They nourish ants and idle doves.
See, you have risen to drive the enemy far off, the *tata*
Not the silo, but the chief organizing the force to forge
The arm; the *tata* head receiving blows and bullets.
And your people are honoured in you. Praise be to your people in
you!
Princess, four cubits tall, shadowy face around your mouth which is
light
Like the sun upon the black pebbles of the shore
You are your people.
The dark earth of your skin is fecund, freely watered by the tempest
of their seed.
You are their wife, you have received Serer blood and tribute of the
blood of the Peuls.
O bloods mingled in my veins, only the naked clapping of hands.
May I hear the chorus of red voices from those whose blood is mixed.
May I hear the song of Africa to come.

VIII

Ah! I am upheld by the hope that one day I shall run before you,
Princess, carrying your message to the gathering of the
peoples.
A procession more splendid even than the Emperor Gongo-Musa
marching towards the glittering East.
O desert shadowless desert, austere earth, pure earth, from all my
pettiness
Wash me clean, from all contagions of civilized man.
May your light which is not subtle wash clean my countenance, your
dry violence bathe me in tempests of sand
And nine days upon nine days, like the pure-bred white *mehari,* may
my lips be chaste from all earthly water, and without speech.
I shall go through the north-eastern land, through Egypt with temples
and pyramids
But Pharaoh who set me at his right hand and my great-grandfather
with his red ears, I leave for you.
Your scholars will prove they, too, were hyperboreans, together with
all the buried greatness of my past.
This solemn procession, no longer four thousand slaves each one
carrying five *mithkals* of gold

But seven thousand new negroes, seven thousand soldiers seven thou-
sand peasants humble and proud
Who carry the authentic riches of my race on their musical shoulders.
Not now gold and amber and ivory but instead the authentic produce
of peasants and men who work for twopence an hour
Instead all the devastations of slave-trading Europe
Instead all the tears dropped through three continents, the black
sweat dropped to richen cane-field and cotton-field
Instead all the hymns they have sung, all the chanting torn by the
muted trumpet
All the joys danced oh! all the exultation shouted.
Seven thousand new negroes, seven thousand soldiers seven thousand
peasants humble and proud
Who carry the riches of my race on their amphoral shoulders
Strength Nobility Openness
And the abandon in delight, like a woman, to the great power of the
universe, to the Love that moves the singing worlds.

IX

In the hope of that day—see how the Somme and the Seine and the
Rhine and the savage Slav rivers are red under the Archangel's
sword
And my heart sickens in the wine-like odour of blood, but I have my
orders, my duty is to go on.
Let me find a little comfort at least that my double loves to go wan-
dering every night.
Toko'Waly my uncle, do you remember those distant nights when my
head grew heavy against the patience of your back?
Or holding me by the hand, your hand led me through the shadows
and signs?
The fields are flowers of glow worms; the stars come to rest on the
grass, on the trees.
All around is silence.
Only the droning scents of the bush, hives of red bees drowning the
stridulation of the crickets
And the muffled tom-tom, the far-off breathing of the night.
But you, Toko'Waly, hear what is beyond hearing
You explain to me the signs that the Ancestors give in the calm seas
of the constellations
The Bull the Scorpion the Leopard, the Elephant the familiar Fishes

And the milky ceremony of the Spirits along the unending shores of
     heaven.
And now see the wisdom of the moon-goddess, see the veils of the
     shadows fall.
African night my black night, mystical-lucid black-brilliant
You rest at one with the earth, you are the Earth and the harmonious
     hills.
O classic Beauty that is never angular, but subtle slender soaring line!
O classic face! From the rounded forehead under the odorous forest
     and the wide oblique eyes down to the gracious bay of the
     chin and
The impetuous leap of the twin hills! Curves of gentleness melodious
     face.
O my Lioness my dark Beauty, my black Night my Black One my
     Naked One!
How often have you made my heart beat like the unconquered
     leopard in his narrow cage.
Night delivering me from arguments and sophistries of salons, from
     pirouetting pretexts, from calculated hatred and humane
     butchery
Night dissolving all my contradictions, all contradictions in the first
     unity of your blackness
Take the child who is still a child, that twelve wandering years have
     not made old.
I bring from Europe only this friend, her child's eyes bright among
     the Breton mists.

Elegy of the Circumcised

NIGHT of childhood, blue Night, blond Night O Moon!
How often have I called to you, Night, crying by the roadside
By the side of the sorrows of my manhood? Solitude—and all about
     us are the dunes.
It was night of earliest childhood, thick as peace. Fear bowed our
     backs under the Lion's roaring.
Tall grasses bowed under the shifty silence of that night.
Fire of branches you fire of hope! Pale memory of the Sun, hearten-
     ing my innocence

Hardly at all. I had to die. I laid my hand on my throat like a girl
   who shudders at the horror of Death
I had to die to the beauty of song—all things drift with the current of
   Death.
See the twilight on the throat of the dove when the blue pigeons call
And the seamews of dream fly with plaintive cries.

Let us die, let us dance, elbow to elbow woven together like a garland
No dress to hinder our steps, but the gift of the promise glows, light-
   ning under the clouds.
Woi! the drum ploughs up the holy silence. Dance. Song lashes the
   blood
Rhythm drives out the fear that has us by the throat. Life holds death
   at bay.
Dance to the burthen of fear, that the night of the phallus may rise
   over our ignorance over our innocence.
Ah! die to childhood, let the poem die the syntax fall apart, let all the
   inessential words be swallowed up.
The weight of the rhythm is enough, no need of word-cement to build
   on the rock the City of tomorrow.
Let the sun rise from the sea of shadows
Blood! The waves are the colour of dawn.

But God, so many times I have wept—how many times?—for the
   transparent nights of childhood.
Midday the Male is the hour of Spirits when every form strips off its
   flesh
Like the trees in Europe under the winter sun.
See, the bones are abstract, lending themselves only to calculations
   with straight edge, compass and sextant.
Life runs through the fingers of man like sand, crystals of snow im-
   prison the life of the water
The serpent of water slips through the helpless hands of the reeds.
Dear Nights friendly Nights, Nights of Childhood, among the seaflats
   among the woods
Nights quivering with presences, brushed with eyelids, peopled with
   wings and sounds of breathing
And with breathing silence, say how many times have I sorrowed for
   you in the noontime of my age?

The poem droops in the sun of Noon, it feeds on the dew of evening
And the drum beats out the rhythm of the sap under the smell of
   ripened fruits.

Master of the Initiates, I know I need your wisdom to break the
    cypher of things
To learn my office as father, as lamarch
To measure exactly the field of my duties, to share out the harvest
    forgetting neither worker nor orphan.
The song is not only a charm, by it the woolly heads of my flock are
    fed.
The poem is bird-serpent, marriage of shadow and dawnlight
The Phoenix rises, he sings with wings extended, over the carnage of
    words.

The Phoenix rises, he sings with wings extended.

The dominant metaphor in the poetry of Léopold Sédar Senghor of Senegal is, explicitly or implicitly, that of the phoenix[1] of
Egyptian mythology, that curious and fabulous creature which
lived for five hundred years, then consumed itself in flames and
was thereby reborn, purified and regenerated, to live for another
five hundred years. A mythic death-purification-regeneration
theme and a concomitant quest for self-identity form the central
focuses of Senghor's poetic work and reproduce in contemporary terms the phoenix metaphor: man's alienation from his
past, and the terrifying loss of identity and sense of cosmic harmony; the attempts to regain identity and therefore dignity by
means of a spiritual, poetic voyage to a historical, often mythical
past, a metaphorical journey to the soul; and the hope for rebirth, a renewal of the individual human in league with the community, a quest for a "civilization of the universal,"[2] where "life
is born again color of whatever is."[3] Senghor's poetry combines
these themes—alienation, renewal, universal brotherhood—into
a progression, an odyssey that is reminiscent in some respects of

1. Headnote from "Elegy of the Circumcised" ("Elégie des circoncis"),
Léopold Sédar Senghor, *Selected Poems,* trans. John Reed and Clive Wake
(New York, 1964), p. 92. All quotations in this paper are from this
translation.
2. L. V. Thomas, "Senghor and Négritude," *Présence Africaine* 54
(1965): 113.
3. "Elegy of the Waters" ("Elégie des eaux"), *Selected Poems,* p. 94.

the philosophical journey of the English poet, William Blake, moving from the pure innocence of childhood into the often repellent but unavoidable world of experience, and finally, hopefully, into a new innocence, an innocence born of experience, a "New Jerusalem."

The poetry of Léopold Senghor explores the impact made by the West on Africa, the effect his own European experience has had on him. He examines the resultant contradictions in his character: Senghor the African, the nostalgic traditionalist, remembering the golden past, cherishing the bold and humane African past; Senghor the western-style intellectual, the Parisian cosmopolite, the Roman Catholic, European educated, European centered. Soukeîna and Isabelle, Africa or Europe—which shall he choose? He learns that he has no choice, and his poetry traces this learning process, from rejection of western ideals to a conclusion that *négritude* has a broad meaning and wide applications. In his love-hate relationship with the West, Senghor does not finally wholly reject the West, although he brings western values under close and critical scrutiny. He realizes that he is not purely a traditionalist African; he concludes that if there is a solution to his dilemma, it is not just an *African* solution. He is indeed repulsed by much that a bankrupt Europe stands for, but he does not seek an insular Africa nostalgically and not very productively turned in upon itself and its past; rather, he recognizes the reality of Europe and the historical fact of Africa's cultural ties with Europe. He finally searches for a synthesis that will partake of both cultures, which will, moreover, have validity not only in Africa but in the West as well. In ministering to an agonized Africa, Senghor also doctors an ailing Europe. *Négritude* ironically becomes a solution for Europe as well as for Africa.

Senghor adopts as his frame of reference the historical and more recent plight of the black man, yet his concern consistently transcends *femme noire* and Joal—these become, finally, symbolic of a more universal preoccupation. Indeed, his racial pronouncements often seem more rhetorical than genuine. This is not to diminish the major role played by the black man in his poetry. He himself is black, and his finest poetry illuminates his

personal experience. The black man, furthermore, is the alienated man par excellence, condemned by the same soul-flattening
reliance on technology and reason which is destroying the white
man, yet simultaneously ostracized from the world of technology
and reason because of his skin color. In the European, American, and colonial African milieux, the black man is a part of a
bankrupt world, yet apart from it: the black man is truly alone.
Senghor is, however, ultimately dealing with a universal problem
which happens to find its most dramatic figure in the black
man.

His argument essentially is this: the "black" man must extri-
cate himself from the "white" man's corrupt world, reestablish
his connections with his past and his rapport with nature, which
is to say with both his own nature (self-awareness, self-identity,
self-esteem) and the world around him. Then, as an equal, he
will reenter the world community, prepared to participate in the
purification of a dying world and to act as midwife to its rebirth.

Color is a major motif in "Neige sur Paris,"[4] a poem in which
Senghor plays almost defiantly, certainly with sarcasm, upon the
word "white" and its usual western connotations of peace, good-
ness, and purity. The poet accepts, for the sake of argument, the
white man's premise that "white is good," and he turns it against
the white man by means of a catalogue of African grievances
and the consequent exposure of the white man's hypocrisy. The
poem is composed in the form of a prayer directed to the white
man's god,[5] and irony is the chief weapon and poetic device as
Senghor assails the corrupt white world, at the same time revers-
ing the European's ethnocentric definitions of "white" and
"black."

God's vengeance and mercy are represented in "Neige sur
Paris" through images of nature: "snow of your peace," which is
also a snow of God's vengeance; "mountain of your peace,"

4. *Selected Poems*, pp. 7–8.
5. Cf. "Prayer for Peace" ("Prière de paix"), *Selected Poems*, pp.
48–51.

"sun of your gentleness," and "hands like dew," all of which
bring God and nature into a kind of unity, the god of the poem
being a kind of God-nature. Man's lack of harmony with nature
is thereby equated to his lack of harmony with God. The whiteness of God's snow purifies and brings peace, and is contrasted
with the powdered, spurious whiteness of the white man's hands
which bring destruction.

The first seven lines of the poem constitute its opening movement, the establishment of the basic image and the immediate
transformation of that image into a symbol. God sends the snow
to purify Paris, to purge it "By white death." So effective is
God's visitation that "even the factory chimneys," symbols of
industrialized Europe, are singing in unison, "Flying white
flags," and chanting "Peace to Men of goodwill." God's snow
has done its work: Europe has been purified, making plain its
surrender to God, and the sterile product of the industrial revolution has been brought into harmony with God—alienated man
has been brought back into a rhythmic union with nature.

Things have been anything but unified prior to this time, however, and the second (lines eight to twelve) and third (lines thirteen to twenty-one) movements of the poem expose what a debased Europe has done to Africa and to itself: it was an alienated, "a divided world . . . a divided Europe. . . ." Spain has
been "torn apart" in a revolutionary war; "And the rebel"
against God disrupted God's peace. Ironically, it is the Jew and
the Catholic—representing the ideological and spiritual bases of
western civilization—who defy God, who fire their "1,400 guns
against the mountain of your Peace." The image suggests man's
assault on God-nature, a Europe out of harmony with God and
nature, a Europe divided against itself.

The poet himself has not been without taint. His heart, filled
with hatred toward the white man, must also be purified by the
"incorruptible cold/By white death." The poet is humble:
"Lord, I have accepted your white cold more burning than salt."
Snow is again the purifier, the cleanser, and the action causes a
burning sensation as it purges the heart of its hatred. That work
accomplished, the poet's "heart melts like snow beneath the

sun." The effect is immediate, and "Under the sun of Your gentleness," the animosity melts away. "And I forget."

Whether or not he actually forgets is of no significance; the
images that follow in the third movement are too vivid, too strin-
gently anti-European to support an attitude of forgiveness. It is
the *process* that is important, as Senghor telescopes the stages of
this metaphorical journey. Forgetting implies forgiveness, on
which the final stage of the odyssey is dependent. Man must first
recover what he has lost, and only then can he forgive, the pre-
lude to deliverance and regeneration. Symbolically, both Europe
and the poet have been brought back into rapport with God-nature.

The poet's inability to forget so easily is suggested by a listing
of grievances, which is the substance of the third movement of
this work. In noting the outrages committed by the white man,
Senghor explains why it is that he and Europe have lost contact
with their spiritual origins, with nature and with God. "Whiteness" is again the motif which binds these several indictments
together: the "white hands," placed in their historical context,
directly and ironically mock the "white snow" images which the
poet has already developed. This tone of irony is a basic element
of the poem: the white hands destroyed Africa and are now in
the process of destroying themselves; the white snow proposes
peace, an end to alienation, a renewed harmony with nature.
These white hands "fired the shots which brought the empires
crumbling," they "flogged the slaves," they even "flogged You"
(that is, God), "buffeted You" and "buffeted me." Those same
white hands "delivered me to the solitude of hatred," are responsible for the poet's sense of aloneness. They "felled the forests of
palm trees . . . in the heart of Africa," and this in the name of
civilization ("railway sleepers"). "They cut down the forests of
Africa to save civilization, for there was a shortage of human
raw-material." This is the barrenness which those white hands
have wrought, and the destructiveness is intensified in the poem
because of the immediate and obvious contrast with that other
kind of whiteness, the whiteness of God's purification. It is a different *kind* of whiteness—in fact, it is not whiteness at all, but a

façade, a mask of whiteness that hides man's viciousness. Those hands are only "chalk-white," they are "powdered painted hands." They represent the very opposite of the white snow of God's peace.

The white man's whiteness is the whiteness of God—to hear the white man tell it; much of the destruction wrought by the European in Africa was accomplished in God's name. Senghor underscores the bitter irony of this, and concludes: if God is whiteness (accepting here the white man's premise), then *your* whiteness is a sham, a shield for deceit and inhumanity. In the process of whipping Africa, the white hands whipped God, and the martyrdom of Christ is here equated to the martyrdom of Africa (the Christian myth of death-regeneration is also relevant in this regard). But the hands whipped God in yet another way —in disrupting the harmony which the African experienced with nature. (Ironically, the white man, in the process, also alienated himself, both from himself, and from that same God-nature he was actively destroying.) Before the coming of the white man, it was nature that commanded Africa: "White hands that felled the forest of palm trees once commanding Africa, in the heart of Africa. . . ." The white man interfered with that natural harmony; he corrupted the innocence of Africa; he cut down those creatures who were close to God-nature: "Straight and stout, the Saras handsome as the first men who issued from Your brown hands." Senghor blurs any distinction between the cutting down of the forest and the "cutting down" of man.

To conclude, civilization (which Senghor mockingly capitalizes), the sterile whiteness, invaded Africa, and destroyed nature, disrupting man's relationship with nature. And again the irony: the white man destroyed nature to save his own civilization, but it is that civilization which is now dying. There is further irony. The poet has been speaking of God's white "snow of peace" and of the white man's "chalk-white hands," then he injects yet another color into the color-sensitive imagery: God's hands are not white, as the white man has insisted, they are "brown hands." The detail achieves significance in this instance because it is immediately contrasted with the Europeans' white hands and with the white snow, and hence cannot be ignored. The poet might have concluded that God's hands are pure white,

not powdery white; this would have been consistent with the
general use of color in the poem. But there is an abrupt color
change. It is possible that Senghor is suggesting here that this
white man's God is in fact closer to the world of the black man
than he is to the world of the white. If so, then this is the crowning irony of the poem. Nature and God are very close, if not
one; the black African, closer to nature, is closer to God.[6]

The fourth and final movement of "Neige sur Paris" deals
with the poet, now cleansed by God's gentle sun. "Lord," the
poet says,

I know I will not bring out my store of hatred against the diplomats
    who flash their long teeth
And tomorrow will barter black flesh.

Again, these are not the words that would be chosen by a man
filled with forgiveness. The poet is not yet cleansed; he is merely
mapping out the way to deliverance. The final movement is concerned with the future, the world after God's peace efforts have
had their effect, after God has dissolved the black man's hatred
and the white man's deceitfulness and penchant for destruction,
and brought them back into union with nature (and therefore
with one another). God's gentleness is generous: it is also applicable "to my enemies, to my brothers with white hands without
snow." Though those chalk-white hands bring anything but
peace, God's "hands like dew" cleanse white and black alike.

While "Neige sur Paris" is more concerned with the havoc the
white man spread throughout Africa, it also contains the seeds
of redemption. That vague promise of deliverance requires exploration, and this is found in the poem, "Que m'accompagnent
kôras et balafong" ("For Koras and Balafong").[7]

6. To the Christian God: "Ah!" says Senghor in another poem,

I know that some of Thy messengers have tracked down my priests like
    game and made great destruction of holy images,
When we could have found an agreement for they were, those images,
    Jacob's ladder from the earth to Thy heaven.

That "agreement" is expressed in the "brown hands" ("Prayer for Peace,"
Selected Poems, pp. 48–51).

7. *Selected Poems,* pp. 12–19. A *kôra* is "a type of harp with between
sixteen and thirty-two strings"; a *balafong* is "a kind of xylophone" (*Selected Poems,* pp. 95, 97).

There are two pasts for Senghor—there is the rhythmic harmony that existed before the white man came to Africa and destroyed it, and there is the innocent luster of Senghor's own childhood, before he was influenced by European civilization. These two pasts blend and become parallel preoccupations in Senghor's poetry, each emphasizing man in union with the cosmos. More important, this concern with the past (of whichever variety) becomes symbolic and completely loses its biographical and racial character.

"Que m'accompagnent kôras et balafong" both intensifies and ameliorates Senghor's attacks on white civilization, the poem betraying the poet's own attraction to Europe while at the same time broadening the condemnation of that society for its bankrupt ideology and its rape of Africa. The promise of hope is elaborated somewhat, but the poem is caught in the dramatic tension that exists within the poet, torn as he is between the two worlds. This conflict is resolved to some extent, but as "Neige sur Paris" was primarily concerned with the present plight of alienated man, so "Que m'accompagnent kôras et balafong" turns to the past and becomes enveloped in a somewhat romantic examination of the concept of *négritude*.

The poem is in nine parts and immediately, at the commencement of the first part, retreats to the past, to the poet's childhood:

By the bend in the road the river, blue among the fields fresh with September.
A Paradise where guard is kept against fevers by a child with eyes bright as two swords.
Paradise, my African childhood, that kept guard over the innocence of Europe.

The use of nature imagery to recreate the poet's childhood is of course intimately connected with Senghor's poetic conclusion that man and nature, woven inextricably together by shared rhythms (man perfectly in tune with the cosmos), represent that perfect time when man felt no sense of alienation. The topic is that lost paradise, the poet's African childhood—Africa and his childhood, the two entities "that kept guard over the innocence of Europe." This comment regarding "the innocence of

Europe" is linked to a second and more complex reference in the second part of the poem: "And I was guided through thorns and signs by Verdun, yes Verdun the dog that kept guard over the innocence of Europe." Two interpretations are possible, and it may be that the two can be held simultaneously; certainly each is compatible with the general themes of the poem. The first reference to the "innocence of Europe" has two possible meanings: it represents the innocence of the poet in Europe, in which case the reference to "my African childhood" is obvious: he is kept from complete contamination, thanks to his African childhood and what it symbolizes; or it suggests that, even though Europe is sterile and corrupt, it is not devoid of hope and the kind of innocence Africa symbolizes to the poet. In this case, the African childhood maintaining its guard suggests that the residual innocence of Europe will be nursed back to health by a regenerated Africa, a theme common in Senghor's poetry.

The second reference to "the innocence of Europe" is more complex. Verdun is, of course, a reference to the devastating Battle of Verdun, fought in the early months of 1916 between the French and the Germans. At that first Battle of Verdun, 350,000 Frenchmen lost their lives, and German losses were almost as great. These losses were incurred between February 21 and June 2 of that year, and by the end of 1916, after even further slaughter, the situation remained very much as it had been at the beginning—no change, except for a ghastly loss of human lives. Part II of the poem deals in part with the poet's European education, and he was guided through those "thorns and signs" by Verdun. The poet seems to be prepared for some incredulousness on the part of his listener: "yes Verdun," he repeats. Why Verdun? Again, the passage suggests two possible interpretations. First, Verdun and its human slaughter are dramatic representations to Senghor of the two great wars in Europe and their meaning: the barrenness of European civilization. It is this revelation that keeps him from becoming completely assimilated into European culture, which preserves his African innocence; it is this memory of bloody and futile warfare which guides him through the thorns and signs of Europe. Second, just as the poet was guided, that same Verdun guarded the innocence of Europe, this seemingly paradoxical statement suggesting again that because of the failures of its own vaunted civilization, a blood-drenched, disillusioned Europe may follow the poet's lead and attempt to reestablish its ties with nature. The inhumanity of war is the most fearful example of man out of tune with nature, and this may be sufficient to reawaken Europe.

What is the substance of the African past? I have already noted that Senghor makes no distinction between his own past and the historical and mythical past of his homeland: it is a part of his poetic design to blend these two pasts. The poet remembers the "fleeting softness at twilight," the tamarind trees "as fresh as a lime," and he considers his rapport with his ancestors, the spirits of the past who inform and enrich the present. He recalls the quiet rhythmic union with nature: "The herdsman's flute" piping "to the slow movement of the cattle"; the drums sounding from across the salt flats, "Beating a rhythm for the line of dancers at the feast of the Dead." The present is thus closely tied to the past, and Senghor describes a world far more desirable than the civilization of Europe ("brighter now than copper from across the sea"). It is not a perfect world, "men died far off as they still do," and that essential harmony was endangered even then.

In Part I of "Que m'accompagnent kôras et balafong," Senghor introduces a leitmotif which he will develop in various ways throughout the work: the fountain of Kam-Dyame, the image of water, of thirst satisfied and not satisfied. It is at the fountain where the poet, naked, flowers adorning his body, "drank your mystical waters out of my cupped hands." The fountain represents the mystical connection with the past, rhythm, the sap within man that rises and struts and dances.

This was his early childhood, and later there were other fountains, the fountains of Europe: his schooling, where the "Latin Muses" were "proclaimed as my guardian angels," but he rejects the shade provided by those muses as being too narrow (the guardians represented by his African childhood and by Verdun exposed for him the emptiness of the Latin muses). His European education did not quench his thirst; those European fountains were insufficient. After partaking in that world of "grilled and salted pistachios," which only served to quicken his thirst, he turned to the past, to another fountain, the "Fountain-of-Ele-

phants, where the stammering water is good," symbolizing as it
does a broader wisdom and a deeper experience—that of his
forefathers who, "with solemn eyes," perceived the very source
of things. So he did not succumb to the muses of Europe; he was
guided through that Scylla and Charybdis by Africa and Verdun. It is true that he has forgotten much of the past to which he
now retreats (it is a distant sound, a "muted trumpet")—"Nothing remains but the black priest dancing/ . . . like the shrewd-
headed Ancestor"—but that is enough. He has retained his innocence and now recalls, if vaguely, the mystical rhythm of his
past.

Part III of the poem introduces the conflict between the two
worlds, and intimates that the poet's innocence has been sternly
tested. The conflict is announced in the child's verse that pref-
aces the section: his mother suggests that he is a white man
"Kissing the prettiest girl," implying that he has compromised
and been won over by the white world. But it is not that simple.
He dislikes the fact that he must choose, "deliciously torn" as he
is "between these two friendly hands. . . ." But he must make a
decision, because friendly though those hands may be, they represent "two antagonistic worlds." Shall it be Soukeîna or Isabelle? Africa or Europe? He "cannot tell now which is my sister
and which is my foster-sister"; he has pleasant remembrances of
each. He protests; he would like to make "those two hands" one.

Still, if he must choose, he chooses Africa, "the verset of
streams and of winds and of forests/The assonance of plains and
rivers"; he chooses "the rhythm of blood in my naked body."
And he chooses harmony, "the harmony of strings and brass
that seem to clash." But the "plains and rivers" are not assonant,
the "strings and brass" do not clash when one is in rhythmic
contact with nature. The poet has made that choice, he has chosen the "Swing swing yes chosen the swing/And the far-off
muted trumpet." In another poem, "Chants pour Signare"
("Elle me force sans jamais répit"),[8] he rejects the music of Europe: "I cannot sing your plain chant that has no swing to it, I
cannot dance it." Dance—rhythm is the essence of *négritude,*

8. From "Chants pour Naett," in *Selected Poems,* p. 59.

enveloping man biologically, emotionally, spiritually, bringing him into harmony with nature and with an Africa that is as real as the beat of his pulse. Europe is out of tune; its music is plain, and the poet cannot dance it. And dance is everything: "She dances, she lives," he proclaims in "Epîtres a la princess" (V, "Princesse, ton épître");[9] his nobleness, he tells the princess, "is to live that land according to that land." It is rhythm, the rhythm of the drums, the rhythm that throbs up within him and possesses him, rhythm with nature:

And from the earth wells up the rhythm, sap and sweat, wave and smell of the damp earth
That shudders the legs of the statue, the thighs that open to the secret
Flows over the buttocks, hollows the loins stretches the belly gorges and hills
Prows of drums. The drums awaken, Princess, the drums awake us. The drums open our throats.
The drums roll, the drums roll, to the content of the heart.

And this drum roll, this rhythm is not only the hope of Africa, it will also resurrect a dead Europe: "the burst of the trumpet [no longer muted] over the snowy graveyards of Europe."

The poet, in almost apologetic tones, speaks in Part IV of "Que m'accompagnent kôras et balafong" of his intimate relations with Europe. But he has already rejected Europe and Isabelle in favor of Africa and Soukeîna, and there is more than mere rejection here. Underlying the comments about Europe is the knowledge that he has something far more desirable than pale occidental offerings: not the arid plains of European knowledge but the fountain of *négritude*, "where the stammering water is good." He "was not always a shepherd of fair heads," teaching in European schools. Not always. There was something that he had long ago, before he taught the white children, before he became a deferential official, the proper colleague, "smiling but rarely

9. *Selected Poems*, pp. 82–84. In *On African Socialism* (New York, 1964), p. 43, Senghor said, "The Negro Africa could say, 'I feel, I dance the Other; I am.' To dance is to discover and to re-create, especially when it is a dance of love. In any event, it is the best way to know. Just as knowledge is at once discovery and creation—I mean, re-creation and recreation, after the model of God."

laughing." It is that primordial state of innocence of which he
speaks, and the memory of his origins intensifies the aridity of
"Old France old University, all the old routine." Age has nothing to do with it; his "childhood is as old as the world and I am
as young as the everlasting youth of the world's dawn." He will
be delivered from the acute sense of alienation, which is
Europe's contribution, by a new sense of his own identity, an
identity which will become known to him through *négritude,* a
reestablishment of contacts with his past, with "The poetesses of
the sanctuary" and the "authentic legend of my race," a new
union symbolized by the rhythmic "sounds of the high *kôras.*"

The essence and lesson of that past are indicated in Part V in
the description of one of the poet's forebears, Koumba Ndofène
Dyouf, a vassal and a governor, important here because the past
makes him a rhythmic counterpart of nature; origins, nature,
and rhythm, all are accounted for as the poet describes the pere-
grinations of this "royal pilgrim," who, accompanied by the
dyoung-dyoungs,[10] gives "ear in the wood to the murmured
grievance," listens to "the prattle of birds," and heeds "the
conch eloquent among the prophetic tombs," that is, the ancestors. While they wept in the evening because their own fragile
peace (the peace spoken of in "Neige sur Paris") is threatened,
there is yet no disruption of that man-nature union; he and his
fellows are "Cousins in peace," continuing their traditional way
of life. The ancestors are symbolic of man's roots, and are important to Senghor's poetry particularly in this symbolic sense:
man's quest for identity will end with a reestablishment of ties
with the past, and hence the emphasis on links with the ancestors. They are a part of the harmony, and once the break with
the past is complete, the harmony too is shattered. The present
blends into the past; the two cannot be separated: "I was myself
the grandfather of my grandfather/I was his soul and his ascendancy."

On "the high pyre" of war (a fracture of God's peace, again
referring to a disruption of man's relations with nature and a
consequent slide toward a state of alienation), the "dusty riches"

10. The *dyoung-dyoung* is "the royal drum of the kings of Sine" (*Selected Poems,* p. 96).

of the past go up in flames. The present is imprisoned ("my house, the wives who have mothered my sons"); the past is destroyed ("Furniture of the sanctuary, solemn masks, ritual garments")—all are consumed. Yet in that smoldering rubble lies hope; the flames of destruction can be transposed, through the effects of *négritude,* into the flame of regeneration, and from the devastation will rise the new phoenix: "Sleep, heroes, in this evening which brings new life to birth, in this night heavy with grandeur." All is not destroyed: "saved is the Singer," the *griot* who creates the poem, embodiment of rhythmic calm. The survival of the singer is all-important, for rhythm is life, and "my pagan sap that rises, struts and dances" will give birth to a regenerated and purified mankind.

The roles of the poet and the poem are essential in this process. "This complex notion" of *négritude,* Sartre has written, "is essentially pure poetry."[11] There is no more appropriate symbol of the agent who will resurrect a moribund Europe and revive a dying Africa than the *griot* who will blow the trumpet "over the snowy graveyards of Europe." The trumpet is the poem. But the poetic word alone is not sufficient: "What makes the *négritude* of a poem is less its theme than its style, the emotional warmth which gives life to words, which transmutes the word into the Word."[12] This statement has meaning only when one considers the emphasis Senghor places on rhythm and the interpretation he gives to it. Without rhythm, the word is sterile: "It is rhythm that lends it [the word] its full effectiveness, that transforms it into the verb. It was God's verb, that is to say the rhythmic word, that created the universe."[13] When Senghor speaks of "the Word," he is not suggesting objective and rational interpretation. It is "intuitive reason"[14] that he is referring to; not necessarily

11. Jean-Paul Sartre, "Orphée noir," in *Anthologie de la nouvelle poésie nègre et Malgache,* ed. Léopold Sédar Senghor (Paris, 1948), p. xxix; "Black Orpheus," tr. John MacCombie, *The Massachusetts Review* 6 (1964–65): 35.

12. Senghor, quoted in Sartre, "Black Orpheus," p. 36.

13. Senghor, "African-Negro Aesthetics," *Diogenes,* no. 16 (1956), p. 33.

14. "Négritude was intuitive reason, reason-embrace, communional warmth, the image-symbol and cosmic rhythm which, instead of sterilizing through divisiveness, fecundated by unifying" (Thomas, "Senghor and Négritude," p. 106).

spoken or written, it is "a certain affective attitude towards the world."[15] It is hence not a reasoned interpretative process, but rather a state of being:

the African Negro . . . does not state that he thinks; he feels that he feels, he feels his existence, he feels himself. Because he feels himself, he feels the Other;[16] and because he feels the Other, he goes toward him on the rhythm of the Other, in order to know Him and his world. It is this soaring of the vital force that the religious and social life of the African Negro expresses, of which literature and art are the most effective tools.[17]

The Word is *négritude,* which is rhythm, which is life. This rhythm is given form in art—in the sound of the drums, in the metrical movement of the poem. This is not to suggest that the form of the poem is the end; the rhythmic beats are illustrative and symptomatic of "the Negro's being-in-the-world."[18] Poetry is not something to be merely read, and drums are not to be simply heard—they are felt, as a part of man's being. It is not a question of searching for the meaning of a poem; what is important is that one feels the poem. One does not ask the meaning of a dance, one simply dances it, becomes a part of its rhythm. As with the dance (and, in a less dramatic sense, the ancestors, the family, nature, the spirits—all the varied facets of "the Other"), man becomes a part of the poem, becomes unified with the poem, feels the poem and indeed becomes the poem, as he is drawn into the work of art by its rhythm. Psychologically, emotionally, rhythmically, aesthetically, man becomes one with the poem. The "message" or theme, if there is one, is felt, and it is more than a mere vicarious experience: it *is* experience. The poem simultaneously expresses in outward form the rhythmic rudiments of man's union with "the Other," but more important, it is an ecstatic heightening of that union. The dance is the most obvious example: the pulsating beat of the blood within man, of

15. Sartre, "Black Orpheus," p. 36.
16. "The Other" is "the external world," including "adult, Ancestor, genius or God." See Senghor, "On Negrohood: Psychology of the African-Negro," *Diogenes,* no. 37 (1962), p. 2; and Senghor, "African-Negro Aesthetics," p. 27.
17. Senghor, "African-Negro Aesthetics," p. 37.
18. Satrte, "Black Orpheus," p. 36.

his throbbing rapport with nature, and of the beat of the drums
—all converge, and while it is true that such an experience is a
symbol of the larger experience, it is at the same time an experi-
ential encounter during which man is most keenly aware of his
identity. So with the poem: the poetic experience is not simply a
microcosm of that larger symphony; it is in itself an experience,
a moment when man's sense of harmony is heightened and
acute, and the harmony itself is complete, perfect. One does not
explicate such poetry: "He has no need to think, but to live the
Other by dancing it. . . . Now to dance is to discover and to re-
create, to identify oneself with the forces of life, to lead a fuller
life, and in short, to *be*. It is, at any rate, the highest form of
knowledge. And thus, the knowledge of the African negro is, at
the same time, discovery and creation—re-creation."[19] Such a
form of "knowledge" is alien to European experience, not because of race but because the European has, through his contin-
ual insistence on rationalism at the expense of feeling, widened
the gap between himself and his origins. He studies rather than
participates in the object, and he thereby misses the point: "It is
a matter of *participating* in the object in the act of knowledge; of
going beyond concepts and categories, appearances and precon-
ceptions produced by education, to plunge into the primordial
chaos, not yet shaped by discursive reason."[20]

In this pantheistic accord with nature, where does man end
and "the Other" begin? The question is irrelevant: the two are
blended into each other, and man *is* "the Other." It is not a matter of talking about stones and the tree and the sky; man is a
part of nature. It is not a question of pronouncing the word;
man *is* the word. Thus, when he considers objects in nature, the
words are more than merely meaningful; the word brings the objects to life, he feels the word, he lives the object in nature. The
word becomes a living thing with him; he feels it because he is a
part of it. He therefore creates rather than interprets (rather, he
re-creates); the word has a living reality for him. Why, then, take
a biology course in the university and dissect the bird and ana-
lyse the flower, and be left with only a handful of bones, some

19. Senghor, "On Negrohood," p. 6.
20. Senghor, "On Negrohood," p. 10.

feathers, and a few wilted petals? As a part of nature, man feels that bird, he is that flower; they are an integral part of his world rather than isolated segments of it. His world is not fragmented; he is indeed a part of all that he sees and meets. He discovers by "participating in the object," by identifying himself "with the forces of life," rather than alienating himself from those forces by test-tube analysis and objective reason.

But this special relationship is reserved for the man who has become. Senghor is concerned with man alienated from that rhythmic state. His problem remains: how can man be brought back into that state? Here, the poem becomes important. For the person who is already a part of the cosmic order, the sound of the drum and the beat of the poem simply reproduce in outward form the rhythm of which he is a part, producing (as I have noted) a heightened experience during which man is most keenly aware of his identity. For the alienated man, the poem can (like the drum) act as a kind of catalyst at the same time that it is itself an experience. It is thus doubly decisive in bringing him back into tune with the universe. As a catalyst, it can strike a primordial chord within that person, and thereby remind him of his past state of euphoric sympathy with nature. It is a reminder of that past harmony, that far-off muted trumpet, just as the ancestors and the glories that were Africa are for Senghor symbols of the lost rapport. He views the past as a symbolic odyssey, an effort to recapture a state of being which has been lost. If the poem—the emphasis on the past in its images, the embodiment of rhythm in its meter—can rescue a wayward mortal and resuscitate a dying society, the poet's role is an essential one. If alienation is, in simple terms, a lack of rhythm between man and nature, then the poem, considered as symbol, can become instrumental in dissolving that unhappy condition.

In Part VII of "Que m'accompagnent kôras et balafong," Senghor addresses the Africa of the past, present, and future. This "Africa," rather than rob the people of their identities (an accusation which the poet immediately rejects), prepares them to survive the onslaughts of those who would destroy that innocence. This is what had protected the poet during the time he spent in Europe. Because Africa was "the member storing

plenty, the barns full to bursting against the days of trial," he
was able to survive. In such difficult times, Africa (négritude,
the primal sympathy) will rise to drive the enemy off; it is the
fortress, "the chief organizing the force to forge/The arm." And
as "your people are honored in you/ . . . You are your people."
(Man is not simply a part of Africa, he is Africa, "Africa" suggesting that natural rapport.) It is this lush fertility and its bold
promise of creativeness, mixing the bloods of all men, these
bloods mingling in the poet's veins, which make him a part of
the totality of humanity. Africa is rhythm—"only the naked
clapping of hands," nothing else is important. This is the promise of that symbolic Africa, it is "the song of Africa to come." In
a word, it is this same "Africa" which signals an end to mankind's torment.

The poet hopes to carry this message "to the gatherings of the
people," thereby preparing the way for the regenerated phoenix.
But before he can carry out his mission of purification, the poet
must himself be purified, and he naturally turns to nature:

O desert shadowless desert, austere earth, pure earth, from all my
        pettiness
Wash me clean, from all contagions of civilized man.

These two lines capsulize Senghor's concept of the initial stages
of négritude: a purgation of the spirit, washing away the contamination of civilization, and a return to the earth. The poet
will return to his roots, find his original identity which is full accord with nature, and reclaim the dignity, now lost, which had
flowed from that accord. Using the imagery of Africa's past to
illumine the present and to embody the promise of the future,
the poet can now set out on his pilgrimage, "together with all the
buried greatness of the past" (not a historical past but a reminder of rhythmic origins—the historical references are mere
symbols of that rhythm), his voyage identical to that of his fore-
bear, Koumba Ndofène Dyouf, bursting with the same promise
and beset by the same dangers. He will march in a procession of
"seven thousand new negroes," regenerated humans, "seven
thousand peasants humble and proud/Who carry the authentic
riches of my race on their musical shoulders." On their shoul-

ders too have been "all the devastations of slave-trading Europe," the agony, "all the hymns they have sung, all the chanting torn by the muted trumpet"—that "far-off muted trumpet." Slave-trading Europe has removed the African from his harmonic past, has muted the trumpet. From those spectacular ruins will rise the "new negroes," the "riches of my race" referring to that regained contact with the past. With "Strength Nobility Openness/And the abandon in delight," this renewed man moves back into harmony with "the great power of the universe, . . . the Love that moves the singing worlds."

This reestablished rapport with the forces of the universe is thrown into stark relief by the abrupt shift, in Part IX of the poem, to the situation in Europe. The poet has already noted that he owes his deliverance not to the European fountains of knowledge, but rather to the fountains of wisdom and feeling which have their source in the African past and which rise and prance and dance within him and are given symbolic form by the rhythmic pulse of blood within his naked body. The waters of Europe flow red with blood: "see how the Somme and the Seine and the Rhine and the savage Slav rivers are red under the Archangel's sword." The poet escaped the fury of that sword because, in Claude McKay's words, he "was in closer biological kinship to the swell of primitive earth life. And maybe this apparent failing under the organization of the modern world was the real strength that preserved him from becoming the thing that was the common white creature of it."[21] A renewed feeling of attraction for this Europe nevertheless wells up within the poet, but he immediately represses it: "I have my orders, my duty is to go on." Still, there is hope, and his love for this destructive Europe leads him to "find a little comfort" in the possibility that his "double loves" may "go wandering every night." There is that dim hope that this torn Europe may, through its attachment to Africa, be saved.

The inner fountain of blood, a symbol of the poet's affinity to nature, has now become a symbol of alienation: those same rhythmic "bloods mingled in my veins" are drained in Europe

21. *Banjo, a Story without a Plot* (New York, 1929), p. 323.

because of war, the primary image of Europe's spiritual bank-ruptcy and consequent sense of aloneness. In the remainder of the poem, by concentrating on the ingredients of his own deliv-erance, the poet proposes a solution for Europe's barrenness. From that sickening sight of European blood-letting, the poet retreats to his past, the sense of union now finding its symbol in "African night." He returns to that first innocence, returns to those "distant nights" when his uncle led him "through the shad-ows and the signs." ("Paradise my African childhood, that kept guard over the innocence of Europe": he never lost this, it was muted but never wholly destroyed; this retreat to the past in Part IX immediately after the description of the bloody graveyard of Europe recalls that other guide mentioned earlier in the poem, the "thorns and signs" of Verdun.) The uncle thereby becomes the vehicle, bringing the young poet back into contact with his past and with nature. It is quiet, the calmness of man in tune with nature—the flowers, the glowworms, the stars, grass, trees, all woven into his being by "the muffled tom-tom, the far-off breathing of the night." The ancestors (representing that past) explain the mysteries of nature (the only worthy education), which means simply that the poet, in harmony with the past, is a part of those mysteries, feels them and thereby has an intuitive understanding of them—this is wisdom, not mere knowledge. All is unified: the poet, his Africa, his past, the spirits, ancestors, nature, and the pulse of the drums. "Africa" is all of this; it is self-awareness.

African night my black night, mystical-lucid black-brilliant
You rest at one with the earth, you are the Earth and the harmonious
     hills.

The fertility of Africa is contrasted with Europe's sterility, the poet speaking of Africa as a princess, as Mother Africa; the poet using sensual imagery to describe her: "The impetuous leap of the twin hills! Curves of gentleness melodious face." It is the memory of this Africa which kept guard over his innocence while he was in Europe: "How often have you made my heart beat like the unconquered leopard in his narrow cage." The poet describes the distance separating "Europe" and "Africa":

> Night delivering me from arguments and sophistries of salons,
> from pirouetting pretexts, from calculated hatred and
> humane butchery.

It is night, "Africa," *négritude,* which delivers him, "dissolving all my contradictions, all contradictions in the first unity of your blackness." The poet is again a child, always a child, reveling in the innocence which is Africa, his protection during his "twelve wandering years."

The poem ends on a brief note of hope, the attempt again to bridge the gulf between the two worlds of "Africa" and "Europe." Though he has now accepted Africa, he has not completely cut his ties with Europe. He has brought back with him "only this friend" (his European wife?), who, like the poet, is yet a child whose eyes, having survived "Breton mists," are still bright, still attuned to "Africa." With this slim hope for a regenerated Europe in mind, Senghor develops the final phase of his odyssey.

Is it realistic to suggest that man can retreat to his past and regain his first innocence? This tormenting question is asked and answered by Senghor in "Elégie des circoncis,"[22] and it completes the phoenix image and again shows close philosophical ties to Blake's poetic second innocence or New Jerusalem. In "Que m'accompagnent kôras et balafong," Senghor sings of his Africa:

> O my Lioness my dark Beauty, my black Night my Black One my
> Naked One!
> How often have you made my heart beat like the unconquered
> leopard in his narrow cage.

This apostrophe is continued in "Elégie des circoncis":

> Night of childhood, blue Night, blond Night O Moon!
> How often have I called to you, Night, crying by the roadside
> By the side of the sorrows of my manhood?

The poet recalls the innocence of childhood, and the ritualistic climax to that sublime state. In *L'Enfant Noir,* the Guinean writer Camara Laye describes a similar ritual:

22. *Selected Poems,* pp. 91–92.

I was growing up. The time had come for me to join the society of the initiated. . . . As soon as the sun had gone down, the tom-tom had begun to beat. . . . Yes, the time had come for me. . . . Towards the middle of the night, our tour of the town and the collection of uncircumcised boys was finished. . . . As soon as our elders had made sure that no intruder was present to disturb the mysteriousness of the ceremony, we left the town behind and entered the bush. . . . Just before we reached the hollow, we saw flames leap up from a huge wood fire. . . . Now that we are on our knees with our foreheads to the ground and our hands pressed over our eyes, Konden Diara's[23] roaring suddenly bursts out. . . . And it is not only a lion, it is not only Konden Diara roaring: there are ten, twenty, perhaps thirty lions.

"You must not be afraid!" I told myself. "You must conquer your fear! Your father told you to overcome your fear!" But how could I *not* be afraid? . . . How I wish . . . How I wish I was far away from this clearing, back in the compound, in the warm security of the house.[24]

Senghor too recalls the fear the uncertainty of that ceremonial night:

It was night of earliest childhood, thick as peace. Fear bowed our
        backs under the Lion's roaring.
Tall grasses bowed under the shifty silence of that night.
Full of branches you fire of hope! Pale memory of the Sun, hearten-
        ing my innocence
Hardly at all.

It is the night of circumcision, when the child will bid farewell to his innocence, and become a man. He is afraid; the entire ceremony seems to be out of harmony with nature; the lion roars and frightens him, this symbol of nature turned hostile suggesting the imminent loss of innocence. Another part of the ceremony is the burning branches, again symbolic of the transformation into manhood; but this fire is a pale imitation of the sun with which, until now, the child in his union with the cosmos has had a special relationship. The elements of the ritual are sym-

23. Konden Diara was "that terrible bogeyman, that 'lion that eats up little boys! . . . This night was to be the night of Konden Diara" (*The African Child,* trans. James Kirkup [London, 1954], p. 80).
    24. *The African Child,* pp. 78–85.

bolic of the loss of that relationship, that initial innocence: "I had to die." As comforting and secure as that childhood world has been, it must now give way to manhood, the world of experience, a world which almost immediately threatens the close man-nature harmony which the child has enjoyed since birth. (The child actually feels himself an integral part of his environment; he has not yet learned to differentiate himself—to alienate himself—from it.) The child is afraid of this transition, and he clings to the primal order:

I laid my hands on my throat like a girl who shudders at the horror
    of death
I had to die to the beauty of song—all things adrift with the current
    of Death.

As with the young Camara Laye, the rhythm of the drums accompanies this ritualistic death. Are the drums not conspiring against the very harmony they formalize by playing a crucial role in this ceremony, the main purpose of which is to remove the child from his harmonious existence? "Elégie des circoncis" emphasizes the fact that Senghor is not so unrealistic as to suggest that man retreat to the innocence of childhood; to do so would be in itself a form of death. Senghor does not deny the importance and inevitability of moving from a state of innocence into a threatening world of experience. What is important is this: first, the symbolic nature of childhood innocence, representing a rapport with nature which is desirable in adulthood as well as in childhood, and second, the hope that man can survive the threats of the world of experience and achieve a new innocence, having its roots and its symbol in that original innocence not only of the child but also of the ancient past which the child sometimes comes to represent. The child must die, but, in Wordsworth's words, "The Child is father of the Man," and, as difficult as the transition is, there is hope. Again Wordsworth anticipates Senghor to an extent:

What though the radiance which was once so bright
Be now forever taken from my sight,
    Though nothing can bring back the hour

> Of splendor in the grass, of glory in the flower;
>   We will grieve not, rather find
> Strength in what remains behind.[25]

Senghor too would find some consolation "In years that bring the philosophic mind,"[26] if this means a renewed and mature rapport with nature.

The boy has to die, and from the ashes of childhood is born the man. The boy begins to feel the change:

See the twilight on the throat of the dove when the blue pigeons call
And the seamews of dream fly with plaintive cries.

The dove and the gull reflect the threatened alienation from the nature which they symbolize, a suggestion that the rites represent a twilight of dreams, a beauty that must die.

It is not death, however, but a life-in-death of which the poet speaks, a life growing out of death; a new innocence and joy are possible, but new hazards can destroy them. It is a more precarious state that the child now enters, but its potential for creativity is profound. "Let us die, let us dance," he cries, and he means, "Let us die, let us live." Life and death are one, "elbow to elbow woven together like a garland," it is a farewell to innocence, an ushering in of manhood. The drums do not simply accompany the transition from innocence to experience, but rather from innocence to the promise of the world of experience, that new innocence. Rather than conspiring against the original harmony, therefore, the drums assure that the transition into the new innocence will be consummated and that man will not be lost in the process, alienated from that rhythmic relationship. While childhood innocence will indeed be lost, the accord with nature will be retained. This is why the drums accompany the end of primal innocence, and it is the rhythmic promise of the drums that drives away the fear:

Woi! the drum ploughs up the holy silence. Dance. Song lashes the
    blood

25. Wordsworth, "Ode: Intimations of Immortality," lines 177–82.
26. "Ode: Intimations of Immortality," line 188.

Rhythm drives out the fear that has us by the throat. Life holds death
    at bay.

Senghor does not despair over the death of innocence; he is ex-
ploring the birth of a new innocence in this poem.

"Let night be resolved to its contrary," Senghor writes in
"Elégie des eaux,"

let death be reborn as Life, like a diamond of dawn
Like the Circumcised when the night unveiled rises the Male, the Sun!

What began as a ritualistic pale imitation of the sun contains the
potential for a complete transformation into the sun (the idea of
being-in-the-world).

Dance proclaims an end to childhood, and acts as a bridge,
harbinger and embodiment of a mature and creative state of innocence:

Dance to the burthen of fear, that the night of the phallus may rise
    over our ignorance over our innocence.

"The night of the phallus": involved in this image are the circumcision rites themselves, symbol of manhood, procreation,
creative potential. The promise represented by the image makes
possible the acceptance, albeit regrettable, of death: "Ah! die to
childhood." The birth of the new from the ashes of the old, the
transmutation of the word into the Word, the metaphor of the
phoenix—all are involved in the symbol of the poem, to which
Senghor again refers:

let the poem die the syntax fall apart, let all the inessential
    words be swallowed up.
The weight of the rhythm is enough, no need of word-cement to build
    on the rock the City of tomorrow.

As syntax and the words are unimportant in the poem, so also
are childhood and manhood insignificant, and to concern oneself
with these specific experiences is to travel a well-worn but ultimately circuitous road (compare Clarence's tortured travels in
Camara Laye's *Le regard du roi*). In childhood and manhood, it
is rhythm that is important; nothing else is needed for the crea-

tion of the future, the city of tomorrow. The poet advises his listener to forget his childhood, and "Let the sun rise from the sea of shadows"—let the man rise from the child, let the phoenix rise from the ashes, let the Word rise from the words. Let a new innocence be born; it must not be stifled by traditional trappings and by idle and misdirected regret for the loss of the past. The essential paradox of this poem, life from death, is understandable only when all aspects of Senghor's poetic art have been considered. It is night, "Night of Childhood," and the waves from that "sea of shadows . . . are the color of dawn."

Neither Senghor nor Blake suggests that this world of manhood, of experience, is as joyous and uncomplicated as that of childhood. The threat to harmony is always very real, and there are times, at midday, in middle age, when the adult looks at himself, "when every form strips off its flesh/Like the trees in Europe under the winter sun," and he despairs, "so many times I have wept—how many times?—for the transparent nights of childhood." He no longer feels himself involved in that cosmic union; rationalism has replaced intuitive reason and feeling. He is alienated from that rhythmic silence that cradled him,[27] and he no longer feels unified with his African night.

See, the bones are abstract, lending themselves only to calculations
        with straight edge, compass and sextant.

He sees himself now as bones which can be counted and studied; he sees a pile of bones rather than a total human being responding rhythmically to the world about him. In such a fragmented state, the poet longs for his childhood, for the completeness experienced by the child. The beat of the drums that carries man from childhood into adulthood can be muted by the burdens of the world of experience, and rhythm—life—is lost:

Life runs through the fingers of man like sand, crystals of snow
        imprison the life of the water
The serpent of water slips through the helpless hands of the reeds.

27. "Nuit de Sine," *Selected Poems*, p. 5.

The flight of the phoenix can thus easily be aborted. And so, in the noontime of his age, the poet longs for those "Dear Nights friendly Nights, Nights of Childhood," when he was not divorced from nature. What seemed so promising has miscarried: "The poem droops in the sun of Noon."

The dangers are present, but they do not preclude fulfillment of the ritualistic promise. While the Word is threatened, "it feeds on the dew of evening/And the drum beats out the rhythm." How does one cleanse from his feet "the mud of Civilization"?[28] The answer is a symbolic return to the past, a reachievement of that rapport with nature which has its most perfect image in the child. Because man has reached his middle age does not mean that his blood cannot still prance and dance. And the poet especially needs the wisdom of the "Master of the Initiates," that he might "break the cypher of things" and "learn my office as father, as lamarch." The poet through the metrics of the poem can then deliver those who have lost that rapport; the muted trumpet is blown and the alienated are restored. In this regard, "The poem is not only a charm," it is life itself, and by it, says the poet-leader, "the woolly heads of my flock are fed." He must grow into manhood, and accept his duties as a father, as a landowner; he must go beyond the child's world, for it is no child's game that he is engaged in. He must feed his flock; the responsibilities of a poet are heavy. To prepare himself, the poet must revitalize himself; only then can he create the poem, which is to say the rhythm, the life-giving ministrations which will save his flock.

As the poem ends, Senghor again demands that we be realistic. We cannot have that world of childhood innocence, that warm womb-like security provided by a pure and untried natural rhythm. The poem, the Word, is not simply a transcendent or mystical concept; it must be as real and as vital as the earth itself. There must be a marriage "of shadow and dawnlight," so that the sun can rise from "the sea of shadows": the child must

28. "The Return of the Prodigal Son," Part IV, line 4, *Selected Poems,* p. 22.

grow into the man, the world of innocence must make way for the world of experience. The poem, the Word, "is bird-serpent"; that is, it is both transcendent and earth-bound. But the serpent also represents creativity; it embodies the seeds of hope. The innocence of childhood, the experience of adulthood, Africa, Europe, the bird and the serpent, dawnlight and shadow, feeling and reason, the combination will produce the new man. It is hence not inevitable that adulthood means an end to innocence; it is not inevitable that Europe means the destruction of Africa; it is not essential that the poem become bogged down in "inessential words," that the body and world are understandable only in terms of the compass and the sextant. One must die to childhood, one cannot return to the past, but one does not thereby have to lose that rhythmic contact with nature. There can be a marriage "of shadow and dawnlight," and from that marriage, "The Phoenix rises, he sings with wings extended, over the carnage of words."

Read on a literal level, Senghor's poems require little explanation. The African, enslaved for centuries and humiliated by the colonial powers, gradually lost his dignity as a man; in the eyes of the white conqueror, he was an inferior being. This was serious enough, but the state of the black man became disastrous when he himself began to accept the white man's premise. One of the most pathetic manifestations of this loss of identity was the concept of the *assimilado:* the black African who tried to become a white European, forsaking his own history and identity, attempting to become what he was not. The experiment was doomed from the beginning, and the African became a double exile: psychologically and physically, he was alienated. Cut off from his origins and adrift in a world in which, because of his skin color, he would always be a stranger, the African was prevented from participating in the world of the present and from aiding in the creation of a more productive future world. The present situation of Senghor's African, then, is one of destruction,

the tearing of self from self

From the tongue of my mother, from the skull of my Ancestor, from
the drum of my soul.[29]

But the plight of the European is even more critical than that of
the African:

It was the year of Discovery. From their eyes they spat a yellow fire.
And the waters of the rivers run with gold and sweat. They
fed the metropolitan capitals to bursting. Naked men were
made slaves and parents sold their children for a guinea piece.
And it was the year of Reason. From their eyes they spat a red fire.
And hatred sprouted in the necks of men in knotted ganglions,
and the soldiers weltered in a mire of blood. Scientists and
executioners received decorations. They had found a way to
kill men twice.
It will be the year of Technology. From their eyes they will spit a
white fire. The elements will separate and come together by
mysterious attractions and repulsions. The blood of animals
and the sap of plants will be turned to whey. The white men
·will be yellow, the yellow men will be white. All will be
sterile.[30]

But Senghor, in his poetry, goes beyond the shores of Africa.
One of the probable reasons for misconceptions arising from the
poetry of *négritude* is that unfortunate word itself. However it is
translated—"blackness," "negrohood," "niggerness"—it leads
one to assume that it is a peculiarly racial (or even racist) concept. Poets like Aimé Césaire and Léon Damas have compounded this confusion; their poetry is uncompromising in its
attacks on white civilization, their artistic images and idealistic
quests marred by an overwrought emotionalism. The subject of
Senghor's poetry is indeed blackness; the error is to stop there,
with the mere personal and historical data and imagery. It is *not*
the theme of the work. "I am not really a Pan-Africanist," Senghor told a London press conference in 1961, "I am a
humanist."[31] And his poetry supports this claim; it is a humanis-

29. "Epître à la princesse III," *Selected Poems*, pp. 80–81.
30. "Epître à la princesse V," *Selected Poems*, pp. 82–84.
31. Quoted in Colin Legum, *Pan-Africanism, A Short Political Guide*
(New York, 1962), p. 95.

tic vision rather than a racial justification that characterizes his work.

A certain shifting of emphasis must take place. *Négritude* must be removed from the racial morass in which it has become steeped, often because of the narrow interpretation of the concept. Artistically, *négritude* must be viewed in an artistic context, its definition not gleaned from secondary political and historical sources.

The concept of *négritude*, while basic to Senghor's poetic design, is not the central theme of the poetry. *Négritude* is, as his poetry emphasizes again and again, self-identity, that rhythmic rapport with the universe, and it is thus an important ingredient in the odyssey which Senghor travels in his poetry. It is the basis, the "rock" on which "the City of tomorrow" will be constructed. This is a goal which is more significant, dependent upon but extended beyond the recovery of one's identity. And Senghor underscores the broad nature of the concept of *négritude;* it applies equally to all races. "[T]his poetry," writes Sartre, "which seems racial at first—is actually a hymn by everyone for everyone."[32] Individual poems by Senghor investigate various facets of this concept, and the consideration of individual poems can confuse the reader as to the poet's overall intent.

Blackness is a symbol, and *négritude* too becomes a symbol which transcends race, a symbol of self-identity. The poet's obvious attraction to Europe and the contradictions and stresses that this attraction invites when joined to his basic involvement with Africa are resolved in *négritude,* and his concern for all men who are similarly involved in a struggle to achieve self-awareness, his vision of a civilization of universal brotherhood, obviously transgress ethnic and racial lines. To attempt to force the poetry into any lesser mold is to overlook the major themes of the work which, in conclusion, can be outlined as follows:

1) Destruction and alienation (the present); 2) Purification and *négritude* (the past); 3) Resurrection and synthesis (the future).

---

32. Sartre, "Black Orpheus," p. 16.

1. Destruction and alienation (the present). Man's present situation is characterized by a terrible sense of alienation. This sense of anonymity and consequent futility is embodied in the symbol of "Europe," which comes to represent a man cut off from his roots, a society sacrificing the macrocosm for the microcosm, emphasizing reason to the exclusion of feeling. Sterile and artificial, constantly engaged in bloody warfare, European civilization is revealed as debased and empty. "Europe" and "whiteness" thus come to represent this state of alienation, symbols which have their roots in history.

2. Purification and *négritude* (the past). Once man recognizes his plight, he can begin his odyssey, and it is a voyage which must go back before it can move forward. Senghor's exploration of the African past and his own childhood (each, as I have suggested, blending into the other) is symbolic of a voyage to the soul. Before one can live a life harmoniously, he must know himself, must accept himself. Many of the images in Senghor's poetry cluster about this childhood and historical past, and "Africa" becomes symbolic, first, of the quest itself, and, more important, of rapport with nature. "Africa" is that perfect world, when one was not alienated from his own nature and from that wider nature about him ("the Other"). "Africa" and "blackness" and the many images that Senghor gathers about these concepts represent the complete man, man as a part of all that he has experienced. "Europe" is a constant threat to "Africa," but many things keep man in contact with that original sense of harmony—the drums and the poem, dance, memories of a childhood innocence, all symbols of that basic state of rhythmic union with the universe. *Négritude* is this process of purification through quest, self-knowledge and acceptance. Only by means of this renewal, this self-discovery, this new dignity, can man be brought back into a productive relationship with his fellows. This hope is embodied in the poem, which is rhythm.

3. Resurrection and synthesis (the future). His identity recovered, man can now become an active participant in his world. He can make certain (the poet is symbolic of this) that all men are delivered from the painful alienation he is now

purged of. With others who have reachieved this sense of identity, he can set about creating a world in which man lives in a state of harmony and brotherhood. In a sense, then, "Africa" (human warmth, feeling) and "Europe" (technology, reason) come into a kind of synthesis, and work together toward a "civilization of the universal."

AFRICAN REACTIONS
IN PERSPECTIVE

Philip D. Curtin

The foregoing essays have dealt with different and diverse circumstances, so different and diverse that a common theme can hardly be expected. This is all the more true, since particular African individuals and groups encountered particular western individuals and culture traits—not a monolithic and inseparable western culture. One common element, indeed, was the African discrimination between different westerners and the aspects of western culture that each seemed to represent. At times, the Africans discriminated between European social classes, as in Sierra Leone, where the "higher type of Englishman" was nearly coterminous with the Victorian middle class whose Evangelical Christianity had been such an important factor in establishing the colony in the first place. In Senegal, the *originaires* also distinguished good and bad French, but the test in this case was political—allegiance to the ideals of French Republicanism. In Gabon, the Fang distinguished European occupational groups—missionaries, merchants, administrators, and so on.

But the West and its people were not simply an array of culture traits and individuals held up for approval or disapproval. The Africans did approve of some aspects and not of others, but they were also capable of being attracted and repulsed simultaneously. The "lower type of Englishman," for example, in the eyes of the Sierra Leone Creoles, was not merely an unpleasant or uncouth person. Part of his unpleasantness in Creole eyes was his failure to measure up to certain European standards of behavior the Creoles had already accepted. A similar ambivalence runs through the attitude of other Africans. The BaKongo acceptance of Europeans as ancestors, and at the same time as dis-

231

ruptive of the proper balance and order in the world, would be
one example. A still more subtle and artistic expression of ambivalence at another level is expressed in the poetry of Léopold
Senghor.

As a further complication, culture is learned. One possible reaction to another culture is to adopt it, but, once adopted, it is
no longer alien. Men like Bishop Crowther and President Senghor learned western culture so thoroughly that they were themselves part of the "West," no longer solely African in outlook or
way of life, even though they might remain African in emotional
identification. The very act of acculturation is, of course, a reaction to the West and a highly favorable one, but it could have
some curious consequences. Bishop Crowther's accounts of his
African travels read, for the most part, exactly like similar accounts by European missionaries of the mid-nineteenth century.
These writings are thus more nearly a part of the western reaction to Africa than an ordinary African reaction to new parts of
his continent.

But assimilation of European culture or some part of it did
not necessarily imply a wholesale approval of the western way of
life, nor did it necessarily take the Africans down a road toward
westernization. As Wyatt MacGaffey has shown, many BaKongo
who were formally Christian and literate in French still held a
view of the world that was basically that of the Kongo tradition.
The cultural borrowings were from the West, but they were rein-
terpreted, in a sense "de-westernized," as part of the borrowing
process. The point here is that the options of culture change
were not simply bilateral. It was not a choice between a "traditional" and a "western" pole, nor even between a "traditional"
pole and one that was "modern" without necessarily being completely western. (For convenience, "modern" can be understood
here to mean any of the variety of different kinds of societies
that are capable of using industrial technology to create a high-
production and high-consumption economy.) In this case, the
BaKongo changed their way of life by borrowing certain features
from the West, but they moved only slightly in the direction of
either westernization or modernization.

Fernandez provides part of the explanation by suggesting that many aspects of western culture are not necessarily modern, are neither necessary nor sufficient conditions of modernization. Christianity may well be one of these, certainly a pre-modern religion in its origins, though one that has survived and accommodated itself to the scientific and technological advances that made the West modern. Here, indeed, was the key to Fang disappointment. The Fang wanted the secret to western power and success in the world, and the West answered with the offer of Christianity—in the honest, if mistaken, belief by the missionaries that Christianity *was* in fact the secret of western superiority.

Behind this simple misunderstanding is a point of crucial importance. The relations between the West and other societies in the world in the nineteenth and twentieth centuries have not been a mere matter of cross-cultural understanding between equals or near equals. They were nothing like the relations, say, between the West and the Islamic world at the time of the Crusades. The western world of the nineteenth century was even then giving birth to the first industrialized societies the world had seen. In the longer run of history, the coming of the industrial age was the most important change in human affairs since the agricultural revolution many millennia before Christ. People in all societies around the world were thus confronted by a major challenge to comprehend the new phase in human history, confused by the fact that it arrived dressed in western clothing. Historians have not yet finished with the problems of sorting out precisely why the industrial revolution came first in the West, or how it is related to western culture, though the industrialization of Japan long ago showed that it was not to be a western monopoly.

In the circumstances of the nineteenth century, however, the confrontation was inevitably one of enormous inequality perceived as such on both sides. It was only natural for Africans to grasp for the secret of western power, to seek it in some aspect of western culture, and to do so without always being able to sort out the essential from the incidental. The theme runs through all of the essays of this volume and comes through even more clearly in a recent study by Veronika Görög of popular

African stories accounting for racial difference.[1] The vast majority of a sample of thirty-seven stories accepted the same error the Europeans made in the nineteenth century: they confused race and culture and assumed that a so-called "white" skin was causally connected with western culture, and a so-called "black" skin was connected with African culture. They also accepted the "fact" of European superiority, symbolized most often by the art of writing. They explained this situation most frequently with an anecdote in which either God or a mortal father set a test for two young men, one black and the other white. The test was usually a choice between two objects or two tasks, and the black contestant was always shown to have made the wrong choice. As a result, he came out technologically poorer, or condemned to an inferior position. These accounts at least had the merit of seeing Africa's weakness as technological. The dominant explanation in the West through the first quarter of the twentieth century was pseudo-scientific racism, tracing "white" superiority to an inborn quality that supposedly produced greater inventiveness.[2]

But the same questions occurred in other societies all around the world, as they too were confronted by the power based on western technology. The African response to the West therefore fits into a very broad pattern of world intellectual history, which can nevertheless be reduced to a few very large categories. First, those who saw the power of industrialization had a basic choice between avoiding or pursuing some such goal themselves—that is, to modernize or not? Then, within both groups, modernizers or traditionalists, other divisions appear.

Modernizers

I. WESTERNIZERS: those who advocated a complete departure from the traditional culture in exchange for western models, in-

---

1. V. Görög, "L'origins de l'inégalité des races. Etudes de trente-sept contes africains," *Cahiers d'études africaines* 8 (1968): 290–309.
2. This theme is taken up in detail in P. D. Curtin, *The Image of Africa* (Madison, 1964).

cluding even the minor details of western fashion along with such major features as science, technology, or religion. Examples tending in this direction outside of Africa are the Kemalist program of westernization in inter-war Turkey, or Hu Shih in China. Others can be found among Latin American writers of the nineteenth century, who contrasted their own "backwardness" with the pace of industrialization in Europe and North America—men like Domingo Faustino Sarmiento who wanted to pattern Argentine progress on that of the United States, or the Comtian positivism of the *scientificos* in Mexico. Generally, however, the most extreme westernizers were not groups but single individuals who tried and often succeeded in crossing from one culture to another. In Africa, the Reverend Philip Quaque of the eighteenth-century Gold Coast was an extreme example. Having lived in England from the age of 13 to 25, he returned to Africa refusing to communicate in his mother tongue without the aid of an interpreter.[3]

II. UTOPIAN MODERNIZERS: those who wanted to depart from the traditional values just as firmly as the westernizers did but preferred a goal constructed by rational imagination to the model of any existing society. The most important examples of this attitude have been in the Communist movement, where the model was not the USSR but a classless society not yet achieved in any country. The separation from the western model is, of course, most complete in Chinese Communism, which rejected Russian Communism along with other aspects of western culture, though it kept its respect for Marx himself, as well as for the achievements of western technology.[4]

III. NEO-TRADITIONALISTS: those who wanted a modern society with industrial technology and high levels of consumption, while

---

3. Some of Quaque's correspondence with the Society for the Propagation of the Gospel in London has been edited and introduced by Margaret Priestley in P. D. Curtin, ed., *Africa Remembered* (Madison, 1967).
4. See Maurice Meisner, *Li Ta-Chao and the Origins of Chinese Marxism* (Cambridge, Mass., 1967).

continuing to preserve some part of the traditional values. The traditional facade should not obscure the fact that this reaction was essentially modernizing. It was willing to pay whatever price modernization exacted, but it preferred to keep whatever change was left over in the coin of the old culture. This tendency contains an enormous variety of possible mixtures of culture. The variety is all the greater, since this position is the most common of all among the intellectual leadership of the nonwestern world today. Examples from Asia and Africa would include several varieties of African Socialism, most Japanese intellectuals since the Meiji Restoration, and the Young Turk movement before the First World War. In time it would range back to the rebellion of Tupac Amaru in Peru of the 1780s, where the leadership claimed to be restoring the Inca Empire, but as a Catholic state that would in other respects be "modern" by the measure of the times. More recently in Latin America, neo-traditionalism has been common in the search for an identity distinct from Europe or the more developed countries of North America. Even here, the kind of sub-culture to be preserved ran the gamut from the Afro-Cubano movement in literature, to an equivalent insistence on their Indian heritage in Mexico after the great revolution of 1910, or a strictly western insistence of Hispanic spiritual superiority over Anglo-American materialism.

Traditionalists

I. ORDINARY CONSERVATIVES: those who wanted to preserve their culture as it was or return to a remembered past before the western impact. Though it must have been one of the most common of reactions, the conservative position has few spokesmen for the literary record. The lack of reasoned and argued response is explicable enough. Most people act from inertia a large part of the time. Intellectuals around the world dealt with the threat of the West only when it seemed serious. If it was serious enough to demand a response, it was serious enough to call for a more thoughtful and complex answer than the simple cry of "change nothing."

II. Utopian Reactionaries: those who wanted to depart from the actual way of life and that of the recent past to seek refuge in a glorified image of a more distant past. Aspects of the Boxer rebellion in China or the mid-nineteenth-century Indian Mutiny would fit in here. Other examples are found in the Saya San revolt in Burma during the 1930s, the al-Wahhab movement in eighteenth-century Arabia, and many of the millennial movements that sprang up in the wake of European conquest. Millennialism, however, is not necessarily reactionary. The Cargo cults in twentieth-century Melanesia were equally utopian, but their millennial dream often centered on the products of western technology.

III. Defensive Modernizers: those who wanted to preserve as much as possible of the traditional way of life, though realizing that the cost of defense was some form of modernization. The distinction between this position and that of the neo-traditionalists rests on the crucial matter of priorities. Both would like to achieve a balance between modern and traditional, but in one case the goal is largely modernization and in the other it is largely preservation. Since priorities can easily shift through time, individuals and political and intellectual movements often passed from one of these tendencies to another. Japanese history provides the classic example in the Meiji Restoration, which began with the battle cry *sonnō jōi* ("restore the throne, expel the barbarians") and then moved on to become a striking example of actual modernization under a neo-traditionalist banner. At times, defensive modernization and neo-traditionalism were allied in the same political movement, as they were in the Indian Congress Party of the 1930s and 1940s, where Gandhi represented one tendency while Nehru stood for the other. In Africa, defensive modernizers have not been very articulate, in spite of a few striking examples like Apolo Kagwa and the Christian revolutionaries in Buganda. This type of response is nevertheless clear enough by implication among important groups like the "Native Authorities" of northern Nigeria. It was probably the dominant response to the West among whole echelons of traditional leadership involved with colonial regimes under one form or another of indirect rule.

One useful kind of cross-cultural comparison would be to examine one type of reaction in detail. It should be possible, for example, to ask whether the circumstances that produced strong movements of a utopian reactionary stamp were similar in different cultural and historical settings. A similar approach has yielded very interesting results in the comparative study of millennial religious movements.[5] Still another comparative perspective on the African examples comes from asking whether any particular type of reaction is dominant at a particular time in a given society, and whether the dominant reactions in that society pass through any recognizable sequence with the passage of time.[6]

Chinese intellectual history after 1800 shows the dominant articulate reaction of Chinese intellectuals as a clear sequence changing through time.[7] Setting this discussion in the categories outlined above, the Chinese began in the first half of the nineteenth century with the reaction of ordinary conservatives, marked by only faint signs of uncertainty and a few movements in the direction of defensive modernization. The dominant slogan during this period was "self-strengthening," and the self to be strengthened (and preserved) was traditional Chinese society and culture, even though the technology for their defense might come from abroad. The ideological rationalization for western

5. See, for example, Peter Worsley, *The Trumpet Shall Sound*, 2nd ed. (London, 1968); S. A. Thrupp, ed., *Millennial Dreams in Action* (The Hague, 1962); Y. Talmon, "Millenarian Movements," *Archives euro- péenes de sociologie* 7 (1966): 159–200; L. P. Mair, "Independent Religious Movements in Three Continents," *Comparative Studies in Society and History* 1 (1959): 113–36.

6. As an example see Nikki Keddie, "Western Rule versus Western Values: Suggestions for a Comparative Study of Asian Intellectual History," *Diogenes* 26 (1959): 71–96.

7. I am indebted to Professor Maurice Meisner of the University of Wisconsin for this paragraph summarizing a presentation at the Belmont Conference where the other contributions to this volume were first discussed.

borrowing was an intellectually corrupted version of the Confucian *t'i-yung* ("essence" and "function") formula, whereby it
was assumed that adopted western science and technology
(*yung*) could serve as the means to protect a traditional Chinese
end, the *t'i* or "essence" of Chinese civilization. From the 1890s
to about 1914, however, the dominant "modernizers" were men
who advocated western ideas and political institutions as well as
western machines. In this generally "neo-traditionalist" era,
some (like K'ang Yu-wei) felt compelled to find Confucian
precedents to sanction far-reaching programs of "westernization" and "modernization"; ideologically, this resulted
in a highly strained and dubious interpretation of original
Confucianism as a utopian prophecy. Others, such as Yen Fu
and Liang Ch'i-ch'ao, achieved a decisive break with the conviction that basic truths and modern answers were to be found in
the traditional cultural heritage and instead identified western
ideas and values as the source of wealth and power of the modern nation-state. As modern nationalists, they were intellectually
committed to the western values and beliefs they felt would contribute to the preservation and strength of the Chinese nation,
even though they retained a deep emotional tie to the traditional
culture. As psychological compensation, they tended to search
for some form of synthesis between the "best" of "eastern spiri-
tualism" and "western materialism." This general process of nationalist alienation from traditional values reached its culmina-
tion in the First World War period among the important group
of intellectuals identified with the "New Culture Movement"
(about 1915–1919) who combined an uncritical acceptance of
western values and civilization with a fiercely iconoclastic rejection of traditional Chinese values. This phase, however, was
brief; it ended with the nationalist anti-imperialism of the May
Fourth movement of 1919 and after. Chinese reactions shifted
once more, and in several different directions. Some, like Hu
Shih, continued to admire the West, but others shifted their admiration from the West that was to western socialist visions of a
"post-capitalist" world that would be. The adoption of socialist
theories, and especially Marxism-Leninism, was a way for nationalist Chinese intellectuals to reject the existing western capi-

talist world that had impinged on China and at the same time to maintain their iconoclastic rejection of traditional Chinese values. This dual iconoclasm was characteristic of the development of Marxism and Communism in China. For the followers of the Kuomintang, however, the shift went the other way—toward a neo-traditionalist revival of aspects of traditional Chinese culture for modern nationalist and politically conservative ends. The Communist victory of 1949 marked the beginning of a new phase; insofar as the traditional cultural heritage was no longer identified with a modern and viable politically conservative foe, it could be "accepted" (in a post-traditional age) as part of the national cultural legacy, dissected and interpreted in terms of Marxist-defined stages of a universal process of historical development.

Needless to say, generalizations at this level are subject to all manner of exceptions and counter-currents, but the main lines are clear. The sequence of reactions passed from ordinary conservatism through defensive modernization and neo-traditionalism to reach a high-water mark of imitative westernization during the First World War. After that, the main thread is less clear, as reactions fell off toward differing kinds of neo-traditionalism, or else to the growing iconoclastic modernization of the Communist movement.

A similar sequence can be detected elsewhere in Asia. In Japan the timing was similar to that of Chinese reactions, from the first "Dutch learning" early in the nineteenth century to the defensive modernization of the Meiji Restoration and on to the faddist copying of the West that reached a peak in the 1880s, the last in some sense equivalent to the Chinese views of the West during the First World War. In Turkey as well a similar sequence can be traced from the first defensive modernization in the late eighteenth century, through the long series of Turkish "reforms" that punctuate the older historical accounts of "the Eastern Question"—in fact a series of different efforts at defensive modernization, adopted with indifferent success. Finally, with the Young Turks of the early twentieth century, Ottoman opinion appears to have crossed over into the neo-traditional sphere. The peak of full and uncritical westernization came only in the inter-war years of Kemal Atatürk, followed by a return to new varieties of neo-traditionalism.

The sequence that appears to be similar in China, Japan, and Turkey is not, however, common to all of Asia. Another kind of sequence is apparent elsewhere in this same period, most clearly in South Asia. There the earliest important moves away from a conservative attitude tended to carry prominent intellectuals toward a very western variety of neo-traditionalism. It appeared in the Hindu tradition with such figures as Ram Mohan Roy in the 1820s, seeking to "purify" Hinduism on the bases of western rationalism and humanitarianism. An equivalent figure for the Muslim community was Sir Seyid Ahmad Kahn, who wanted a "modernized" Islam and western style of education. Their successors, however, tended to move in a traditional direction. In the Muslim community, the *khalifat* movement of the First World War was followed in political life by M. J. Jinnah and the Muslim League of the inter-war period. The reversal of really full confidence in the West came earlier among Hindus; in the mid-nineteenth century Dayananda Saraswati was calling for religious purification by a return to the Vedas. Among the politicians, B. G. Tilak and then Mohandas Gandhi are representative of a trend toward defensive modernization.[8]

These generalizations have many and obvious exceptions, but they represent the consensus of opinion on the intellectual history of these countries. They were noticed more than a decade ago by Nikki Keddie: "In countries without direct colonial experience but with contact with the West intellectual leaders have tended increasingly to drop traditional values and adopt Western values. In colonial countries, however, an early trend toward identification with the West has been reversed by many thinkers and met by reaffirmation of modified traditions."[9] The Keddie

8. For authoritative Indian assessments of these tendencies see J. Nehru, *The Discovery of India*, 2nd ed. (London, 1947); N. V. Sovani, "The British Impact on India," *Journal of World History* 1 (1954):857–82; 2 (1954):77–105.
9. Keddie, "Western Rule," pp. 80–81.

hypothesis, in short, seems borne out by Japan, China, and Turkey as noncolonial countries, in contrast to India under the British Raj.

The pattern of early and uncritical approval of western culture, followed by second thoughts and finally some form of neotraditionalism—the Indian pattern—was also broadly true of African experience. It is very well illustrated by Spitzer's discussion of the Sierra Leone Creoles. James Fernandez's discovery of a similar sequence of reactions among the Fang is a further confirmation, important in showing that this sequence in Africa was not merely the case among a narrow group of western-educated intellectuals.

In other parts of Africa, a westernizing tendency is visible as an early reaction to the European presence on the coast. With a few individual figures like Philip Quaque, it began in the middle of the eighteenth century. It then became dominant in the early nineteenth, where it found its most extreme examples among such western-educated Christian missionaries as Abbé Boilat of Senegal or Bishop Crowther of Nigeria. Later in the century, the same uncritical acceptance of western values appeared again among the first generation of "school people" in the Cape Colony—John Tengo Jabavu would be a representative leader. Around 1900, however, the early westernizers were joined by a new generation that was more critical of the West and more interested in preserving its own culture. This group would be represented by J. Mensah Sarbah or S. R. B. Attoh-Ahuma of the Gold Coast, Sir Apolo Kagwa in Uganda, or Rev. Nehemiah Tile in South Africa. The neo-traditional tendency they introduced continued to be dominant to the end of the colonial period and beyond, though some moved on down the road toward extensive modernization, as Kagwa did in his later career.

Africa, then, seems to fit the "colonial" pattern, but Africa was not really colonial when many of these men were first exposed to the West. The European jurisdiction over trading forts, or even towns like Saint-Louis du Sénégal, had not yet turned into full colonial administration before the 1880s. Crowther, Quaque, and Kagawa were at least adolescents when they first entered European political jurisdiction.

The Latin American experience also seems to suggest that the Keddie hypothesis is not quite accurate as stated. The intellectuals of Latin America were, of course, western in culture from 1800 onwards. Even so, their reactions to the more developed West fit the pattern of nonwestern reactions. But the pattern they fit is the "colonial" reaction, similar to that of Africa and India. From the 1830s to the 1890s, Latin American intellectuals tended to be critical of their own culture and to hold up the United States and northwest Europe as models, often for quite uncritical imitation. From the 1890s into the twentieth century, however, the new generation shifted from westernization to a local equivalent of neo-traditionalism. The drive for modernization continued, but it was now accompanied by glorification of whatever African, Indian, or Hispanic tradition provided a separate Latin American identity.[10]

On a world-wide basis, then, Keddie's two opposing trends are visible, but no longer so obviously associated with a colonial experience or lack of one. They seem to be more closely associated, instead, with a special form of relative deprivation—"a negative discrepancy between legitimate expectations and actuality," seen from the point of view of the deprived.[11] The relative deprivation for the nonwestern world of the early industrial era was simply the maldistribution of information, material resources, and technology that began in the nineteenth century to reach ratios of difference unheard of in recent human history.

The intellectual reactions appear to have varied with the way the new fact of western superiority was received, that is, with the degree of relative deprivation it suggested to each society. A strong sense of relative deprivation tended to push people toward neo-traditionalism or even imitative westernization, simply to narrow the gap. If the western lead seemed less threatening, the reaction could be less dramatic. A strong sense of comparative

10. Leopoldo Zea, *The Latin-American Mind* (Norman, Oklahoma, 1963); W. R. Crawford, *A Century of Latin-American Thought* (Cambridge, Mass., 1944).

11. D. F. Aberle, "A Note on Relative Deprivation Theory as Applied to Millennarian and other Cult Movements," in Thrupp, *Millennial Dreams*, p. 209.

deprivation came early in Latin America. By the 1830s industrialization was well under way in Europe, but Latin America had barely begun to recover from nearly two decades of endemic civil war. Similar contrasts came early to Indian observers; India was largely under British rule at the time Ram Mohan Roy began to write. The western-educated Africans of the coastal trade enclaves had equal reason to see a wide gap between their own technology and that of the Europeans, but recognition of the gap came more slowly in the Ottoman Empire and in East Asia, if only because these societies retained a sense of security, power, and self-sufficiency that reflected the realities of an earlier century.

While the contributors to this volume have dealt with such diverse circumstance that rigorous comparative analysis using their detailed findings is not possible, they nevertheless support and help to modify hypotheses at a much higher level of generalization. It is hoped that future research along some of the lines taken here will make it possible to develop comparative perspectives that can take account of smaller pictures and the special nuances of the African scene.

INDEX

ABAKO, 60, 61, 74
Abeokuta, Nigeria, 78, 87, 92, 93
Acculturation: Fang, 11; and cultural dilemmas, 37; defined, 43; and appearance of legends, 43; mentioned, 8, 180, 232
l'Action Sénégalese, 167
Adeyemi, King of Oyo, 83
Affonso I (Nzinga Mvemba, King of Kongo), 51, 69
Africa, in Senghor's poetry, 202, 203, 204, 206, 207, 210, 212, 216, 218, 219, 229, 230
African Communists League, 175
African independent churches, 26
African models of the universe, 20
African socialism, 235
Africanization: defensive vs. offensive, 95; defensive, 106, 117; of Creole dress, 114, 115; of Creole names, 114, 115; of Creole history, 117, 118, 119, 120, 122, 123; mentioned, 113
Afro-Americans, 136
Afro-Cubano movement, 236
Afro-French community, Senegal, 99
Akan, 23
Alafin of Oyo, 90
Alake, 95
Alienation, in Senghor's poetry, 215, 217, 226, 229
Allègre, Adrien Edgar, 169*n*
Allovalues, defined, 38
Al-Wahhab movement, Arabia, 237
America: BaKongo view of, 55, 56, 62; mentioned, 122
American Council of Learned Societies, ix, x

American Presbyterian Mission (1889), 6
Americans: BaKongo view of, 58, 61; delegation to Pan-African Congress, 174
Americo-Liberians, 136
Ancestors: and BaKongo view of Americans, 58; in Senghor's poetry, 211, 215
Angrand, Armand, 140*n*, 168
Angrand, Joseph, 148*n*, 168
Anti-colonialism, BaKongo, 60
Anti-Semitism: among *originaires* (Senegal), 162, 163
Antonine cult, 68, 72
Arabia, al-Wahhab movement, 237
Argentina, 235
Arogangan, Alafin Awole, 84–85
Art, Fang, 9
Ashanti: British defeated by, 119; mentioned, 102
Assimilado, concept of, 226
Assimilation: among Senegalese, 150, 154, 156, 170, 184, 185; in Senghor's poetry, 226; mentioned, 171, 232
Assimilés, 156
Atatürk, Kemal, 241
Atlantic Ocean: BaKongo view of, 55; mentioned, 3, 50
Attoh-Ahuma, S. R. B., 242

Bâ, Alpha, 140*n*
Babylon, 122
Badagry, Nigeria, 77
BaKongo: compared with Fang, 3, 49; historical background, 50; response to Christianity, 50, 67, 68, 69, 71, 72; view of western

Educated elite, Sierra Leoneans, 75–76, 79

Education: primary (Gabon), 4, 5; western, 5, 101, 110, 126, 168, 208, 210; in the Congo, 67; of Africans in Europe, 76, 101, 154, 167; ethnocentric, 118; used as a weapon against Europeans, 119; C.M.S. Grammar School, 126; Sierra Leonean Creole view of. 133; Senegal, 146, 166, 167, 185; Catholic, 162, 166, 185; French, 163, 179; Muslim, 166; mentioned, 214

Egba: United Board of Management, 94–95; mentioned, 78, 87, 88, 91, 92, 94

Egypt, in Sierra Leonean Creole history, 119

Egyptians, 121, 122, 129

"Elegie des eaux," 223

"Elegy of the Circumcised": reprinted, 197–99; textual criticism of, 219–26

Elite: acculturated, x; educated (Fang), 4; educated (Sierra Leone), 75–76, 79; Senegalese, 154; urban, 140, 142, 145, 150, 165, 186

England. See Britain

English. see British

Enguta, Ntuma Ondoua, 40–41

Equatorial Guinea, 3

Ethiopia, 121

Ethiopians, 122, 127, 129

Europe: in Senghor's poetry, 202, 203, 206, 207, 210, 217, 219, 224, 229

European world view, 23

Europeanism, 111

Europeanization: Sierra Leonean Creole attitude towards, 101, 107, 112, 115; Blyden's view of, 112; mentioned, 81, 96, 108, 124, 130, 135, 232

Europeanizers: defined, 130; Sierra Leonean Creole, 130, 132

Europeans: trading posts and forts, 75; and the Bwiti cult, 46. See also Westerners

Evangelical Christianity, 231

Evangelization, effect on Fang, 45

Evus (Fang witchcraft spirit), 18, 21, 25, 41, 43

Experience: representations of, 7–10, 14, 15, 16; Fang representations of, 8, 10, 16, 17, 40, 47; in Senghor's poetry, 213, 214, 221, 222, 224, 226

Faduma, Orishatukah (William J. Davis), 113, 114

Faidherbe, Genéral Louis Leon César, 163, 164, 170

Fang: contact with missionaries, 3, 16, 22–26 passim, 45; and western education, 5; religion, 5, 9, 19, 25, 29, 38; sense of time, 6; European view of, 7, 9; social organization, 8, 9, 16, 17, 33, 34, 35, 38; social models, 8, 10, 16, 17, 20, 40, 44, 47; legends, 9, 43; art, 9; responses to western culture, 11, 13, 14, 29, 30, 46, 48, 233; acculturation, 11, 37; impact of western culture, 11, 18, 37, 44, 45, 47; palabra house, 11–14; jurisprudence, 12, 13; proverbs, 13, 24, 38, 46; view of science, 19, 20; response to Christianity, 20, 26, 28, 30, 31; witchcraft, 21, 25, 41; values, 23, 34–38; view of Bible, 26, 28; categorization of people, 26, 40, 41, 46, 231; sequence of reactions to the West, 28–29, 40, 41, 242; assertion of own culture, 29; concept of social disorder, 36, 37; compared with Ba-Kongo, 49. See also Bwiti cult

Faraday, Michael, 19, 46

Faulkner, Enoch, 114

Fernandez, James W., 232–33, 242

CPSIA information can be obtained
at www.ICGtesting.com
Printed in the USA
FFHW010616131219
56917172-62553FF

9 780299 061241